GREAT
JOCKEYS
of the
FLAT

ILLUSTRATIONS page 1, Fred Archer; 4, Derby 1973; 6, Steve Donoghue; 8, Pat Eddery/Pebbles; 10, Alan Munro

AUTHOR'S NOTE

In a text covering 200 years one must either write a little about a lot of jockeys or a lot about a select few. I prefer the latter approach. Accordingly, the spotlight has been thrown on the outstanding jockey (arguably) of each generation. An élite group emerges consisting of eight key personalities, one, roughly, per quarter century. These eight individuals then act as figureheads around which other notable exponents of jockeyship can be incorporated in lesser detail. Lastly, one further chapter examining today's rising stars seems permissible and advisable: if the last 200 years is any guide, by the time this book appears we may be acknowledging one of them as the latest addition to the jockeys' hall of fame.

Michael Tanner

Published in Great Britain by Guinness Publishing Ltd, 33 London Road, Enfield, Middlesex

Design and layout: Amanda Sedge

Typeset in Bembo by Ace Filmsetting Ltd, Frome, Somerset
Printed and bound in Italy by New Interlitho SpA, Milan

'Guinness' is a registered trademark of Guinness Publishing Ltd

A catalogue record for this book is available from the British Library.

ISBN 0-85112-989-7

THE GUINNESS BOOK OF

GREAT
JOCKEYS
— of the —
FLAT

A celebration of two centuries of jockeyship

MICHAEL TANNER

GERRY CRANHAM

GUINNESS PUBLISHING

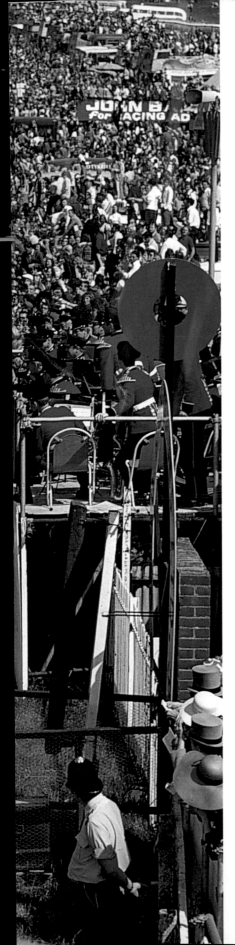

CONTENTS

FOREWORD

I am delighted to write the foreword to this magnificent tribute to jockeys and jockeyship, which covers the last two hundred years of race riding in this country. For most people the principal interest in horse racing is betting on it. In the unending and frustrating struggle to beat the bookmaker, the punter inevitably looks to the horse's human partner for inspiration – and then so often, only a few minutes later, looks to him again to take the blame for the punter's own mistaken judgement. In the eyes of the racing and betting public, the jockeys are usually the stars or the villains of the piece. Often their performance is misunderstood, underestimated or simply unobserved by the 'experts' in the grandstand. For the owners and trainers who employ the jockeys, the relationship is, if anything, even more fraught; it is only in the strictest sense that jockeys are employees, for they can, of course, be much more than that: advisers, confidants, lasting friends and, sadly, sometimes lasting enemies.

Naturally this book concentrates principally on the successful jockeys and their remarkable exploits. It is fascinating to read the many different explanations of great jockeyship contained herein, and from the evidence of this book and the very wide and authoritative sources quoted by Michael Tanner, it is clear that there is not one explanation of greatness nor a single formula for success.

During the span of this book every aspect of racing has changed dramatically. It may be nowadays that fewer jockeys live life to the extremes of their predecessors and more of them have happier and successful careers after they have given up race riding, but that does not alter the principal lessons that we learn from reading of all these remarkable men, which is that jockeyship requires skill, dedication, physical prowess and, above all, courage. It is a dangerous and difficult profession whose rewards are great but whose risks are greater, and those risks are not limited to the racecourse. Jockeys are and always have been very public figures; the object of admiration from many and envy from a few, they are an obvious target for the villain and thus inevitably a number have fallen victim to temptations of the flesh and of the will. Certainly this is no portrait of perfection; Mr Tanner has rightly depicted the warts and worse of some of history's leading jockeys. He is right to do so because, against this background of temptation and of the frequent physical abuse the jockeys have had to endure, their immense courage and professionalism stand out bold and clear.

This book is a celebration as well as a valuable historical account. I am sure that it will be read with pleasure by many racing enthusiasts for years to come and I hope that the splendid photography and illustration will attract others not perhaps already fascinated by racing. British racing has a proud heritage no better exemplified than in these pages through the deeds of so many great jockeys.

Marquess of Hartington
Senior Steward, The Jockey Club

PROLOGUE

Having ridden the winners of more horse races (8833) than anyone else on the planet, Bill Shoemaker is worth heeding on the subject of jockeyship. The world's winning-most jockey identifies a number of key features: 'Balance, intelligence, the ability to switch the whip from one hand to the other and back again, making the right moves most of the time, and a rapport with horses. Most of the outstanding riders have all these qualities.'

In a sport where the horse is king, the jockey provides the most overtly influential human contribution. Whatever the weight accorded the contribution of breeder, owner or trainer, it is the jockey who constitutes the second most important factor in the racing equation. 'Jockeyship,' wrote leading trainer Charles Morton in 1930, 'must necessarily make all the difference in the world to a horse. The veriest novice in Turf matters understands, of course, the difference between a horse being handled by a grown man and a little apprentice but very few people realise the comparatively vast gulf that lies between an ordinary jockey and a super horseman.'

In a 60-year career Morton had seen that gulf bridged by the likes of Fordham, Archer, Cannon, Sloan, Maher and Donoghue; his predecessors extended similar acknowledgement to Chifney, Buckle and Robinson, just as those who came later would nominate Richards, Smirke and Wragg, Piggott, Eddery and Cauthen for induction into the halls of greatness. For despite the intervention of 200 years, the skills which elevated Sam Chifney above his peers are the self-same ones which clearly single out Steve Cauthen as a master practitioner. The uncanny ability to achieve and maintain perfect balance so that weight appears to be taken off the horse's back; the uncanny ability to transmit confidence down the reins and through the bit so that the horse realises his tender mouth will not be abused whatever exertion is asked of him. Revelling in this freedom the horse can use himself to the full, responding to every request from the saddle; horse and man are as one, the living embodiment of the mythical centaur.

Consummate balance and exquisite 'hands', however, are present in considerably more jockeys – often instinctively – than can ever hope

PROLOGUE

to traverse that chasm to greatness, for there exists one other priceless gift bestowed by God. From Chifney to Cauthen all jockeys have been blessed with a body well below normal size and weight, but not all have been blessed with the intelligence to maximise its usage on the back of a horse during a race. What use is balance or hands if the brain proceeds to mismanage them? At around the same time as Morton was airing his views on the difference between an ordinary jockey and a super horseman, another champion trainer, Richard Marsh, chose not to mince words as to the reasons underlying such a distinction. 'It is the gift of brains which makes the jockey. Jockeys are born and seldom made. They have been given the brains which enable them to do the right thing at the right time. They have no time in a race for hesitation. Their brains must act quickly.'

We all sense what is meant by the description 'good jockey', even though the required criteria might not trip off our tongues so fluently as they do Shoemaker's. Yet this has not always been the case. According to Taplin's Sporting Dictionary of 1803, 'To say in one district that any man is "a good jockey" means no more than that he is a good horseman. In another, to say he is "quite a jockey" is to communicate an idea that he is very little, if any, better than a swindler and exceedingly well qualified to jockey any person with whom he has a transaction. Horsedealers, till within the last half century, passed under the denomination of jockeys in every market town and country fair in the kingdom.' This uncompromising and uncomplimentary view of jockeys was echoed in Brown's Turf Expositor of 1829 wherein the author admitted they were 'honester men than trainers' but divided them into three classes, 'namely Southern, Northern and dirty'.

However, the jockey was no different from any other skilled artisan in that he approached his work according to the mores of contemporary society. As the term 'jockey' gradually came to be associated more with 'horseman' than 'swindler', a deeper interest in, and appreciation of, his skills began to develop. Arguably more significant than the jockey's character were the riding style and tactics he employed, because these were increasingly the principal factors that determined the outcome of races. Part of the Turf's fascination is that in spite of an inherent tendency towards conservatism, evolution and change have inexorably made their presence felt. The techniques of jockeyship are a case in point. Many a saddle has been flung across horseflesh since the days when stirrups dangled below a horse's belly and races culminated in a frenzy of whip and spur after a funereal opening gambit, yet by constantly refining their methods the 'Knights of the Pigskin' have played their part in stimulating the thoroughbred to run faster. As the 20th century draws to a close we are witnessing the fruits of innovations popularised by Sam Chifney and Tod Sloan at the end of the 18th and 19th centuries respectively.

FRANK

FRANK

Previous page: Bill Arnull and Tom Goodisson, winners of 16 Classics between them in the early 19th century.

Frank Buckle brought respectability to race-riding. Although no record of winners ridden was officially kept, it can be stated without fear of contradiction that Buckle was the jockey nonpareil during the opening quarter of the 19th century and when he retired, in 1831 aged 65, he had 27 Classic victories to his name, twice the number accumulated by any other man then active. It would be over 150 years before Buckle's record of 27 (though he almost certainly rode two more which were uncredited) was overhauled by Lester Piggott.

For all his artistry in the saddle Buckle's universal acclaim stemmed from his unquestioned honesty in an age of open corruption and flouting of the rules. 'He has left behind him not merely an example for all young jockeys to follow,' ran his obituary, 'but proof that honesty is the best policy, for he died in the esteem of all the racing world and in the possession of a comfortable independence acquired

'The Governor': there was nothing flash or big about Frank Buckle except his heart and his nose.

from his profession. What the Greek said of Fabricius might be said of him – that it would have been as difficult to have turned the sun from his course as to have induced him to deviate from his duty.'

Buckle had no side to him. Jockeys were allowed to bet, yet he frequently rode against his own money in a finish of heads rather than succumb to the temptation of financial gain by feigning exertion (a feat he could have accomplished quite easily) in narrow defeat. In truth Buckle was not reputed to be the most intelligent of men. Many averred that if they turned him once round after a race he would not remember anything about it, and that if he was turned round twice he would forget even what horse he had ridden.

Be that as it may, Buckle needed no instruction in the arts of equitation. It was the decided opinion of rival jockey John Day that if you threw him up in the air in any part of the country he would be certain to fall on a horse at the post, all ready to begin; and he brought his horse with such energy at the finish 'that the very plates flew into the air'. There was nothing flash or big about this Pocket Hercules except his heart and his nose, while his courage matched that of the bulldog invariably at his heel. This combination of integrity and artistry in a man saluted by an adoring public as 'The Governor' made him the first authentic riding hero.

> *A Buckle large was formerly the rage*
> *A Buckle small now fills the sporting page.*

Prior to the emergence of Buckle jockeys had not enjoyed such a high profile. Contrary to the views expressed by Taplin and Brown there *had* been jockeys of honesty and skill – but seldom were the two qualities fused. The most unsalubrious and disreputable elements, Brown's 'Dirty Class', were to be met 'in Westmoreland, Cumberland etc. and are remarkable for their slovenly, dirty and unworkmanlike appearance . . . It is no uncommon occurrence to see these wretched apologies for jockeys ride in dirty jackets, dark greasy corduroys and gaiters of similar complexion.' The other Northern jockeys were scarcely smarter, particularly in comparison to their Southern counterparts who 'much to their credit appear on horseback with a neatness and cleanliness bordering on elegance'. The distribution of wealth in pre-industrial England played some part in all this; the North–South divide is no modern phenomenon.

Once racing became more organised and serious a pursuit, owners eschewed partnering their own horses in favour of putting up grooms. In keeping with their lowly status these embryonic jockeys were not only dressed like servants – right down to the crested buttons on the master's frock-coated livery – but were treated as such. If your master happened to be the King you were a lucky jockey indeed. As early as 1530 the Privy Purse expenses of Henry VIII record payments for doublets and caps in black satin to be worn by the 'boys that runs the

*Jockeys of the North (**above**) of England recorded for posterity by Anson Ambrose Martin. An intense rivalry existed between the two.*

geldings'. Black caps appeared the norm until around 1762 when certain members of the Jockey Club came 'to the resolution and agreement of having the colours annexed to the following names worn by their respective jockeys for the greater convenience of distinguishing the horses in running and also for the prevention of disputes arising from not knowing the colours of each rider'. However, the old order died hard. The St Leger meeting of 1821 featured a race for jockeys wearing three-cornered cocked hats and in a similar event at Goodwood jockeys so attired were allowed 7lb.

Brown's Northern jockeys were rough diamonds in ways other than dress. To the charge of slovenliness could be added another far more heinous crime – an uncultured approach to race-riding which often verged on the dangerous. 'Crossing and Jostling' was for long allowed on the English Turf and advertised in race conditions; outbreaks of fisticuffs were not unknown. Indeed, such belligerence was considered by some to constitute a valid and integral weapon in the jockey's armoury. Both one's opponent and his mount were regarded fair game, the avowed intention being 'to cut out their eyes' according to one scribe. Nor was it unheard of for the spectators to join in the fun. Until 1838 mounted spectators were permitted to

mingle with the runners in the home straight. Of course, as many of the crowd had ridden to the meeting and very little of the track was fenced off, it was only natural that overexcitement led to these displays of exuberance. During one Newmarket race attended by Charles II, some of his party could not resist participating 'at the utmost speed scarcely inferior to the racehorses'. An even more bizarre sight was afforded by one young jockey being accompanied throughout the race by his father who rode alongside giving advice and instruction. Needless to say, as the winning post loomed collisions between participants and non-participants multiplied and the resultant bedlam had to be seen, and heard, to be believed.

Rough or not, Northern jockeys proved remarkably successful and in the opinion of that most celebrated early Turf chronicler The Druid (Henry Hall Dixon), 'it is to Yorkshire that we have to look for the germs of real saddle science' because the pioneer of professional jockeys, John Singleton, was born at Melbourne, near Pocklington, in 1715. As a 10-year-old boy he learnt to ride on the shaggy young racehorses which often ran loose among the cattle he tended on the common lands of Ross Moor, above Melbourne. This literal horseplay led to employment as a groom to Mr Wilberforce

Read of Grimthorpe. The relationship prospered. Of middle size with
a broad chest, a strong arm and a quick eye, Singleton possessed a
cool head and ample nerve. In 1737 he walked the filly Lucy 120
miles to Morpeth (sleeping under haystacks), won the Plate and
secured two others at Stockton and Sunderland before returning to
Grimthorpe. By 1751, however, Singleton was based in Newmarket as
trainer and jockey to the Marquis of Rockingham. The most vaunted
animal Singleton partnered for the Marquis was Bay Malton whom he
rode to victory over Herod, Turf and Ascham at the Newmarket First
Spring Meeting of 1767. 'This race brought together a larger number
of people of all ranks than had ever before been seen at Newmarket.
The Tykes backed Bay Malton freely and won thousands.' A
delighted Rockingham presented Singleton with a specially
commissioned gold cup adorned by figures of horse and rider.

Singleton's position as Rockingham's jockey was later filled by
another John Singleton, who may or may not (the more likely case)
have been a relation. This second Singleton achieved everlasting fame
on 24 September 1776 when he rode Rockingham's filly Alabaculia
(though she was unnamed at the time) to victory in the Three-Year-
Old Stakes over two miles at Doncaster – in other words the
inaugural St Leger. A period in France managing the stable of the
Duke of Orleans was curtailed by the imminence of Revolution and
Singleton resumed riding in England, taking his last mount at Chester
in 1784. As would many another jockey down the years, Singleton
found life out of the saddle increasingly bleak and he spent the last
five years of his life in Chester Workhouses. Curiously, there was to
be a third jockey bearing the name John Singleton. Before going to
France, the second John had married the daughter of Rockingham's
stud groom, Lund, but then did Turf historians no favours by
christening his son John. Lund's brother was a surgeon and it was
intended that the boy should become his apprentice. However, the
lure of the Turf proved irresistible and young John ran away to
Newmarket, where he entered the Duke of Bedford's stables. He
thrice rewarded his patron in the Classics, winning the 1791 Oaks on
Portia, aged only 17, the 1793 Oaks on Caelia and the 1797 Derby on
the unnamed Fidget colt. Singleton's Yorkshire associations were
rekindled in 1802 when he won the St Leger on Orville for Lord
Fitzwilliam, who had inherited the Wentworth estate of his uncle, the
Marquis of Rockingham. Two months later, at the age of 26,
Singleton was dead, 'highly respected, esteemed and lamented' by
everyone at Newmarket.

Some Yorkshire-born jockeys who shone without forsaking the
white rose county for pastures south were the three Johns – Mangle,
Jackson and Shepherd – as well as Ben Smith, George Searle and his
two lads Bill Pierse and Garbutt; the second of whom, The Druid
assures us, 'had a fine seat but no head, and although very resolute on

rough horses, he was so severe that owners and trainers hardly liked at last to employ him'. Befitting their birthright these Tykes amassed 20 victories in Yorkshire's own Classic. In fact Mangle would have added another St Leger had not his mount Zango been disqualified after passing the post first in 1789. Mangle had no reputation for losing gracefully; in his youth he'd been tagged 'Crying Jackie' because of his propensity to burst into tears in such circumstances. He went on to train at Ashgill and Brecongill, near Middleham, where one of his jockeys was John Jackson, who won no fewer than eight St Legers between 1791 and 1822. Jackson did his darndest to get off Theodore in 1822. 'What!' he groaned with tears running down his cheeks in the style of his own guv'nor. 'Ride such a cripple as that?' The 'cripple' won by four lengths. However, just one of these distinguished Yorkshire jockeys – Shepherd – won a Derby and then (1806 on Paris) only in 'exile' after Lord Foley had persuaded him to train and ride his horses at Newmarket for a salary of £200 per annum.

John Shepherd was not alone in following the 'brass'. Selby's Dick Goodisson also drifted to Newmarket where his 'flash of lightning style at the post' impressed the Duke of Queensbury; so much so that the Duke left him a legacy of £2000. This Goodisson could always put to good use as he was wont to go about the town carrying £500 in ready cash. His reason for running such risk was that he had once been unable to cover a tempting bet to this amount and did not intend to miss any further opportunities. Coarse in language and attire, Goodisson, known as 'Hell-fire Jack', nevertheless won the first three renewals of the Oaks.

Bill Pierse won just a single St Leger (that of 1793 on the aptly named Ninety-Three) though he twice landed the Oaks. Excessively short legs rather spoilt his seat. In early life Pierse had played Tom Thumb in a travelling theatre and once, when visiting a friend, he was overheard struggling to clamber into a high bed: 'I can't get in,' he cried. 'Do give me a leg up.' But he was a powerful finisher. 'The flexor muscle of his arm was a wonder of anatomy,' marvelled The Druid. 'He could hold anything breathing with those fat little hands.' Pierse never betted – in his world money was far too valuable to spend. Apart from the Bible it was said the only book he ever read was Adam Smith's *Wealth of Nations* which he would study for hours on end. Equally parsimonious was Ben Smith, who came to share with Jackson many of Mangle's runners. It was said of Ben that he would have ridden all night if there had been anyone to put him up; and on one occasion candles were tied to the posts at Carlisle and he rode in a hack race for a fee of half a crown. Smith was a quiet, simple-minded character, much given to outrageous malapropisms which had listeners in stitches. He was always sprucely dressed in snowy white cravat, black coat and cream breeches and gaiters. Pluck he possessed in abundance. Just as the horses were about to start for a four-mile race at York in August 1796, one lashed out and broke Smith's leg. Overcoming the pain Smith stayed in the pigskin and won the race. All six of his Classic successes were in the St Leger, the last two after another accident that would have finished a lesser man. At Chester in 1814 a drunk strayed onto the course and collided with Smith's mount, resulting in the drunk's death and a broken collarbone and severe arm and shoulder injuries for Smith. Ever after Smith was obliged to whip underhand.

The first jockey to record a victory in each of the five races which came to be known as the Classics was another Yorkshireman, William Clift. The 2000 Guineas (1809) and 1000 Guineas (1814) were not inaugurated, of course, until some time after the St Leger (1776), Oaks (1779) and Derby (1780) and initially were not so highly regarded as the three longer events, but Clift took the first running of the colts' mile on Wizard while Charlotte's victory in the fillies' equivalent completed a Classic collection begun by Waxy (1793 Derby), Pelisse (1804 Oaks) and Paulina (1807 St Leger). In many respects Clift personified Yorkshire's favourite type of son. He rose from humble beginnings as a shepherd boy via the hardest of paths, yet doffed his cap to no man: when the Duke of Dorset requested the jockey's opinion of a horse of his which had just been successful Clift replied, 'Hang me! You see I won; that's enough for you.' No wonder Clift's contemporaries spoke of him as 'a wild, uncultivated Indian'.

For all their inestimable qualities the Northern jockeys, from Singleton to Clift, could not hold a candle to Sam Chifney. That is to say in terms of skill; when it came to honesty it was another matter entirely. Brown described Southern jockeys as follows: 'They appear on horseback with a neatness and cleanliness bordering upon elegance; their performance is, for the most part, of a superior order to their rivals of the North; they are illiterate, ignorant men, with little exception; though in private they affect a mysterious but plebeian importance and would willingly be thought a sort of semi-gentleman, which, however, their very attempt to assume such a character renders impossible.' Much of this description fitted Sam Chifney like a glove. He dressed like a mannequin, nurtured an ego the size of a house and was as bent as a paper clip. But he was also instrumental in transforming race-riding from a ritual slogging match to a mounted chess game and for that he will be eternally fêted.

The career of Norfolk-born Chifney began around 1770 when he was apprenticed to Foxe's stable at Newmarket, though in typically vainglorious fashion he insisted, 'riding I learned myself'. His modestly-titled autobiography *Genius Genuine* bragged: 'By 1773 I could ride horses in a better manner than any person ever known in my time and in 1775 I could train horses for running better than any

Sam Chifney, 'Genius Genuine', on Skyscraper, his single Derby winner.

person I ever yet saw.' Standing about 5ft 5in, he experienced little difficulty in reducing his natural weight of 9st 5lb to 7st 12lb during the summer. 'With the exception of Frank Buckle,' observed The Druid, 'perhaps no man was ever so exactly built for his profession.'

Peeling away the conceit, there was, it must be admitted, a lot of truth in what Chifney had to say about himself. He had taken the trouble to indulge in a spot of analysis. He rode so long that he hardly seemed to rise in the saddle, but rather than sit back throughout a race he constantly adjusted his seat to relieve the weight on his partner's back. 'Suppose a man had been carrying a stone in one hand,' he argued, 'would he not find much ease by shifting it into the other?' He further relaxed his mount by riding with loose reins. 'The first point in riding a race is to command your horse so that he runs light on his mouth; it keeps him better together, his legs are more under him, his sinews are less extended, he has less exertion and his wind is less locked. I maintain that a horse with a good mouth will run faster and more cheerfully on a gentle rein than when being asked to take part of the rider's weight into his mouth. In a close finish the horse accustomed to gentle use of the reins will run better than the one persistently terrorised by rude pulling of the reins . . . In these moments of greatest excitement he should be enticed to ease himself an inch at a time as his situation will allow. This should be done as though you had a silken rein as fine as a hair and were afraid of breaking it.'

In the words of The Druid, 'Paganini had not more complete mastery of the violin' than Chifney exercised over a horse's mouth. This gift was strikingly revealed by the instance of Knowsley in a King's Plate at Guildford in 1800. The horse had run away with every jockey who had ridden him, but when Chifney was handed a heavy curb-bridle with which to restrain this notoriously hard-puller he took one look and replied imperiously, 'Take that silly gimcrack away and bring me a plain snaffle.' The partnership – on Chifney's terms – was successful and was so again at Winchester shortly afterwards. Chifney's touch was equally evident on the idlest of animals, such as Eagle. He had advised the Duke of Dorset to buy the horse from Sir Frank Standish and run him for a King's Plate at Newmarket. The deal was done, much to the delight of Standish who told Dorset not to back the horse 'for a halfpenny' as no jockey had yet been able to get the best out of him. 'I'll let Sir Frank Standish see whether I can get him out or not,' snorted Chifney, 'and what's more, I'll neither use whip nor spur to him.' Eagle won by a neck without ever feeling 'whip nor spur'. Eagle could count himself lucky: Chifney was not above resorting to spurring a lazy horse in the brisket. 'I find when it comes to the last spring I can get a head there when I can get it nowhere else.'

Besides these refinements Chifney introduced recognisable tactics to race-riding. Not for him a breakneck gallop from flagfall. Newmarket grew familiar with the sight of Chifney saving his horse for a decisive late swoop – the famous Chifney 'Rush' was born. There were as yet no Newmarket Classics for Chifney to win and he seldom trekked north (even though his tactics constantly bemused and exasperated the local jockeys) but he made his presence felt at Epsom where he won a Derby and four runnings of the Oaks, the undoubted highlight being the 1789 victories of Skyscraper and Tag which made him the first jockey to land the Epsom double.

Chifney's mode of dress belied his profession for he was much addicted to wearing ruffles and a frill 'whenever he took silk of an afternoon', while lovelocks hung down from beneath his cap and bunches of ribbons adorned his boots. The cultivation of this dandified, foppish image became more understandable once Chifney had entered the Prince of Wales's circle in 1790. Prinny paid Chifney a retainer of 200 guineas to ride his horses, a huge sum by the standards of the day, but in this glamorous liaison lay the seeds of

Chifney's downfall. The Prince Regent's extravagant lifestyle brought him many enemies who constantly sought sticks with which to belabour his reputation. In his conceit and deceit Chifney offered them two extremely large and powerful pieces of wood.

The blows were struck in October 1791. Chifney, it was alleged, had pulled the Prince's Escape in one race at Newmarket in order to obtain a better price for another 24 hours later. Sir Charles Bunbury intimated to the Prince that no members of the Jockey Club would henceforth make matches or run horses in any stake where Chifney rode. Though hardly short of faults himself, the Prince refused to take the easy option by making a scapegoat out of his jockey, who everyone knew (including His Royal Highness) was perfectly capable of stopping a regiment of cavalry. The Prince sold all his horses and deserted the Turf for five seasons. To his maligned jockey he promised: 'You shall have your 200 guineas a year all the same. I cannot give it to you for your life, I can only give it to you for my own. You have been a good and honest servant to me.'

Genius Genuine naturally provides a full account of the Escape scandal and although vulnerable to the charge of whitewashing the whole affair, the explanation offered by Chifney suggests he might, on this particular occasion, actually have been innocent. Escape's story really begins in June that year, when he was laid out to win the Oatlands Stakes, Ascot's new race and the most valuable in the country. Five days beforehand Escape was tried with the Prince's three other entrants for the Oatlands at the race distance and weights. Escape beat Baronet a neck but Chifney, who rode Pegasus in the trial, believed Escape would have won more comfortably had he been waited with; accordingly, Chifney scurried off to back Escape for the Oatlands. On the Sunday before the race Chifney got a message from the Prince to meet him at the stables. The royal quartet were stripped for inspection and the jockey 'instantly saw Escape was not well to run and I was very certain that his chances for the Oatlands were all done away'. With Prinny's permission Chifney switched to Baronet, backed him (at 20–1) for all he was worth and got him home the winner by half a length. 'The Oatlands Stakes was won chiefly by the stratagem and ability of a boy whose name is Cheffney,' commented *The Times*. The Prince reputedly won £17 000 from bets on Baronet; Escape, meanwhile, had finished down the field. It seemed he was an in-and-out performer who could not be counted upon to keep his condition for any length of time.

Escape did not run again until October when he won two matches on the 3rd and 5th at Newmarket. On Thursday 20th, however, starting a 2–1 on favourite, he and Chifney finished last of four behind Coriander, Skylark (whom he'd beaten in the spring) and Pipeator over two miles; on Friday 21st, Chifney and Escape (5–1 this time) met Skylark again in a field of six over four miles and won

Chifney on Baronet – a portrait by Stubbs from Lord Halifax's collection. The painting itself stirred up almost as much interest as Chifney's alleged shenanigans on the horse and its royal stablemate Escape, as it was the first known representation of the 'flying gallop' style which would become the norm in the 19th century.

easily. Pandemonium ensued and Chifney was hauled before a Jockey Club enquiry to explain the discrepancy in form and declare any bets he made on both races. Chifney maintained that Escape was a stuffy horse who had not had a good sweat since his race three weeks earlier and, in any case, preferred the longer trip of four miles. He had not backed him on the Thursday but, in the belief that the race had brought him on, he wagered 20 guineas over the following day's longer distance. Bunbury, who effectively conducted the enquiry, was unimpressed. Despite the convincing nature of Chifney's explanation he remained absolutely certain the jockey was crooked through and through, and that his pernicious influence should be expunged from the Turf. Chifney was hoisted on the petard of his own making.

Chifney reverted to type. He sold Prinny's annuity for a lump sum of £1260 and left Newmarket for London where his autobiography eventually appeared at the outrageous price of £5. Misfortune had not

dimmed Chifney's arrogance. 'If the Jockey Club will be pleased to give me 200 guineas I will make them a bridle as I believe never was, and I believe never will be, excelled for their lightweights to hold their horses from running away.' Neither Bunbury nor his colleagues took the bait (though the Chifney bit ultimately became standard equipment in stables throughout the racing world) and Chifney was left facing a £350 bill from a saddler named Latchford. When no payment was forthcoming Latchford had Chifney committed to the Fleet Prison for debt. And it was here, for the want of £350, that the first truly great jockey died on 8 January 1807, aged 53. He was buried in St Sepulchre's, Holborn. His widow and six children had good cause to rue the Escape affair which had so reduced the family circumstances; the wounds took an age to heal. One of the Chifney boys, William, only seven at the time, swore revenge on Colonel Leigh, one of the men who had called his father a cheat. Eleven years later he proved true to his word, thrashing Leigh to within an inch of his life. William Chifney was sent to gaol for six months. On release he went on to train five Classic winners; his younger brother Samuel rode nine. Chips off the old block, both. More would be heard of the Chifney name.

In May 1783 a 16-year-old boy modelling himself on Chifney walked the bay colt Wolf onto the Rowley Mile having weighed out, for the very first time, at 3st 13lb. For all his alleged lack of intelligence Frank Buckle possessed sufficient wit to realise where the line must be drawn in his conscious imitation of the 'Genius Genuine'. Francis Buckle was the son of a Newmarket saddler who came of an old Westmoreland family that claimed links with a Lord Mayor of London in the reign of Queen Elizabeth. On the death of his parents when he was 12, Francis was entrusted to an aunt whose exemplary standards of truth and honour he always considered instrumental in the formation of his own outlook on life. Buckle saw no future in his father's trade and became apprenticed to the Hon. Richard Vernon, the trainer of Wolf.

Vernon had been impressed by the lad's riding in private trials. He was tremendously strong for one so tiny; in fact throughout his long career Buckle was always able to keep his weight in check without recourse to wasting, and on his final mount drew 8st 7lb with ease. Nevertheless, the end of every season was celebrated by a feast, with a goose as its centrepiece. Buckle's almost superhuman stamina was legendary. Most jockeys were obliged to travel to meetings on horseback, with saddle and the rest of their accoutrements strapped to their back. Buckle thought nothing of making the 92-mile round trip between his farm at Orton Longueville, near Peterborough, and Newmarket just to ride in a trial – and be back home for tea at six o'clock. So renowned was his endurance that on the day he retired the public clamoured for a match between him and the noted long-

FRANK

Right: *A true son of the North, Yorkshireman Bill Clift (far left) pictured with his last Classic winner, the Duke of Portland's Tiresias whom he brought home in the 1819 Derby.*

Below: *Buckle aboard Violante, in his opinion the best horse he ever rode.*

distance rider Squire Osbaldeston, 'To ride for 25 days or till either of them dropped.'

Buckle's forte was to wait. Whatever the distance of a race he preferred to hold up his horse for the late rush popularised by his mentor, a strategy demanding immense nerve and precision timing which was not always appreciated. 'If I win by the length of my arm, won't that do as well as winning by a couple of lengths?' he once asked connections before a race. 'Nay, lad. Thy fine finishes shorten a man's life. What's the use of having a nag that's fit to run if you don't make use of him?' Buckle's tactics were admirably suited to the match races which were an integral part of any meeting in the 18th and 19th centuries. One of the most famous in which Buckle participated took place at the Newmarket Craven meeting of 1799. Buckle rode the North's Hambletonian against Diamond, partnered by Dennis Fitzpatrick, for a purse of 3000 guineas. Newmarket town was full to the brim; every bed had been bespoken for weeks. The Heath was abuzz with excitement and the amount of betting was unprecedented, so that when Buckle jumped into the saddle Sir Harry Vane-Tempest, the owner of Hambletonian, clutching what seemed the solitary calm and firm hand for miles in his own fevered grasp, exclaimed: 'I would give half my fortune, Frank, for such a nerve as yours.' In a tremendous battle over the 4 miles 1 furlong and 138 yards of the Beacon Course, Hambletonian won by 'half a neck' in a time of 7 minutes 15 seconds. However epic a contest this was, Buckle himself later professed to fonder memories of his match-racing on the bay mare Violante, who he always insisted was the best horse he ever rode. Possibly love blinded his judgement. Violante had been turfed out of Lord Grosvenor's stud as useless and was for sale at £50. Buckle immediately bought her, but in the light of the jockey's keenness Grosvenor begged out of the deal.

Not that Buckle had matters all his own way in match races facing opponents of the calibre of Fitzpatrick, Clift, Jem Robinson, the Chifneys, the Arnulls and the Edwards clan. One-eyed Harry Edwards, for instance, was a phenomenally strong finisher. However, vision was not all Edwards lacked, for he was entirely devoid of scruples and he would 'rather nobble for a pony than make a hundred by fair means'. The Arnulls – brothers John and Sam and the former's son Bill – won twelve Derbies between them and were somewhat more trustworthy. Bill, a fearless albeit unsophisticated rider, was probably the best of the three. He was fond of a practical joke although he was never sure to see the funny side if he himself was the victim. When a colt named Hokee Pokee was led past him one day he asked the lad its name and on being informed rushed off to the trainer in a fit of pique insisting that the lad had been taking liberties. If there was one thing Bill Arnull liked more than a joke it was money. His friends used to tell him that he would go without food

FRANK

Above: Buckle with Colonel Henry Mellish, for whom he won the 1804 St Leger on Sancho.

Previous page: The fearless albeit unsophisticated Bill Arnull, sat on Andrew.

for a month if he saw his way to a sovereign. For one of such miserly inclination it seemed slightly perverse that he should wind up an overseer of the poor.

Buckle's historic affinity with the Classics began in 1792 with a Derby victory on Lord Grosvenor's John Bull. Before the Earl's death in 1802, Buckle presented him with further Epsom success through Daedalus (1794 Derby), Nike (1797 Oaks) and Bellina (1799 Oaks). An even more fruitful association commenced once Buckle began riding for Newmarket trainer Robert Robson – 'The Emperor of Trainers' – whose principal patrons were the 3rd and 4th Dukes of Grafton. Buckle is credited with having ridden eleven Classic winners for the two Dukes and although the jockey is not named it seems inconceivable that it was not he who partnered Catgut (1818) and Tontine (1825) to their victories in the 1000 Guineas. The year Tontine walked over, Buckle is listed in the Racing Calendar as the rider of two winners for the 4th Duke at the Guineas meeting, one of them on the very afternoon of the 1000. This tally would be higher still had the Graftons overcome a reluctance to challenge for the St Leger, or the Guineas been founded early enough for the 3rd Duke to have taken an active interest. As it was, Robson and the 4th Duke assisted Buckle to the Guineas double on four occasions. The jockey also twice secured the Epsom double, though in these instances he was not wholly dependent on his major employers. In 1802 he won the Derby on the 3rd Duke's Tyrant and the Oaks on Mr John Wastell's Scotia. Neither horse was strongly fancied to begin with yet Buckle backed them to win and win they did, thanks to his consummate judgement. In the Derby Buckle ignored the furious pace set by Young Eclipse and Orlando, convinced the pair would come back to the field in the straight. As they tired he made his late run. Having witnessed this successful coup the public plunged on Scotia and she started favourite for the Oaks. Only five opposed the grey filly but Buckle had to pull out all the stops to gain the day. Three times she appeared beaten; each time Buckle nursed her back into the fray and 'with knee and thigh and tightened rein' he snatched the race out of the fire by a head. Seasoned judges swore they had never seen a finer piece of riding. The sporting public's admiration for Buckle's skills knew no bounds, a fact amply demonstrated by the publication of the following jeu d'esprit:

> *Tho' long by the beaux reduced to disgrace*
> *The Buckle's the gem and the pride of the race;*
> *For lo! the bold jockey's neat dext'rous strokes*
> *Have crowned him the conq'ror of Derby and Oaks*
> *When backed by his rider's consummate address,*
> *The high-mettled racer feels sure of success.*
> *Eclipse was the horse of all horses that ran,*

FRANK

Frank Buckle, laid to rest in a sumptuous tomb befitting the first of the truly great English jockeys.

But whatever be our horse, now Buckle's the man.
Oh! where is a match for a treasure so rare?
Look round the wide world, and ye'll ne'er find a pair;
For, trained to the Turf, he stands quite alone,
And a pair of such Buckles was never yet known.

Buckle rode his last Classic winners in the Guineas of 1827 (Turkoman and Arab) at the age of 60. 'Buckle is now grown old,' declared Brown when summing up his jockeys in 1829, 'and does not often appear, otherwise I place him at the head of the list.' If he did 'appear' Buckle endorsed Brown's opinion. At the second Newmarket October meeting of 1828 the antics of Lord Exeter's mare Green Mantle down at the post would have unsettled many a jockey years Buckle's junior, but 'The Governor' sat tight and won the ensuing race. Unfortunately, his last ride – Conservator at Newmarket on 6 November 1831 – was not a winning one. After weighing in for the umpteenth but last time, he donned his voluminous white cape-coat, strapped his racing saddle across his back and headed home to Orton Longueville. Buckle did not enjoy a full retirement in pursuit of his numerous pastimes: breeding cattle, greyhounds, bulldogs and fighting cocks or hunting with the Hertfordshire Hounds when, they said, he would invariably fall off at every fence. He died on 5 February 1832, scarcely three months after last wearing silk, and lies buried beneath a sumptuous tomb in his parish churchyard.

No better rider ever crossed a horse;
Honour his guide, he died without remorse.
Jockeys attend – from his example learn
The meed that honest worth is sure to earn.

The 1821 Derby – one Buckle did not win. He and the Duke of Grafton's Reginald chase Gustavus (Sam Day) through the crowds that broke onto the course.

JEM

JEM

As the 1820s slipped by, Frank Buckle's pre-eminence was increasingly challenged by Jem Robinson. A rider of comparable honesty, Robinson made fewer mistakes and fewer enemies than the other claimants to Buckle's office. The same could be said about his own successor, Nat Flatman, who concluded the first half of the 19th century as the first officially recognised champion jockey. However, whether these two were the supreme jockeys of their time remains highly debatable. The Chifney torch, for example, burnt bright in the hands of Sam's son Samuel, who in terms of sheer talent outshone everybody. He was successful but not so spectacularly as he ought to have been, for like his father he owned a self-destruct button and had a fatal tendency to press it. To the scourge of dishonesty – apparently endemic to the make-up of a Chifney – was added the tyranny of the scales, because in this respect the son was not the image of the father.

Previous page: Jem Robinson aboard the 1827 St Leger winner Matilda. His skilful handling of the fidgety animal earned him a gift of £1000 from one admirer.

Right: Robinson wearing the light blue and purple sleeved jacket of the Duke of Rutland in which he won the 1828 Derby on Cadland.

All of Bill Scott's formidable repertoire proves useless as Cadland beats The Colonel in the re-run of the 1828 Derby.

In Samuel Chifney's lazy eyes, wasting was akin to the Chinese water torture. To a lesser degree these character deficiencies surfaced in his nephew Frank Butler and one or two, certainly dishonesty, were to be found lurking in the character of John Barham Day, who succeeded Buckle on most of the Grafton horses and got to wear the royal jacket of George IV when Old Sam's former employer resumed his Turf career. Day was decidedly strait-laced compared to the sociable, hard-drinking Butler and positively pious in comparison to the latest in the long line of firebrands to emerge from the hard school of Northern jockeys: Bill Scott was rough, tough and dangerous to know. Indeed, his best friend was the bottle; then again, it may have been his worst enemy for not only did it lead him to an early grave but it also rendered him so hopelessly incapable during the 1846 Derby that his mount, Sir Tatton Sykes, lost a Classic he should have won easily and thus missed inclusion in the history books as the first winner of the Triple Crown.

Born into a family of Newmarket farm labourers in 1793, James Robinson spent 13 formative years in the stable of Robert Robson where he absorbed countless lessons in the arts and crafts of race-riding from Frank Buckle. On many an occasion young Jem would promise another lad 'half his plum-pudding on Sunday' to dress over his own horse so that he might nip across the Heath and watch the master in action. Pretty soon he was cutting his teeth in matches against his idol – and beating him. 'Try that on somebody else next time,' muttered the old champion after Robinson had bested him in an early encounter. Their greatest confrontation involved the Ardrossan colt and Abjer on 15 October 1821 and resulted in a dead heat. Robinson rarely employed a high or vigorous whip action but he

Chifney

Wheatley

was ruthless when he so chose. Of all jockeys riding he could 'punish a horse most in the least time', according to John Day; on this famous afternoon Lord Exeter's Ardrossan colt received the full treatment. A week earlier the horse had savaged Robinson prior to a trial and afterwards, with no jockey in the vicinity on whom he could vent his spleen, bit off his lad's thumb. The wild colt never forgot the thrashing he received at Robinson's hands. Two years later the jockey visited Exeter's stud and was persuaded to enter his stall. 'We've got him as quiet as a lamb,' said Exeter, whereupon the beast stole one glance at his former chastiser and promptly tried to maul him.

Although Robinson's total of Classics fell three short of Buckle's record, no one, not even his mentor, can match the nine victories he achieved in the 2000 Guineas. Nor were the six Derbies he collected at Epsom bettered (Steve Donoghue's six included two wartime substitutes at Newmarket) until Lester Piggott drove Roberto home in 1972. The Guineas were just beginning to assume greater prominence in Robinson's heyday. For instance, in 1826, when Buckle sent an inscribed whip over to Germany to be offered as a challenge prize, an attached letter detailed his Epsom and Doncaster Classics but merely referred to 'all the good things at Newmarket' as a seemingly insignificant afterthought.

The first of Robinson's 24 Classics came in the Derby of 1817 aboard Mr John Payne's Azor. His instructions had been to 'go as fast and as far as you can', which he did to such effect at the top of the Hill that the 50–1 shot became the longest-priced winner of the Derby to date. Seven years later a second Derby winner, Cedric, formed the first leg of an eccentric treble, for Jem had bet £10 at odds of 100–1 that he would win both Epsom Classics and get married within the week. After Cedric made nearly all the running to land the Derby, the bet looked like coming unstuck at the second hurdle. Robinson's partner in Friday's Oaks was the 1000 Guineas heroine Cobweb, a red-hot favourite at 11–8 on. At a crucial stage of the race, the gag she was wearing became entangled with her bit; in a trice the unflappable Robinson leant forward and removed the contraption, enabling them to sail serenely on to victory. No odds were available for the last part of Robinson's wager but one imagines his marriage to a Miss Powell was the one cast-iron certainty in the treble and he safely pocketed his £1000 without further anxiety.

Robinson's best Derby winner was probably his sixth and last: Cobweb's son Bay Middleton in 1836. A beautifully proportioned thoroughbred, Bay Middleton possessed a vile temper which, along with a doubtful leg, kept him off the track as a two-year-old, but so promising did he seem that he was still heavily backed for the Derby. Robinson was asked to tame him. On arriving at the yard he was greeted by the colt's trainer, James Edwards: 'Thank God you've come. He's bolted with everybody. We'll gallop him in the morning.'

Forewarned to all Bay Middleton's devices, Robinson told the colt's lad to hold him fast by the head until he was safely seated. Bay Middleton had other ideas and before Robinson could do anything about it the increasingly fractious animal had stamped on its lead rein, broken it and shot off in the direction of the Cambridge Gap. Slowly but surely Robinson's hands began to work their soothing magic and by the end of his career as a three-year-old Bay Middleton was comparatively docile. He won the 2000 Guineas and the Derby and was undefeated in seven starts.

This imperturbable streak in Robinson's nature undoubtedly paved the way for his victory in the 1828 Derby on Cadland. In the race itself they had run a dead-heat with The Colonel, partnered by Bill Scott. As the tension rose prior to the rerun Robinson remained as phlegmatic as ever. 'Stop a minute,' he called to the lad who was leading him out of the paddock, 'just let's have a pinch of snuff first.' Robinson knew he would need all his wits about him at the post. Racing's bad-boy excelled himself: Scott gave breath to every oath in his formidable lexicon in an effort to rattle Robinson. It all came to nought because he was comprehensively outmanoeuvred. Robinson made the running until the distance where he took a subtle pull which fooled Scott into thinking he was beaten. Allowing The Colonel to pass, he then brought Cadland with a mighty rush on the post to win by a neck.

Cadland's triumph offered the perfect illustration of Robinson's technique for, as The Druid observed, 'He had so many dodges that the jockeys always declared that neither he nor they ever knew when he was beat. Four strokes in the last 20 yards was his way of popping the question.' Adoption of more forcing tactics occasionally got Robinson into trouble, for instance on George IV's favourite mare Maria in a match against Tom Thumb at Egham in 1828. In trying to win from the front, Robinson was caught napping on the last bend when his rival, in the words of Theo Taunton, 'rushed past him like a whirlwind, Robinson being so amazed that he pulled Maria short up for a moment and only won on the post by a short head by dint of the most resolute riding. The King was furious.' Robinson was less fortunate on the St Leger winner Rockingham during a match for the King's Plate at Goodwood in July 1835. At the one furlong mark he was a dozen lengths ahead of Lucifer, whose situation appeared so hopeless that his trainer, standing nearby, loudly instructed his jockey to pull up. Overhearing all this, Robinson began to ease the 7–2 on favourite, only to suffer the mortification of seeing Lucifer, whose jockey had either not heard or bravely chosen to ignore his employer's orders, dash past a few yards from the line.

Truly outstanding riders can successfully adopt all manner of stratagems, however, and Robinson was no exception. In the 1827 St Leger he gave a virtuoso performance to make virtually every yard on

Previous page: When Ben Marshall painted this study in 1818, Sam Chifney junior (left) had just won his first Derby on Sam and Jem Robinson (right) had just won the 1000 Guineas and St Leger on Corinne. Will Wheatley (centre) enjoyed no Classic success that year but won five altogether.

Matilda. She was of such a fidgety disposition that Robinson rode her without spurs and she was a minute creature compared to the Derby winner Mameluke (partnered by Robinson at Epsom) who chased her all the way up the straight and at one point even seemed to have stolen a narrow lead.

> *By heaven the mare*
> *Just on the post her spirit rare*
> *When Hope itself might well despair;*
> *When Time had not a breath to spare;*
> *With bird-like dash shoots clear away,*
> *And by half a length has gained the day.*

Robinson's riding was universally lauded and it is said a Scottish admirer, one Captain Dowbiggin, thrust a plain envelope containing £1000 into his hands as he was sitting at tea that evening. With riding fees at £3 per mount (and £5 for a win) gifts like that were always welcome in the Robinson household where it was a case of easy come, easy go as far as money was concerned. Robinson commanded, of course, a much larger fee in the big races: £100 to ride in a match, for example, or in a Classic; successful owners would then be expected to show their gratitude with a cheque for £500. But the Robinsons lived high on the hog. Once the season finished they headed for rented accommodation in London and indulged themselves. For their Newmarket home Robinson had constructed a fine red-brick cottage (which subsequently became part of Machell Place) but, frankly, Robinson was a trifle silly with his money. He gave away and threw away so much that, but for the generosity of the Dukes of Rutland and Bedford, his retirement might have been as ignominious as the elder Chifney's. Even so, according to his obituary, 'He was perfect.' His reign was brought to a close when a two-year-old called Feramorz threw him before the start of a match at Newmarket in 1852. The colt swerved, a stirrup leather snapped and Robinson smashed his thigh, leaving him with one leg four inches shorter than the other and a permanent limp for the remaining 13 years of his life.

Robinson's expression rarely betrayed his hedonistic inclinations. His long face, doleful eyes and bulbous nose presented the most lugubrious and melancholy of countenances. Although he could not alter the features he was born with he did – like his great friend and rival Sam Chifney Junior – constantly interfere with his metabolism. At 5ft 6in Chifney was a head taller but he was a reed beside Robinson who was fairly broad-chested for one so small. Both were obliged to lose prodigious amounts of weight before the start of each new season. Robinson's winter extravagances invariably saw his weight balloon to 9st 10lb but he was capable of dropping 24lb inside four weeks if necessary. Wasting of this order involved swallowing

JEM

When this likeness was drawn, Sam Chifney junior had yet to become 'the long, thin, lazy lad'.

physics and enduring marathon walks in heavy clothing and, not surprisingly, Robinson was often discovered in a faint and taken home in a cart.

Above and beyond their battle with the scales, Chifney and Robinson were united by bonds of mutual respect and admiration. It was on Chifney, rather than Buckle, that Robinson principally modelled his riding. 'He hasn't Sam's fiddling,' he would say of his old guru if pressed to draw comparisons: 'You might as well look for a rat as for Chifney. First find out what he's doing and then beat him.' For his part, Chifney initially regarded Robinson as only moderate but eventually he confided to his brother that 'he's taken to riding like the very devil'. In point of judgement and knowledge of pace there was little between them, but in the 'Rush' Chifney exuded power to Robinson's elegance. The Ascot Gold Cup of 1832 provided one study of opposites; Chifney on Rowton and Robinson aboard Camarine, 'the best mare I ever rode'. The field more or less walked the opening furlong before Chifney broke into a slow canter and, completely out of character, decided to go on. However, he kept the pace pedestrian until the final straight and when Camarine was forced wide as the tempo increased it seemed his tactics were about to succeed. Then Robinson's whip began to crack, the mare tenaciously closed the gap and after the two horses flashed across the line in unison the judge opted for a dead heat. Robinson's objection was overruled and a rerun ordered in which, said *The Times*, 'Camarine crept up very cleverly and won by two lengths.'

Camarine's was one of six victories Robinson recorded in the Gold Cup. That of 1835 was, in his opinion, courtesy of the greatest horse he ever rode – Glencoe. The partnership had won the 1834 2000 Guineas but finished only third in the Derby to the massive Plenipotentiary. In the Gold Cup neither he nor Glencoe broke sweat. 'A glance at Robinson's seat foretold the result,' wrote Taunton. 'Next to the rails this superb horseman was skimming over the sod as light and graceful as the dolphin shoots away from the shark.'

One of Glencoe's Gold Cup victims was Shilelagh, a costly failure for the Chifney brothers since they had also backed him heavily in the Derby in which he finished second. Neither really recovered: Will sold up and left Newmarket and although Sam rode on and won the 1843 1000 Guineas on Extempore, a gap of 18 years separated that Classic from the previous success, evidence indeed of the slump in

Voltaire (right), one of Chifney's four runners-up in the St Leger, alongside Rowton (Bill Scott) who beat him by half a length in 1829.

Chifney's fortunes. The record books can be cruel arbiters and the name of Sam Chifney the younger does not loom large in their pages: his talent was not converted into the kind of concrete achievement that stands the test of time. As with his father, the reasons for this sad state of affairs lay in a badly flawed character.

No other 19th-century jockey could have commenced a career in the pigskin with greater advantages than Samuel Chifney the younger. He had the most artful jockey in the land for his tutor and one of the country's richest men as his patron. By his sixth birthday Sam was out on the Newmarket gallops twice a day, seated on the Prince's Kit Karr and receiving tuition from his father on a 300-yard course specially marked out on Warren Hill. Here father and son ran race after race, taking turns to make the running or wait and utilise the 'Rush'. 'By the powers, it's not fair,' joked Dennis Fitzpatrick on witnessing these lessons, 'Buckle and I will be having Sam and Sam-son down on us soon.' As a result of such expert repetition the Chifney Rush was brought to the very peak of perfection in the hands of Young Sam and led to its ultimate appreciation by a much wider audience.

When he turned 13 Chifney was sent to the stables of his maternal uncle Frank Smallman who trained for the Earl of Oxford at Bampton Park in Hertfordshire. So many victories were gained in 1800–1 by 'waiting till they had ridden to a standstill and then pouncing on them at the post' that the Prince of Wales was persuaded to engage Smallman as his trainer, thus enabling Chifney to don the royal silks worn so conspicuously by his father; he received a retainer of £8 per annum. Chifney proclaimed his heritage in the Claret Stakes at the Newmarket First Spring Meeting of 1805 riding Lord Darlington's Pavilion. Ranged against the duo were the winners of the previous year's Derby (Hannibal), Oaks (Pelisse) and St Leger (Sancho) partnered respectively by Messrs Arnull, Clift and Buckle. Pavilion's chances seemed accurately represented by his odds of 7–1; Sancho was favourite at 6–4, Hannibal 3s and Pelisse 5–1. To everyone's astonishment, Pavilion waited on Sancho until Chifney produced him like a rabbit out of a hat to win by a head. In a later match, riding Florival, Chifney savoured the satisfaction of besting Buckle on Petronel and on his debut at York he outrode Jackson, Clift and Pierse.

The first of Chifney's nine Classics came on Briseis in the 1807 Oaks, but his riding of another filly, Manuella, in the 1812 Derby raised more than a few eyebrows and hinted at things to come. A number of sound judges believed Chifney deliberately stopped the filly, a suspicion hardly dampened when she won the Oaks (with Pierse riding) at odds of 20–1.

If the activities of the Chifney brothers were usually conducted to the refrain of jiggery-pokery, no one could complain they played out of tune when it mattered. One patron who believed they could do no

JEM

The looks of a choirboy belied Bill Scott's habits.

wrong was the 23-stone squire of Riddlesworth, Thomas Thornhill. He named his Scud colt after the jockey, who repaid the compliment by getting Sam first past the post in the 1818 Derby to net the owner £15 000 in bets. Twelve months later the triumvirate of owner, trainer and jockey won the Oaks (and £20 000 in bets for the squire) with Shoveler, a daughter of Scud; and in 1820 the filly's full brother Sailor won the Derby. Thornhill was so grateful to his jockey (Sailor had won him another £23 000) that he bequeathed Chifney his home and stables.

Chifney's display on Wings in the 1825 Oaks may well be interpreted as his apogee. Tontine had set off at a scorching gallop and it was solely due to Chifney's innate judgement of pace that he was able to steal up inch by inch and win in the last three strides. The 'Rush', in fact, could only be accomplished successfully if Chifney had, as it were, 'won' his race out in the country. St Francis, for instance, was in Robinson's estimation one of the shiftiest and idlest animals ever to set foot on a racecourse. One afternoon Chifney rode him. 'Come back with me and I'll show you a treat of your uncle's riding such as you never saw yet,' the watching Robinson shouted to Frank Butler. 'He's got St Francis in hand today and I know what a slug he is.' Chifney somehow cajoled the ornery critter through the early stages before rousing him to victory. And he could most definitely lay into a horse. In a driving finish at York in 1826 he brought Memnon on the scene, in The Druid's phrase, 'with a stroke of the whalebone which might have been heard to Bishopthorpe'.

In neither flesh nor spirit did Chifney possess the wherewithal to recover from Shilelagh's defeat in the 1834 Derby. He hated the perspiring walks along the Dullingham Road which were so necessary to control his weight, far preferring to meander the lanes with a gun under his arm and his favourite yellow and white pointer, Banker, at his heels; or, alternatively, just to sit on his farm watching his pet foxes cavorting in their pen. At one stage Sir Tatton Sykes engaged Chifney to ride the Sledmere horses at £100 a year, but the jockey seldom appeared on the gallops. A hack would be sent over to Malton to meet him off the Newmarket coach and regularly returned riderless. He was even prone to keeping his own brother waiting two hours on Newmarket Heath. Chifney's indifference cost him hundreds of winners, including the 1838 Oaks and St Leger for Lord Chesterfield, whose retainer he had declined even though it required him to ride only his lordship's best animals. Having finished second in four St Legers, missing that winning ride on Don John should have upset Chifney but he was not disturbed one iota. In fact, as his weight became more troublesome he was rarely seen in action outside of Ascot, Epsom and Newmarket; in his entire career he only won twice at York and once at Doncaster. 'It was no wonder,' remarked *Bell's Life*, 'that he so often departed up the North Road like a Knight of

JEM

the Rueful Countenance.' However, as Thornhill's generosity testified, few bore 'the long, thin, lazy lad' any grudge. His Newmarket home – Cleveland House in Old Station Road – was built for him by Lord Darlington. Chifney's swansong came on Thornhill's Extempore in the 1000 Guineas of 1843. He sweated off 12lb in order to ride her and won by a head; in the Oaks they could not fend off the challenge of Poison, ridden by none other than his own nephew Frank Butler. 'The Old Screw', as Chifney was now inelegantly called, took just a handful of mounts in 1844. He twice had the pleasure of riding Extempore to victory in match races against opponents aided by Jem Robinson, and he took his final tours of Epsom on Elemi in the Derby and Example in the Oaks. He retired to Hove (on the strength, it was rumoured, of a pension from Butler) and was last seen on a racecourse at Brighton in 1853, a year before his death. His tombstone denoted a man of nationwide fame, for upon it were just the words, 'Sam Chifney of Newmarket'. Yet, 150 years later, this very brevity carries undertones of a career unfulfilled.

The last occasion Chifney attended Epsom was to see his nephew win the 1853 Derby on West Australian. 'I only touched him once with the whip and I was glad to get him stopped,' said Butler; three months later 'The West' won the St Leger to secure the first Triple Crown. In most circumstances Butler could, and would, 'stop' anything, but though he had accepted a bribe to do precisely that at Doncaster – he'd been suspected of stopping another potential Triple Crown winner in Cotherstone ten years earlier – the colt's trainer,

Frank Butler on West Australian, the first winner of the Triple Crown in 1853.

Above: Scott alongside Touchstone on whom he won the 1837 Ascot Gold Cup.

John Scott, had got wind of the plot and warned him of the dire consequences. 'The faster they'll go, the sooner it will be over; they'll wonder what's coming when I lay hold of them,' Butler predicted. 'The West' won in a canter by three lengths. In stark contrast to his uncle, Frank Butler was of the hail-fellow-well-met variety who liked nothing better than a sing-song and a joke. Nevertheless, he learnt much from Sam, and not all of it honest. He was apt to overdo the waiting, as for example when Springy Jack failed to catch Surplice in the 1848 Derby, but on the other hand he had few equals in a rough race. Only a rider of his immense strength could have forced Daniel O'Rourke past the judge ahead of Barbarian in the 1852 Derby. Butler only really came to the fore after 1843 when Bill Scott fell out with his brother John, 'The Wizard of the North', who trained 40 Classic winners: all Butler's 14 came during his last 11 years in the saddle and 10 of them were for Scott's Whitewall stable, in Malton. Besides being the first Triple Crown jockey, he earned a further slice of Turf history by winning the same Classic – the Oaks – four times in a row (1849–52), a feat achieved by just three other riders: Buckle

JEM

Yorkshire baronet Sir Tatton Sykes leads the colt named in his honour, on whom Scott ought to have landed the first Triple Crown.

Nat Flatman was the first officially recognised champion jockey, in 1846 with 81 winners.

in the 1000 Guineas (1820–3), Robinson in the 2000 Guineas (1833–6) and Bill Scott in the St Leger (1838–41). However, there was a price to pay: a diet of champagne and toast was all he might swallow if he were to manage 8st 7lb. His strength began to ebb away, the year of the Triple Crown proved his last and three years afterwards he was dead at the age of 38.

Although his portraits make Bill Scott resemble the kind of choirboy whose good habits that regular churchgoer John Barham Day would have admired enormously, the truth of the matter proved otherwise. Scott resorted to extreme examples of verbal abuse and intimidation that in the world of cricket has come to be termed 'sledging'; he was also wonderfully adept at bending his elbow whenever a drink hove into view. Yet his needling failed to unsettle Robinson before the rerun in the 1828 Derby, while his addiction to the bottle also backfired on him at Epsom 18 years later. He had won the 2000 Guineas on his own horse Sir Tatton Sykes (purchased from the Yorkshire baronet and originally called Tibthorpe) and backed him for the Derby as if the result was already known. A morning at the brandy bottle had done its worst by the time Scott reached the start, where his behaviour and language knocked the performance of 1828 into a cocked hat. As the race began Scott was still cursing the starter (for which the jockey was fined £5) and Sir Tatton Sykes was left fully 60 yards. By some miracle the horse recovered all the ground bar the neck which enabled Pyrrhus the First to win the day.

In addition to these flagrant displays of drinking and uncouth behaviour, Scott took precious few steps to conceal his dishonesty. In the 1840 Derby he backed his mount Launcelot to win a fortune.

JEM

Overleaf: Four racing portraits by John Frederick Herring. The Run In *(top left) shows West Australian (centre foreground) with the spotted colours of Voltigeur immediately behind and the tartan jacket of The Flying Dutchman second from the right. The same horses feature in* Saddling *(bottom left) and are among ten involved in* A False Start *(top right). West Australian, The Flying Dutchman and Teddington are prominent as they are shown* Returning to Weigh *(bottom right).*

Having got to the front close to home, he was thunderstruck to see Little Wonder launching a challenge which he realised Launcelot could not repel. 'A thousand pounds for you if you stop him,' he screamed to Little Wonder's young jockey Macdonald, but the boy replied, 'Too late, Mr Scott, too late!'

William Scott was a native of Chippenham, near Newmarket, but he made his name in the North where he was initially apprenticed to James Croft at Middleham. His breakthrough occurred in 1816 through Filho da Puta's victory in the Doncaster Cup. Town Moor was an apt venue for the 19-year-old jockey's first big success because his record here, particularly in the St Leger, became second to none. Between 1821 and 1846 he won nine St Legers, a total still unequalled. When it came to race-riding Scott's attitude was simplicity itself: 'Only give me a good horse and quicksilver be hanged', which could roughly be translated as 'grab the rails and make the running'. At Doncaster especially he liked to ensure the pace was severe to the top of the hill, arguing, 'If you can't get a pull and go on again, you'll never win; what's the use of condition if you don't use it?'

Scott's love affair with the St Leger dates from 1818 when he finished third on The Marshal. For two weeks the following year Scott actually believed he'd won his first St Leger. Of the field of 19 who faced the starter, five – including Scott on Sir Walter – were left behind. The race was won by Antonio but the stewards declared a false start and ordered the race to be rerun. Ten horses complied (Antonio was not among them) and Sir Walter prevailed. Unfortunately for Scott the inevitable appeal to the Jockey Club by the owner of Antonio resulted in the 'first' race being deemed perfectly legitimate. So Scott was denied, though not for long.

Flatman up on Colonel Peel's Orlando, the 1844 Derby winner. Running Rein was in fact first past the post but was subsequently exposed as a 4-year-old.

GREAT JOCKEYS OF THE FLAT   47

GREAT JOCKEYS OF THE FLAT 49

*Scott (**above**) and Flatman (**right**): two vastly contrasting characters.*

Previous page: The eagerly awaited rematch between The Flying Dutchman (Charles Marlow) and Voltigeur (Nat Flatman) sees Marlow bring his mount home by a length.

Jack Spigot broke the ice in 1821. By all accounts the colt despised Scott and showed anger even at the sound of his voice. At Doncaster he had to be blindfolded before Scott could get on him. Further triumphs came at regular intervals. Those of The Colonel (1828) and Launcelot (1840) were some compensation for their Derby defeats and that of Satirist (the fourth member of the 1838–41 quartet) over the Derby winner Coronation was considered to be one of the high spots in Scott's entire career. For once he did not make the running, electing to track the favourite until pouncing below the distance to win by a head.

Scott rode 14 Classic winners for his elder brother John, in whose opinion the Derby of 1835 constituted the jockey's finest hour. With a furlong to go he and Mündig were running neck and neck with Ascot. On the line Mündig had just got his head in front; a stride beyond, Ascot showed in front. Scott confessed he had never ridden a more ferocious finish and had had to shout across at Nat Flatman to keep his horse from hanging onto him. One shudders to think of Scott's reply had the roles been reversed. The parting of the ways between the Scott brothers happened around the time of the 1843 St Leger. Bill Scott now verged on alcoholism and although he rode John's Cotherstone to success in the 2000 Guineas and Derby, Frank Butler replaced him at Doncaster.

Indeed, it was touch and go whether Scott rode Sir Tatton Sykes in the 1846 St Leger. Supervision of the colt's training at Scott's Highfield stable, near Malton, was entrusted to William Oates and his father, but their biggest headache was ensuring the jockey, not the horse, got to the Leger start in a fit state. The younger Oates was so anxious in this regard that he turned up ready to ride Sir Tatton Sykes himself should Scott's condition threaten a repetition of Derby day. Wasting and drinking were visibly taking their toll of Scott's constitution but somehow he kept body and soul together and won his ninth St Leger by half a length. 'Halfway up the distance,' recorded The Druid, 'Bill fairly dropped forward onto his neck from exhaustion and couldn't drive him at all.' He would not ride in another St Leger and died a fortnight after Surplice defeated his brother's Canezou for the renewal of 1848. Despite his dissipation Scott died a rich man: investments in several collieries had made him worth over £100 000.

Bill Scott's coarseness of character and riding style enabled him to bridge the gap between the jockeys of North and South, whose rivalry had persisted since Chifney Senior first gave the Tykes a glimpse of his exquisite horsemanship at the turn of the century. Northerners empathised with Scott's bluntness and warmed to him. Nat Flatman was a totally different character altogether and despite enjoying extensive patronage from Northern owners he never reached the heights of public adoration colonised by Scott. However stuck-up he may have seemed, Elnathan Flatman was modest, dependable, honest and discreet, a clutch of qualities which, in 1846, made him eminently suitable to become the first officially recognised champion jockey with 81 winners. He retained his title in each of the next six seasons, achieving his highest total of 104 in 1848.

Unlike many of his contemporaries there was nothing ostentatious about Nat Flatman. Remarked The Druid: 'We should call him rather a good jockey by profession, than a great horseman by intuition. He seldom did anything brilliant but his good head and fine patience served him, and he rarely made a mistake as regards measure in the last few strides. A tremendous finish, when a horse had to be ridden home from below the distance, was not his forte; and it put him all aboard if he had to make the running. His thighs were so short that he hadn't sufficient purchase from the knee to use a sluggish horse and if he had a free goer he was a little apt to overdo it.' With his large doe eyes and long broken nose suggesting the visage of a circus clown, Flatman, it must be said, lacked the charisma often associated with a champion sportsman.

Flatman's trump card was his weight: a natural lightweight, he was barely 11lb heavier at 50 than he was at 20. However, this only worked in his favour once he'd carved a reputation, because owners and trainers did not regard 'Tinies' worth the extra lead in the saddlecloth. Flatman received no ride in public until he was 19 and, arguably, his star only began waxing after the filly Pickle had landed an almighty gamble in Ascot's Albany Stakes of 1834. Ascot was a lucky course for Flatman and provided him with nearly 100 winners, a staggering total when one remembers there was only a single fixture each season. In 1845 he won a dozen races and in 1847 he won eleven, for instance, although he won the Gold Cup only once, on Alarm in 1846 when the race was temporarily known as the Emperor's Plate.

Flatman must have harboured mixed emotions concerning Alarm. Prior to that Ascot success, he and the bay son of Venison won the 1845 Cambridgeshire, the first leg of the Autumn Double which Flatman later completed on The Baron in the Cesarewitch, a riding feat duplicated by only three others in 150 years. Five months earlier Alarm had very nearly killed Flatman at the start of the Derby. Another horse attacked Alarm, he threw Flatman and commenced flailing and kicking at anything that moved. Luckily, Flatman ended up in a ditch, bruised but in one piece. Flatman's good fortune at the start of this Derby was only once repeated at the finish. He never passed the post first in either the Derby or Oaks but in 1844 he had ridden Orlando to be a three-quarter-length second to the notorious Running Rein, who was subsequently identified as a four-year-old masquerading as a three-year-old; a month after the race, the 1844 Derby was awarded to Orlando and Flatman.

Nat was associated with a Derby winner of greater renown, however. His Northern affiliations saw him get the ride on Voltigeur in two of racing's most famous encounters. Forty-eight hours after Voltigeur (ridden by Job Marson) had added the St Leger to his victory in the 1850 Derby, Flatman was asked to partner him in the Doncaster Cup against The Flying Dutchman. The four-year-old 'Dutchman' had won all his ten races which included the Derby, St Leger and Ascot Gold Cup. Voltigeur was also unbeaten. Nothing else dared face them. It was said the elder horse had been off his feed, had not been trained seriously for the Cup since no opposition was expected and he had to concede 19lb to Voltigeur. These obstacles may or may not have been insurmountable but the additional handicap imposed by his jockey Charles Marlow in the face of a peerless match-race rider like Flatman eliminated any chance he did hold. By the time Marlow mounted The Dutchman (a 4–1 on favourite) he was as tight as a tick. 'I'll show you what I've got under me today,' he cried, blatantly disobeying his orders to ride a waiting race in favour of setting a lung-bursting gallop. The Dutchman held on for as long as he could but Flatman brought Voltigeur through inside the final furlong to win by half a length.

> *Ye backers of Aske's Voltigeur, boast not too much his strength:*
> *Though The Flying Dutchman lost the race, 'twas but by half a length;*
> *Doubt as ye will, his heart is still as strong as Spanish steel,*
> *And o'er Knavesmire 'gainst that verdict he will enter an appeal.*

The rematch demanded by poet and public alike took place for £1000 a side on Tuesday 13 May 1851 over two miles of the Knavesmire. The Dutchman, declared Admiral Rous, would now concede only 8½lb. On this occasion the betting was even and Flatman, uncharacteristically, made the pace. Moreover, The Dutchman stripped the fitter and Marlow was sober. Strive as he might, Voltigeur could not lose his dark shadow, which came through to win by a length amid a cacophony of sound that would have reduced the walls of Jericho to instant rubble.

Flatman's career was terminated by an horrific injury sustained after he had ridden Golden Pippin in a match at Newmarket on 29 September 1859. As he dismounted, the filly lashed out and struck him a fearful blow in the body. He never really regained his health and died the following August, aged 50. One of his last requests was that he should not be buried in Newmarket cemetery and he was instead laid to rest beneath the tower of All Saints' Church.

Flatman and Robinson may have lacked the sparkle of a Chifney or a Scott but they made far more admirable role models. So developed was Flatman's sense of propriety that he refused either to divulge information arising from trials in which he'd participated or to accept a retainer greater than £50. Times were a-changing; the Jockey Club was asserting itself and the conduct of jockeys came under closer scrutiny than ever before. In 1844 the foul-mouthed and devious Sam Rogers was warned off for three years even though his principal patron was Lord George Bentinck, the most influential and powerful member of the Jockey Club.

Nobody could promote the likes of George Fordham and Fred Archer as plaster saints, but the laurel of champion jockey first worn by the whiter-than-white Nat Flatman was invariably destined to adorn the brow of an individual possessing more than a modicum of integrity.

GEORGE

GEORGE

George Fordham in his pomp must have been a joy to behold. Racing would be a pretty dull affair without opinion, as is reinforced by the age-old debate concerning the best jockey of all time. Posterity's assessment of Fordham the jockey tends to be coloured by the overpowering personality and tragic demise of his arch-rival Fred Archer, yet whatever conclusions are reached by present-day historians, the jockeys and trainers of the Victorian era were of virtually one accord – George Fordham was in a class of his own.

Henry Custance: 'In speaking of one whom I consider all round to be the finest jockey I ever saw or rode against, it is needless for me to say that I refer to my dear old friend George Fordham. It is quite impossible for me to mention all the fine races I have seen him ride.'

John Osborne: 'There's been a lot of good jockeys. Jem Robinson was a good jockey and so was Fred Archer . . . I am inclined to think Fordham was the best; you never quite knew where you had him.'

Tommy Heartfield: 'Archer was a fine horseman, without a doubt, but I should certainly say not in the same class as Fordham. Everybody, when speaking of greatest jockeys, always used to put Fordham in a corner by himself and then they talked about the others. I never knew how he could make horses win races that nobody else could.'

Fordham's standing among his fellow jockeys was complemented within the ranks of the training fraternity.

Charles Morton: 'I think that I would rate him a greater jockey than Archer. Not only was he more skilful but he possessed the greater finishing power and one could count the number of races he threw away on the fingers of one hand.'

Richard Marsh: 'For Fred Archer I had the greatest admiration as well as respect. He had some uncanny means, I thought, of imparting extra vitality to his horses . . . yet, on the whole, I am inclined to name George Fordham as the greatest all-round jockey I have ever known. He was a master in judging pace in a tight fit, and no one knew where the winning post was better than he did.'

Besides Morton and Marsh two other champion trainers in John Porter and Mat Dawson also went on record as believing Fordham to be Archer's superior. 'He had beautiful hands,' said Porter, 'and horses that stronger men could do nothing with went kindly enough for him.' The statistics almost speak for themselves: 16 Classic victories highlighted by a record total of seven in the 1000 Guineas; 14 times champion jockey between 1855 and 1871, a figure second to Richards'; a seasonal record of 166 winners in 1862; 2587 winners altogether, placing him ninth on the all-time list and second only to Archer during the 19th century; six winners (from seven rides) on one card, at Stockbridge on 18 June 1867, a feat in this country beyond every Flat jockey except Archer, Richards, Alec Russell and Willie

Previous page: 'The Demon'. George Fordham, by common consent the greatest jockey of the Victorian era.

GEORGE

Carson. Fordham dead-heated in his seventh ride and lost the run-off.
The final word might rest with Mat Dawson, the man largely
responsible for Archer's own success: 'Undoubtedly, George Fordham
was the best of the jockeys that have come within my knowledge.'

Even Archer himself confessed a grudging respect for the one man
(whose photograph flanked his fireplace) he could never quite fathom
on the racetrack. 'Fordham was cluck-clucking at his mount for the
whole of the race. I thought I had him beaten two or three times in
the two miles. But with his infernal cluck-clucking he was always
coming again. Still 200 yards from home I supposed I had him dead
settled. I'll cluck-cluck you, I thought – and at that moment he
swoops down on me and beats me easily.' Fordham continued to
exasperate Archer right to the bitter end. In his last full season of
1883 Fordham rode just 77 winners to Archer's record 232 but the
veteran kept rubbing his junior's nose in the mire. On 10 May Archer
was engaged to ride Reputation in a match over five furlongs against
Brag, partnered by Fordham. 'That old devil always terrifies me in
matches at Newmarket,' Archer told the Duke of Portland. 'Nobody
knows what he's up to. They're about right when they call him the
"Old Demon".' Archer had already lost one match to Fordham that
week and was determined to set matters right. 'Mind the old man
don't do you again,' some mischief-maker jeered as he came out onto
the course. 'I will be halfway home this time before the old
gentleman knows where he is,' retorted Archer. Unfortunately for
Archer this barb was reported to Fordham, who quietly set about
making an utter fool of him. He duped Archer into thinking he had
stolen an advantage at the start and could afford to show his hand.
Reputation was giving a stone to Brag and ought, by rights, to have
been conserved for one short run at the death. Fordham waited for
Archer's horse to blow up and then produced Brag to win by a neck.
The humiliation was too much for Archer. He stormed into the
weighing room and slung his saddle at his valet William Bartholomew
(known as 'Solomon') saying: 'I can't beat that kidding bastard!'

Fordham took immense delight in 'kidding' whether he was riding
against Archer or young greenhorns. Races still tended to be run in
snatches with the pace only quickening towards the finish; at this
crucial stage Fordham would feign distress and 'cluck' at his horse,
encouraging the unwary to make their efforts prematurely. Then, just
as the victim sensed triumph, Fordham would pounce, to the
amusement and financial gain of his countless supporters who,
understandably, christened him 'The Kidder' and 'The Demon'.
'Archer would win races with 10lb in hand and make it appear that he
had got 21lb in hand,' insisted Heartfield. 'Fordham would win a race
with 10lb in hand and make it appear he had got home by the skin of
his teeth. Old Fordham was a man to sit and nurse 'em; yet he was a
powerful jockey at the same time.' Richard Marsh concurred: 'He

would win a race by a head and carry 7lb more on the same horse and still win. You never knew after years of careful observation what he had in hand.' Fordham's was a totally instinctive genius which he was incapable of explaining. 'Well, don't you see, I just went up and, er, don't you know, I, er, just managed to win,' was all trainers ever elicited from him.

Although horses were still subjected to severe punishment from whip and spur, Fordham frequently rode with neither. To the apprentice mounting Don Juan prior to the 1883 Cesarewitch he said: 'Dear me, what a pretty whip that is, my boy, but what a pity it is that these pretty things lose so many races. Don't you think that you had better leave it behind?' – whereupon he placed it in his pocket and walked away. Don Juan proceeded to oblige. Fordham's reluctance to strike a horse (except in the last few strides), his judgement of pace and lightness of touch combined to make him the ideal partner for a two-year-old. 'When I get down to the post on these two-year-olds and I feel their little hearts beating under my legs I think, why not let them have an easy race, win if they can but don't frighten them.' This humanitarian philosophy found especial favour with fillies, as is evidenced by the female of the species providing Fordham with 13 of his 16 Classic victories.

Much of Fordham's deception resulted from his rather ungainly seat. He used very short leathers and leant forward in the saddle with his shoulders hunched above the horse's withers, onto which he directed his weight; his body eventually slewed round until it was almost sideways. Or as John Osborne put it: 'He used to get all out of a horse. Archer and Fordham had two different styles altogether – as different as possible. Fordham rode short and Archer long. Fordham rode more with his hands than Archer. Fordham didn't punish his horse so much and you never knew you were done with Fordham until you got past the post.' However unattractive Fordham's premature version of the 20th-century 'crouch' may have appeared, John Porter believed the Fordham style to be 'the happy medium . . . that should be taught and encouraged. The position enabled him to drop into the saddle and control a horse when in difficulties and drive him straight home at the finish of a race.'

By these velvet subtleties Fordham developed powers of conveying human will to the equine, which became the envy of all. One example from 1866 may here suffice. Mr James Merry's two-year-old colt Marksman was generally regarded as a bit of a rogue. In Goodwood's Findon Stakes he ran unplaced behind Friponnier and Bismarck, to whom he was trying to give 5lb. Fordham watched the race and was so convinced Marksman had not shown anything like his best form that he urged Merry to run the colt in the Molecomb Stakes the following day and to put him up. Merry was not keen on the idea. Marksman would meet Bismarck at exactly the same weights

Tom French, destined for a short life only, who showed Fordham a clear pair of heels in the 1870 Derby.

and risk another spirit-sapping ordeal. Fordham persisted and at length was allowed to have his way. Odds of 5–4 were laid on Bismarck, while 5–1 was obtainable about Marksman. The tables were completely turned. Marksman won in a canter. 'There, that'll give him confidence,' said The Demon. Marksman won twice more that season and in 1867 was only beaten a neck in the Derby.

Fordham did not ride Marksman in that Derby. Instead he partnered the 6–4 favourite Vauban (on whom he'd won the 2000 Guineas), who finished third. Fordham could not match Archer's success in the Derby: he was unplaced on the 4–1 favourite Tournament at his first stab in 1857, and in 22 attempts he only won the race once. One possible explanation of this moderate record is that he hated taking the kind of risk which so often proved necessary during the hectic descent of Tattenham Hill. The course itself posed no problems. After all, he did win five races for the Oaks but the pace, number and generally poorer quality of the runners in the fillies' Classic seldom generated the tense hurly-burly of a Derby. Fordham's solution was to avoid trouble down the Hill by going clear in the hope of keeping something up his sleeve for a successful exhibition of 'kidding' in the later stages – no simple ruse to execute in a Derby. It failed on Vauban (although to be fair to Fordham, the horse's stilty forelegs were ill-adapted to the undulating track) who tired a furlong out, as it had on another warm favourite, Lord Clifden, four years previously. 'No one but me knows how good this horse is,' the normally reticent Fordham had observed beforehand.

There were no less than 34 false starts before the 1863 field was permitted on its way in appallingly wet weather, but Fordham soon held a handy position and led Macaroni into the straight. Unforgivably Fordham made that most elementary of errors: he looked round for signs of danger. Macaroni's jockey was Tom Chaloner, no mean exponent himself of the wiles of jockeyship. He and Macaroni had won the 2000 Guineas and now they seized their chance to win a Derby. Lord Clifden's narrow advantage diminished as Fordham, awakened to the threat, transferred his whip from one hand to the other. The favourite faltered once, then, sensationally, once again as he trod on a piece of orange peel and Chaloner forced Macaroni up to win by a head. The judge said the only difference between them was that Lord Clifden's head was down and Macaroni's up as they flashed past the post. Fordham was inconsolable. He had arranged to dine that evening with friends at Carshalton. On the way over he and his companion were assailed by Oldaker, the Clerk of the Course at Harpenden, who called out that he had lost heavily on the Derby thanks to the jockey pulling the favourite. Fordham's temper, usually so even, finally snapped. He vaulted from his hack and set about his accuser with his whip. On arrival at Carshalton he could not be persuaded to enter the dining room and, refusing all

Fordham's only Derby success in 22 attempts – Sir Bevys, one of his worst ever mounts.

offers of food and drink, he just sat outside on the stairs sobbing his heart out.

Fordham's Epsom torment scarcely abated. The year after Vauban's defeat, he was up on a fourth favourite in the shape of Lady Elizabeth, who had won a dozen races for him as a two-year-old. But she was now a spent force and never looked like winning. The worst blow of all occurred in 1870. Merry's brilliant colt Macgregor had spreadeagled his opponents in the 2000 Guineas when ridden by John Daley. A raging favourite for the Derby at 9–4 on (the shortest odds in the race's 90-year history), here at last was a horse that seemed destined to change Fordham's luck. Macgregor's legs, however, were not his strongest points: he had not run as a two-year-old partly due to a weakness in the suspensory ligament of his off-fore. On the morning of the Derby Fordham and Tom French, the rider of the Guineas third Kingcraft, went for a stroll. French spotted a horseshoe, picked it up and tossed it over his shoulder, exclaiming, 'George, I shall beat you today!' In the weighing room before the signal to mount, Fordham looked pale and sat nervously biting his nails. 'You never know; there's no such thing as a certainty,' he mumbled to well-wishers. Indeed, there isn't and wasn't. Fordham was hard at work on the favourite a long way from home and could only finish fourth to Kingcraft and the omniscient French.

It was thus somewhat ironic that Fordham should win his single Blue Riband on one of the worst horses he ever rode in the race. Sir Bevys had little to commend him for the 1879 Derby. He was a smallish dark-brown son of the 1871 Derby winner Favonius out of a stoutly bred mare; not unexpectedly, therefore, he struggled to break his maiden as a juvenile. However, a trial over 1½ miles shortly before the Derby, in which he gave 18lb and a beating to decent middle-distance handicappers, provided his owner Baron Lionel de Rothschild (who ran his horses in the *nom de course* of 'Mr Acton') with some crumbs of hope. Extremely heavy conditions further boosted the 20–1 shot's chances of making his stamina pay dividends. Fordham skilfully avoided the more treacherous ground and with the first two in the Guineas, Charibert and Cadogan, all at sea, the rank outsiders Palmbearer and Visconti chased Sir Bevys across the line. Few people admitted to backing the winner but one who did so was Poet Laureate Alfred Tennyson who had a bet of £100 to £5 because, he explained, 'Sir Bevys was the hero of one of my early poems'.

Fordham's miserable Derby experiences were positively upbeat in comparison to his fortunes in the St Leger: 22 appearances, three seconds, two thirds and no victory at all. In 1862 he was beaten a head on the 3–1 favourite Buckstone, but the bitterest pill to swallow came in 1868. Fordham had won three Classics on the wonderful filly Formosa – the 2000 Guineas (a dead heat), 1000 Guineas (by three lengths) and the Oaks (by ten) – but just before the St Leger she went amiss and he begged off her to ride Paul Jones. Inside the last 100 yards Formosa cruised past Paul Jones to win by two lengths. Although Fordham had 11 more cracks at the Leger, the neck defeat of Martyrdom one year after his rejection of Formosa was the closest he ever came to victory.

Fordham's career can roughly be divided into two parts: pre-Archer and post-Archer. All Fordham's championships and two-thirds of his Classics came before Archer opened his own accounts in 1874. The years of virtually unchallenged supremacy were over, and the latter period, punctuated by temporary retirement in 1876 and 1877, was one lit up by a simmering rivalry with Archer which often boiled over into open conflict.

George Fordham was born in Cambridge on 24 September 1837 and at the age of ten he was sent to the stables of Dick Drewitt in Middleham, where his uncle was travelling head-lad. Drewitt moved to Lewes and Fordham had his first ride at Brighton on 24 October 1850 on his master's Isabella. He weighed 3st 8lb which was increased to the necessary 5 stone with heavy clothing and a large saddle; the future 'Demon' trailed in last. However, at the equivalent Brighton meeting of 1851 the 14-year-old Fordham gained his first success, on Hampton in the Trial Stakes for two-year-olds on 9 October. Soon afterwards an accident befell Fordham which nearly cost him his life and certainly scarred him for life. Miss Nippet, a horse he was exercising in Drewitt's strawyard, threw him and his foot slipped through the iron, suspending him by the knee. The filly panicked and dragged the defenceless youth round the yard, trying to kick him as she went. Fordham sported an enlarged knee joint until his dying day, but perhaps more importantly, this sickening experience may have undermined his confidence and led to his safety-first policy around Epsom.

The following year welcomed Fordham's first major success: the Cambridgeshire on Little David. The horse started at 33–1 and ran into Newmarket before its tiny pilot (still only 3st 12lb) could pull it up. Little David was owned by a Mr W. Smith who, it was said, only read three books in his life – the Holy Bible, the Sporting Calendar and the Duke of Wellington's Despatches. Smith presented his jockey with a Bible and a gold-headed whip inscribed 'Honesty is the best policy'. Fordham went from strength to strength and in 1854 won another prestigious handicap, the Chester Cup, on Epaminondas. His mounts quickly became popular with punters: Army officers about to embark on foreign service, for example, were wont to leave commissions to back every horse he rode for a tenner. They were well advised to do so. In 1855 Fordham became champion jockey at the age of 18 with 70 winners.

Another fan of Fordham's was the wealthy American Richard Ten Broeck who had recently shipped a string to England. In the 1857

Cesarewitch Ten Broeck's Prioress was involved in a triple dead-heat. Her American jockey Tankerley carried the can and was replaced by Fordham in the run-off which Prioress duly won. The association blossomed. Not that it was all plain sailing. One day at Newmarket Fordham was caught napping on Amy, the medium of a spectacular Ten Broeck wager. Fordham's gloom plumbed the depths reached on the night of Lord Clifden's Derby. Ten Broeck wrote his jockey a kindly letter, however, telling him to put this solitary mistake out of his mind as he was certain he had won him a great many races he ought not to have done.

The season of 1859 was a significant one for Fordham since it heralded his initial Classic success. He won the 1000 Guineas on Mr William Stirling-Crawfurd's Mayonaise before switching to Lord Londesborough's Summerside to land the Oaks. The pick of the many fillies Fordham rode to victory in Classics were Formosa and Stirling-Crawfurd's Thebais, on whom he achieved the 1000 Guineas–Oaks double in 1881. Meanwhile Fordham gained compensation for his lack of success in the Derby by twice winning the French equivalent, on Gabrielle d'Estrees (1861) and Suzerain (1868); he also won the 1880 French Oaks on Versigny. At this time, though, the Grand Prix de Paris outranked every race in France and Fordham recorded a hat-trick of wins via Fervacques (1867), The Earl (1868) and Foxhall (1881). The last named belonged to another American, James Keene, and was rated the best three-year-old of his generation, but his chances of proving the point were dashed by his not being entered for the Classics. Consequently, the Grand Prix was Foxhall's heaven-sent opportunity to show his class. Fordham was engaged. Their principal adversary was the English colt Tristan (later to be the last of Fordham's five Ascot Gold Cup winners) with Archer up. The distance of 1 mile 7 furlongs was a tough examination for a three-year-old in June but Fordham elected to make the running; Foxhall had plenty of stamina and guts. He needed plenty of both, because Archer brought Tristan with a determined challenge inside the last 50 yards. To no avail – Foxhall and Fordham held on by a short head.

No champion concedes his title without a struggle and Fordham was not about to accept lightly the loss of his crown in 1874. The Ascot meeting of 1875 witnessed an early skirmish between him and Archer. In the Ascot Derby, Archer rode the 1000 Guineas and Oaks winner Spinaway while Fordham was up on Gilbert, a horse that required a lead. 'The Kidder' went straight to the head of affairs, dictated the pace for a while and then dropped away as if beaten. Archer went on, exactly as Fordham wished; Gilbert perked up with someone to follow and, catching hold of his bit, ran on once more to catch and finally beat Spinaway by three parts of a length. Archer was not amused.

During Fordham's two-year absence Archer quickly grew

GEORGE

'I do not think Archer will
ever take a liberty with
George again.'

accustomed to getting his own way. Other jockeys became frightened
by his intimidatory tactics. Not Fordham. Memories of all the old
duels were rekindled when 'The Demon' made his comeback on a
horse trained by Tom Jennings called Pardon, in the Bushes Handicap
at Newmarket on 23 April 1878. To avoid the ballyhoo, a nervous
Fordham obtained permission to mount Pardon down the course.
Though Custance kept him company Fordham's resolve gradually
began to weaken. 'Cus, I wish I hadn't got up,' he moaned. 'Look at
these kids; I don't know one of them.' Custance tried to lift his
friend's spirits: 'My dear George, don't you trouble about that; they
will soon know you when you get upside of them, especially at the
finish.' The one jockey Fordham did know, of course, was Archer,
and it was he who won the race – by three lengths from Fordham. It
struck Custance that Fordham had not overexerted himself, which he
attributed to his being weak and out of condition but he questioned
him about it all the same. Fordham's reply spoke volumes: 'You don't
think I was going to let him beat me a neck the first time I rode,
which he would have just done.' 'The Kidder' was back all right.
Custance hurriedly sought out Jennings to report this conversation
and persuade him to run Pardon in the Bretby Plate later in the
afternoon. The trainer agreed; Pardon won. 'I never heard anyone
receive a greater ovation than George Fordham did on his return to
weigh in that day,' wrote Custance.

The fur soon began to fly again. At the start of the Royal Hunt

Cup Archer began badgering Fordham. 'The Demon' waited for the flow of invective to subside before quietly hissing, 'You have taken a liberty with me, Mister Archer, and I will teach you to act differently. I may not do it now; I shall probably wait till you are on something that you fancy yourself about; you must not take a liberty with George.' The moment arrived, as Fordham knew it must. Archer was riding Silvio, one of his Derby winners, in a race where Fordham made the running. Eventually Archer decided to move. 'Pull out! Pull aside!' he bellowed. Fordham did nothing of the kind. Archer then attempted to come round, so Fordham did pull out. 'I thought I saw some better ground in the middle of the course and made for it,' he afterwards explained innocently. In all that he did there was not the slightest room for objection and yet he had most assuredly prevented Archer from winning. Never was Archer so thoroughly paid with his own coin. 'I do not think Archer will ever take a liberty with George again,' said Fordham.

Whatever malevolence Fordham displayed in his harsh treatment of Fred Archer, he possessed many appealing characteristics as a man, not least of which was his kind-hearted nature. During Goodwood week, for instance, there was nothing he loved more than arranging races for the children at East Dean and distributing half-crowns to not only the winners but also to every other competitor. On another occasion, after he had lost a small race by a head to a horse owned by the widow of his old guv'nor Dick Drewitt, he turned to Sir John Astley and said: 'Well, you know, Sir John, Mrs Drewitt has not been able to pay her rent and all through the race I could not help thinking of that damned rent, and you know, I ought just to have won.'

Apart from this unique instance Fordham's honesty was unimpeachable. When he learnt that the Woodyates trainer William Day, as a means of placating the owner, had cast aspersions on the way he had ridden The Happy Land in the 1858 2000 Guineas, Fordham – still only 20 – reported Day to the Stewards of the Jockey Club and refused to ride for him ever again. Captain James Machell was another who lived to regret making a similar insinuation. He greatly admired Fordham and put him up whenever he could get him. One afternoon he had a huge gamble in a seller, against the wishes of Fordham who told him that the horse was not good enough. The horse drifted in the betting and was easily beaten, prompting Machell to misguidedly accuse Fordham of not trying. Fordham immediately severed their relationship. 'That damned horse,' a repentant Machell later admitted, 'was no good and I lost the best jockey in the world.' In fact, Fordham would ride against his own money if need be. Custance records a match at Newmarket in which he rode Trovatore (4–1 on) against Fordham on Lady Peel. 'I have told a friend of mine to win a bit on yours,' said Fordham going to post. And yet, in a cliffhanger finish, Lady Peel beat the favourite by a short head. 'Nor do I think I ever saw Fordham more pleased with himself although he had lost £20 by winning,' said Custance.

Fordham's reputation also survived the notorious 'Spider and Fly' scandal of 1868. The previous season Fordham had exercised his genius with two-year-olds to register 12 wins from 13 starts on Lady Elizabeth. The liaison between the flighty filly and the sympathetic horseman seemed one made in heaven. However, this purity needed to withstand the shadiest possible influences because Lady Elizabeth was trained at Danebury by the devious John Day Junior (brother of William and son of John Barham) for Henry, 4th Marquis of Hastings, whose reckless gambling had seen him fall under the spell of the infamous moneylender Henry Padwick. By 1867 Hastings' health and fortunes had begun to nosedive, and despite Lady Elizabeth's herculean efforts he was heavily in debt and looking far older than his 25 years. He sold all his horses except the filly and The Earl, a decent but backward colt who had nevertheless won four times as a two-year-old. Hastings' immediate rescue depended upon Padwick; his ultimate salvation lay in Lady Elizabeth winning the Derby. But the filly wintered badly. Her arduous juvenile campaign, concluded by a short-head victory over the three-year-old Julius in a £1000-a-side match, had broken her. She grew nervous and irritable. She had been backed to win so much money in the Derby that Day was afraid to try her and confirm his worst fears. A stream of fictitious reports from Danebury as to her continued prowess saw her line up for the Derby as the 7–4 favourite. On a warm afternoon she sweated profusely and even tried to buck Fordham off. In the race, won by Blue Gown, she was never seen with a chance.

Ten days later Fordham won the Grand Prix de Paris on The Earl, which really put the cat among the pigeons. He had beaten Blue Gown earlier in the season yet Padwick had persuaded Hastings to scratch him from the Derby at the eleventh hour. Admiral Rous, racing's unofficial conscience, reacted angrily. In a letter to *The Times* he maintained Day and Padwick knew in March that Lady Elizabeth had lost her form. 'Lord Hastings has been shamefully deceived . . . I state that he stood to win £35 000 by The Earl and did not hedge his stake money. Then you will ask, "Why did he scratch him?" What can the poor fly demand from the spider in whose web he is enveloped?' Hastings strongly refuted any suggestion that he had been duped and the 'Spider', Padwick, and Day instituted libel suits against Rous. The case never came to court. Lady Elizabeth never won another race; The Earl broke down and missed the St Leger; Hastings was dead within six months. The taint of corruption never left Day. Only Fordham walked away without a stain on his character.

Fordham was far too unsophisticated to become an active party in a carefully planned deception. His was a rough and ready, take-it-or-leave-it code of conduct. He spoke as he found. When the Duchess of

Montrose, who changed her jockeys with unfailing regularity, dismissed him, he quickly informed the *Pink 'Un* newspaper which reported cryptically, 'The Duchess of Montrose has requested Fordham to send in his cap and jacket. He did so instantly, for fear the Duchess might change her mind.' Yet Fordham was devoutly loyal to his owners and never discussed with one owner the horses of another.

Meanness was another human frailty Fordham had no time for. The only thanks he got from one miserly owner after winning a valuable race was £5. Once again Fordham awaited an opportunity to repay this injustice. Eventually he beat a horse belonging to this skinflint by a short head. As he came back to unsaddle, he said in a voice loud enough for his victim to hear, 'Look sharp – I think I am a bit short of weight.' The owner swallowed the bait and rushed gleefully into the weighing room only to have the chagrin of seeing Fordham pass correctly. 'Quits,' said the smiling jockey. As it happened, Fordham had little regard for money: at one time he was offered and refused a retainer of £1500 a year.

Fordham eschewed the high life that surrounded racing. In winter he was a devotee of the hunting field and he was an exceptionally able shot, while of an evening there was nothing he enjoyed more than whist, at which he was an expert. Racing rarely entered his conversation and he refused to let his son have anything to do with the sport. Practical jokes were more his cup of tea, especially whenever he stayed with the Brighton vet John Mannington for the races. One year the local riding school had just hired a new riding-master, who was considered a bit above himself. Mannington and Fordham decided to bring him down a peg or two and it was arranged that Fordham should enroll as a pupil. He was seated on a pony and, much to the riding-master's disgust, adopted every conceivable position he was expressly told to avoid. At last the instructor got Fordham to sit fairly straight so that he could trot up and down the school. 'Well, I think you have done enough for today,' the beetroot-faced tutor said patronisingly. 'You can tell your papa if you get on as well tomorrow as you have done today, you will be able to go out with the other pupils on Thursday on the cliff.' Needless to say, Fordham did not return and much laughter ensued at the riding-master's expense.

Fordham's other willing ally was Custance, who once extricated him from a tricky situation in a game of cricket. Fordham had agreed to a single-wicket match with a bookmaker called Jackson for £5, he to play with a bat and Jackson to use a broomstick. However, the bookie produced a flattened hedge-stake with which he proceeded to strike Fordham's bowling all round the playing area. Defeat and the loss of the bet were imminent. Presently Jackson hit the ball right out of the ground into an adjacent orchard. 'Now, my boys,' said

Fordham to the crowd of small admirers watching the game, 'if you find the ball I will give you five shillings.' Custance assured him it was safe to offer them ten; the missing object was now in his pocket. With the ball lost, the match was declared a draw and the bookmaker was thwarted.

Fordham was himself the hapless victim on a visit to Paris. He went into a hairdresser's where, being unable to speak the language, he gesticulated his desire for a haircut. The coiffeur took him at his word – or lack of them – and left his head as bare as a cannon ball. On returning to Newmarket Fordham had to endure the numerous taunts of his friends eager to know from which gaol he had just escaped.

Fordham's major failing – one shared with so many of his contemporaries – was drink. Before the 1872 City & Suburban at Epsom, Henry Woolcott, the trainer of Fordham's mount Digby Grand, entered the paddock carrying a bottle of port with which he hoped to stimulate the animal's somewhat faint-hearted racing instincts. Fordham insisted he test the vintage first and took a swig; Woolcott followed suit. The dregs, contended the jockey, were so minimal as to make no difference to the horse, so he polished off the bottle himself. Climbing aboard Digby Grand he went out and won

John Wells, already champion jockey at the age of 19, aboard his first Classic winner Virago, in the opinion of many judges the finest filly of the 19th century.

the race. But by 1875 things had begun to get out of hand. Fordham was a tired man. He had accumulated enough money – why not retire and enjoy life a little? Without more ado he went home to Slough and the comfort of dry gin.

It is a curious paradox that some Victorian jockeys did not eat enough while others drank too much. Perhaps an excess of the latter compensated for deficiency in the former. Fordham, however, was not a patch on Jem Snowden, who succeeded Bill Scott as the North's champion tippler. Snowden vowed he would willingly give £5000 to be able to stop drinking but many Northern trainers swore he was better value drunk than most riders were stone-cold sober. William l'Anson, the Malton trainer for whom Snowden won the 1864 Derby and St Leger on Blair Athol and the 1880 Oaks on Jenny Howlett, rated him the best jockey he ever saw. But Snowden's legs were hollow and when he hit the bottle hard he clearly aspired to Oscar Wilde's dictum, 'Work is the curse of the drinking classes,' and just didn't ride at all. He once turned up a week late for Chester races, remarking: 'Things seem quiet for race time.' On being put right, he shouted incredulously, 'Then where the hell have I been for seven days?' In his cups Snowden often displayed a waggish line in humour, delivered in a rich Yorkshire accent. Due to partner a good old plater named Aragon at Catterick he tottered into the paddock quite the worse for wear to find the horse being fitted with hood and blinkers. 'Naa, naa, tak it away,' he implored, 'bleend horse and bleend jockey winnet dee.' All the paraphernalia was removed forthwith and Aragon won his race. Snowden died flat broke at the age of 45.

If alcohol did not destroy the Victorian jockey he was often driven to an early grave by the unremitting struggle to satisfy the low weights still in vogue. For instance, in the year of Fordham's first 'retirement' the winner of the Royal Hunt Cup carried 7st 4lb, the Lincoln and Cesarewitch 6 stone and the Cambridgeshire 5st 13lb. Tom Chaloner succumbed at the age of 47; the unscrupulous John Charlton, who achieved everlasting notoriety by pulling the Derby and Oaks heroine Blink Bonny in the 1857 St Leger, was 33 when he died of consumption in 1862; Tom French, Archer's predecessor as first jockey to Mat Dawson, also indulged in constant wasting that ultimately precipitated the onset of consumption which killed him, aged 29. All these three won Classic races but none of them was ever champion jockey. John Wells, on the other hand, won eight Classics and was twice champion (1853–4) before wasting caught up with him in 1873 at the age of 39.

The sheer tragedy of Wells' case can be gauged from the fact that at the commencement of his colourful career he was nicknamed 'Tiny', and he could still do 6 stone during his first championship season. Although Fordham supplanted him as champion jockey, Wells continued to be in demand and he celebrated a lucrative collaboration with Sir Joseph Hawley's animals by winning the 1858 2000 Guineas on Fitzroland and the Derby on Beadsman. In 1859 he won Sir Joseph another Derby on Musjid: 'Not one jockey out of 50 who cared a straw for his life would have dashed through the mob of horses that shut him in as he did,' declared one observer of the ugly finish to the race. Hawley never paid Wells much of a retainer but he always looked after him with presents. When Wells won him a third Derby on Blue Gown (1868) the baronet gave the entire stakes of £6800 to his jockey.

Custance's description of 'Brusher' Wells, as he eventually became known, ran thus: 'I think Wells was the tallest and biggest man I ever saw ride 8st 7lb. He was an extraordinarily good pedestrian and would bet that he walked eleven miles in two hours with four suits of sweaters on. He was a very strong man on a horse and used to lap his long legs round them at the finish. He always sat well back in his saddle, kept fast hold of the horse's head, and was a very resolute finisher. Take him altogether I think he was a good jockey.'

Blue Gown's trainer, John Porter, trusted Wells implicitly – 'there was not sufficient money in the Bank of England to bribe him to ride a crooked race' – but the jockey fell foul of both trainer and patron as a result of his unavailing effort to 'do' 8st 10lb on Blue Gown in the 1867 Champagne Stakes. In order to lose some pounds Wells marched off to see friends who lived in a village four miles out of Doncaster. Instead of returning immediately, however, he was talked into staying the night and sat up into the small hours playing a convivial game of cards. His chances of making the weight were blown sky high. Hawley was a tetchy character and Wells could ill afford to displease him by declaring overweight, so he committed the cardinal sin of touching the floor with his toes to prevent the weights rising. After Blue Gown had won his race Wells was not so lucky. John Doyle, a jockey with a score to settle, had spotted this old dodge and, following him back to the scales, saw Wells attempt to complete the deception by dropping a small saddle cloth prior to weighing in. Doyle waited till Wells sat in the chair and then made a great play of handing over the errant cloth: 'Here! You weighed out with this, so you must weigh in with it.' Wells was a good 6lb overweight. Now his ordeal really began. 'Get out! I'm ashamed of you,' roared Admiral Rous, sending the cringing jockey on his way with a cuff to the back of the head. Sir Joseph's response was also unequivocal: Wells did not wear his colours again for over a month. 'I got more weight off during the 20 minutes I was in that room than I did in the course of any walk I ever took,' confessed Wells after his carpeting by Hawley.

'Brusher' had developed into quite a character, particularly with regard to his dress. Custance recalled him exercising Hawley's Pero Gomez before the 1869 St Leger wearing an Alpine hat with several

Opposite: Wells in the colours of Sir Joseph Hawley which he wore successfully in five Classics. The confident look is typical of the man.

GEORGE

GREAT JOCKEYS OF THE FLAT 73

feathers, a suit made from Gordon tartan and a pair of red morocco slippers. 'Everyone roared with laughter. Wells, however, didn't mind a bit . . . I asked him where his hat came from. He turned round and said, "You would like to know, wouldn't you, so that you could get one like it." I answered: "If I did, I would be complete and get a monkey and an organ with it." ' Wells' usual riposte to such jibes was to quip: 'My tailor makes my clothes for nothing. It is not often he comes across a figure like mine to fit them on.' None of this vanity bothered Hawley. 'I don't care how he dresses; he is a good enough jockey for me.' The 1869 St Leger was the last great day for Wells. His life was being slowly sacrificed to wasting and he only had four more years to live. He had been careful with his money, investing some of his savings in a steel pen factory which ensured his parents were generously provided for after his death.

George Fordham's investments in foreign stock, by contrast, landed him in dire financial straits. He sought deeper refuge in the gin bottle and was in a sorry state when Sir George Chetwynd visited him in the winter of 1877–8. 'What do you want to go on like this for? You are not an old man,' he railed. 'Why not come back and ride again?' Replied The Demon: 'Me? Why, if I tried to sit on a horse now I would fall off.' Chetwynd persisted and finally Fordham was browbeaten into staying with Henry Woolcott at Beckhampton where he could 'dry out' and regain fitness on the gallops. The ploy worked and led to that highly-charged reappearance at Newmarket in April

The nadir of Fordham's Derby fortunes as his mount, the 9–4 on favourite Macgregor, can only finish fourth behind Kingcraft and Tom French in 1870.

1878 with Fordham riding 10lb lighter than when he had departed the stage. Commented The Druid: 'Fancy, Fordham, with all his knowledge and experience and able to ride at 7st 5lb; it seems like a gift from heaven.' The 'gift' lasted until Fordham carried his racing saddle into the weighing room at Windsor after riding Aladdin into fourth place in the Park Plate on 14 August 1884 – six days after his only other ride of the season had run unplaced at Lewes. The Demon's fire had been extinguished for good. During this Indian summer of six seasons Fordham added a further 482 winners to his tally, including five more Classics – notably, of course, his solitary Derby on Sir Bevys. It might have been six because he had originally agreed to ride Scot Free, who easily won the 1884 2000 Guineas, until finally deciding he was no longer up to the task.

However, the magic had persisted throughout the last full season of 1883 when he won the 1000 Guineas on Hauteur and the Ascot Gold Cup on Tristan – not to mention the humiliation of Archer in the Brag–Reputation match. Perhaps the truest exhibition of vintage Fordham came in the Jockey Club Cup at the Houghton Meeting. Charles Morton called Fordham's victory on Ladislas 'the finest horsemanship I have ever seen. He had been riding for fully 30 years but he still remained the incomparable master of his craft. The people who were present at Newmarket on that occasion witnessed an epic battle they never forgot to their dying day.' Fordham and Ladislas had three opponents: Corrie Roy (Charlie Wood), winner of the race in 1881 and the 5–2 on favourite; the St Leger-winning filly Dutch Oven, partnered by Archer; and Faugh-a-Ballagh (Fred Webb), winner of the Alexandra Plate at Royal Ascot. 'Fordham on Ladislas gave them something to remember. He dropped down on Charlie Wood in the last 50 yards and beat him a head amid a turmoil of excitement. The redoubtable Charles, never at a loss on such occasions, remarked to me after the race: "What do you think of that? You never know where he is on the course. He ought to be somewhere else," mentioning a place slightly warmer than Newmarket.'

With the relish of a master torturer Fordham's final winner was at the expense of Archer in the Brighton Cup on 31 October. He and his trusty confederate Brag beat Archer and the odds-on favourite Geheimniss by five lengths. Fordham died at Slough on 12 October 1887, a fortnight after his 50th birthday. His lungs had taken too much of a pasting. It was said of him that he made just two mistakes in his life – looking round in Lord Clifden's Derby and heeding the advice of a French financier. Little was made of a single fact which clearly showed his enviable wisdom, namely that he steadfastly refused ever to vote in any parliamentary election. He was laid to rest in the churchyard of St Laurence at Upton, Slough. The silver plate on his coffin said all that needed to be said: ' 'Tis the pace that kills.'

FRED

FRED

Fred Archer rode like a man possessed; if Fordham had genius in his hands, Archer had the devil at his elbow. Whether or not a Faustian deal had been struck will never be known but on 8 November 1886 any such dues were paid in full when Archer was driven to placing the barrel of a revolver into his mouth and pulling the trigger. He was 29 years old; he had ridden 2748 winners (including 21 Classics) from 8004 mounts for an unapproachable winning percentage of 34.3, and won 13 jockeys' championships, eight of them with totals exceeding 200, including as many as 246 in 1885.

The last of Archer's Classic victories was gained on Ormonde, whose trainer John Porter has left the following thumb-nail sketch of the jockey's character: 'His whole heart and soul were in the business he had in hand. He was almost invariably the first to weigh out, the first at the starting post, the first away when the flag fell, and, as the record shows, very often the first to pass the winning post. I am afraid he was not too scrupulous. Very masterful, he generally had pretty much his own way, especially in minor races. If he did not want a horse to run, he never hesitated to suggest to the owner that he should keep the animal in the stable that day. In short, Fred Archer was a powerful personality as well as a brilliantly successful jockey.'

Porter's last sentence strikes at the quick of the Fred Archer story. He outgrew his profession. On the occasion of his first visit to Thirsk racecourse in 1884, for instance, his safe arrival was announced in the market place by the town crier.

> 'Gentlemen! This is to give notice that F Archer, the celebrated horseman, has arrived in this town, and that he will ride the winner of the Foal Stakes. Gentlemen! Come and see the wonder of the world. God Save the Queen.'

Archer won the race, naturally. The news of his death was felt far beyond the narrow confines of racing. In London, special editions of the evening papers were issued; crowds thronged Fleet Street to buy them and omnibuses stopped to allow passengers to read the billboards. So anxious were Victorian commuters to obtain copies that silver coins were being given for the sheets as fast as the paper lads could extricate them from the bundles.

> Fred Archer's dead. The words ring out
> O'er verdant plain and valley wide,
> And ears distended hear with doubt
> The news that he no more will ride.
> His last race done he sleeps in peace,
> And what may now his requiem be,
> When all his efforts sadly cease?
> He rode right well and gallantly.

Previous page: Archer on Ormonde, arguably the best horse he ever rode, though not according to Archer himself. Yet had it not been for his love of 'the tin' Archer might have ridden the colt in the 2000 Guineas and thus won a Triple Crown, the only riding honour to elude him.

In tram or train Archer's death was the sole topic of conversation. No greater interest could have been aroused had he been the Prime Minister or a member of the Royal family. Indeed, if truth be told, in life he had frequently been treated as such. Once, at Ascot, the special first-class train was waiting at the platform ready to pull out, bursting with dukes, lords, MPs and the elite of society all impatient to get underway. Why was the train being held? For Mr Archer, of course. When he took his seat in a theatre, 'No king could have had a greater reception,' according to the Hon John Boscawen. And like a king Archer had his courtiers. Women, in particular, flocked to him. 'The way in which some women ran after Archer was amazing,' wrote Lady Hastings, who was herself probably smitten with the jockey's gauche charm. The ageing Duchess of Montrose could not conceal her passion for the man 40 years her junior. She pursued him from gallops to racetrack and showered him with invitations to her home and the theatre. It was widely believed she wished to marry him. 'I don't think I had better do it,' Archer was alleged to have told Captain Machell. 'And anyhow it would not make me the Duke of Montrose.' Despite the considerable pressure resulting from all this adulation, the majority of contemporary opinion (though John

The extent of the Archer legend can be gauged by the memorabilia associated with his name: here, matchboxes and cuff links.

FRED

Osborne said of Archer, 'He became so conceited that no man believed more in Mr Archer than Fred Archer the jockey') stated that Archer rose above it. 'A very large income, the unbounded confidence of employers and public might help to turn less ordinary heads, but Fred Archer quietly goes his own way and studies diligently to improve his calling,' wrote a correspondent of *The World* in 1879; and 38 years after Archer's death, the Hon George Lambton said, 'Even when quite a boy he was courted and flattered by every kind of man and woman, and early in life he became the idol of the public . . . and yet he never suffered from that prevalent and disagreeable complaint "swollen head". I think the shrewd, hard common sense of Mat Dawson, for whom he had the greatest affection and respect, was a great help to him.'

Archer's *raison d'etre* was to ride more and more winners. The story that the young jockey was once found in tears because he could not ride both winners in a dead-heat may be apocryphal but it serves to illustrate Archer's attitude to his chosen profession. This unquenchable thirst for success is all the more remarkable when one considers the physical handicaps Archer overcame. When he entered Dawson's Heath House stables as an 11-year-old in 1868 he weighed barely 4st 11lb; in his first championship season of 1874 his minimum weight had risen to 6 stone and by the close of the decade he struggled to do 8st 7lb. As a tiny boy he had been taught to box by his father William, the steeplechase jockey, which was just as well. The delicate apprentice who was afraid of the dark was soon bullied by the older boys, but the bravery which took him over the drystone walls of the Cotswolds around his Cheltenham birthplace gradually enabled him to surmount this painful obstacle. The Dawsons had no children of their own and Archer was the perfect surrogate. He invariably snaffled the biggest slice of Mrs Dawson's cake (she called him 'the little cat') distributed after Sunday service; he also worshipped blackberry jam. Weight gain was the inevitable outcome, especially as he grew to around 5ft 10in in height. During the winter he filled out to 11 stone. Unfortunately, he was a poor walker and could hardly run at all. With his weight-reducing options thus limited, drastic measures were called for. Heath House had a turkish bath for the horses: Archer used it more than they did. A Newmarket doctor, JR Wright, prepared him a special purgative which earned immortality as 'Archer's Mixture'. One tablespoonful of this noxious brew was enough to consign anyone to the nearest lavatory for 24 hours. Archer drank it by the sherry glass and went on about his business. The only thing apt to induce a similar reaction from Archer was the very sight and smell of food. He once bolted from a dining room on seeing a steak and kidney pie. His own diet during the season largely consisted of castor oil, a biscuit and a small glass of champagne at midday. If he ate a good dinner of an evening his weight shot up by 3 or 4lb. 'It's all right, Mr Dawson; I promise you I shall be 8st 10lb by 3 o'clock,' the Duke of Portland overheard him say at Goodwood one morning. 'You see, my medicine hasn't acted yet; and I shall sit in my turkish bath and no doubt elsewhere until it's time to go to the races.' In October 1886 this regime enabled him to lose 6lb in two days on a visit to Ireland but he failed to make the 8st 6lb on St Mirin in the Cambridgeshire upon his return. It cost him the race (he was beaten a head) and at the end of a chilly afternoon, the rigours of which he was trying to keep at bay with the thinnest of silks and an empty stomach, his undernourished constitution finally began to cave in. A fortnight later he was dead.

Archer made a lot of money. Retainers and presents from grateful owners (and gamblers) pushed his annual income towards £10 000 in the 1880s. His riding fees alone would amount to nearly £2500. His first retainer with Lord Falmouth was a nominal, and inviolate, £100 but the Duke of Portland and Lord Hastings paid him £2000 jointly, the Duke of Westminster £1000, and Lord Alington £500. On top of this came the owners' presents, £1000 for a big win (while one professional gambler gave him £2000 in a single year) and whatever he won betting – and he certainly indulged, even if he was not part of the notorious 'Jockeys Ring' to which Sir George Chetwynd alerted the Jockey Club in 1884. He was known to have heavily backed St Mirin for the Cambridgeshire (his betting book for the season was currently showing a loss of £30 000) which proved fatal in more ways than one. Although at one time he was thought to be worth a quarter of a million his will was proved at £60 000, which to some degree contradicts the popular conception (partly cultivated) of him being a penny-pincher. 'That damned long-legged, tin-scrapping young devil,' is how Dawson was to describe him, 'tin' being the Victorian slang for money.

Nevertheless, 'The Tinman' must not be pilloried as a cold, ungenerous fish. According to his sister Alice: 'Fred had a great deal of character. He was gentle, but he took no liberties himself and no one ever thought of taking one with him. And he was always so quiet. There was never any ranting and raving. He would also rather be two minutes early than two minutes late. Fred knew we were short of money. At first he would send postal orders for a few shillings whenever he could spare them. Later it ran to fivers and, lastly, big sums. Mother and father always owed long bills and Fred always paid them.' Archer's generosity extended to close friends. Before he departed on a trip to America in November 1884 he gave a blank cheque to his lifelong friend Herbert Mills. 'You may want money or be in difficulties while I am away and if you are you will be able to fill in this.' Any jockey down on his luck could always count on a fiver from Archer and every winter he used to throw a ball for his weighing-room colleagues.

FRED

Although Archer resembled the devil incarnate astride a horse, the act of swapping silks for a suit of clothes instantly transformed him into the guise of an unobtrusive bank clerk on a lunchtime stroll down Threadneedle Street. Lambton described a young man of about 5ft 10in in height, with a marvellously slim and graceful figure and remarkably small hands and feet. His eyes were a cold blue-grey and the expression perennially sad, 'the shadow of melancholy in his face which indicated a side to his nature never far absent even in his brightest days,' not being helped by pronounced front teeth over which his lips did not quite meet. One physical feature betrayed his profession: the round-shouldered stoop which all tall jockeys inevitably develop. He'd have made a poor bank clerk, however. Due to his riding, Archer had scarcely learnt to read or write when he left home, much to the consternation of his mother Emma. 'Let the lad alone,' William Archer would bark, 'he'll make more out of his riding than he ever will out of his book-learning.' Archer did attend Mrs Dawson's night school during his early years in Newmarket, but though many who came into contact with him believed that in another life he could have entered Oxford or Cambridge, he grew up poorly educated and seldom bothered to even write his own letters, for example.

It was often said that although Archer's father had been a good enough jockey to win a Grand National, the vital quicksilver which differentiated Fred from his rivals came from Emma Archer. 'She was a big, fine-looking woman with handsome aquiline features – people always used to say she must have had some good blood in her veins,' said one neighbour. 'One's first impression of Archer would have been that of a gentleman by birth.' Indeed, some sections of Victorian society subscribed to that view exactly, naming his father as Lord Wilton, with whom he frequently stayed when hunting from Melton Mowbray: Lord Rosebery annotated the margin of his copy of Archer's biography with such an opinion. For all the inestimable qualities the short, squat former jump jockey William Archer passed on to his second son, the mien of a gentleman could not be numbered among them. In spirit Fred was his mother's boy; by profession he was his father's successor. In the taut, self-contained and highly introverted personality which grew out of the conflict between a mother's all-consuming love and a father's lofty expectations lay the seeds of not only unmitigated ambition but also the depression which eventually killed him.

Whatever the source of his genius Archer was soon riding in pony and donkey races. At the age of eight, mounted on a pony, he lost his first match, against a donkey. Lessons were redoubled and deadly serious. Said a friend of the family: 'Old Billy Archer threw bits of grass and turf at young Fred and his language was something awful. I don't think Fred was ever afraid of the pony.' Not even a broken leg sustained out hunting prevented the boy's relentless progress towards his destiny. Pony races were now being won and a hunting acquaintance, a Mr William Le Terriere, happened to be a friend of Mat Dawson. Father and son spent a week at Heath House in February 1868 at the end of which the canny Scot declared: 'He will do, Archer, you may leave him.'

It would appear trite to suggest that the relationship between trainer and apprentice was akin to father and son, yet equally, not to acknowledge the possibility would constitute a grave omission. Dawson's apprentices customarily received wages of five guineas in their first year; Archer received seven. 'Mark my words,' Dawson confided to a friend, 'I have a wonderful boy here who will do marvellous things.' Archer prospered, absorbing the lessons of Dawson's right-hand man 'Jockey' Swift – 'I taught Archer pretty well all he knew and I was a bit too good for him' – and studying the methods of Tom French. Some of his fellow apprentices were thrown (one was actually killed) but nothing could dislodge Mrs Dawson's 'little cat'.

Archer's apprenticeship finished at Christmas 1872 and Dawson presented him with a gold watch inscribed 'For good conduct'. Said Archer, 'I value this more than anything I have and shall keep it as long as I live.' Champion jockey or not, Archer always remained in awe of the master of Heath House. In his *Memories of Racing and Hunting* the Duke of Portland records a visit in 1882: 'Archer was talking to someone and for that reason did not, as usual, hurry to open the gate for us, whereupon Mat indignantly said, 'Archer, mon, where are your manners; are you no' going to open the gate?' Archer ran to do so at once. At the time, Archer was quite possibly earning £8–10 000 a year and was the idol of the public, but old Mat stood no nonsense from him or anyone else. Every evening he attended at our stable inspection and Mat insisted upon his standing strictly to attention like any other boy when anybody spoke to him.'

The future champion got his first ride on the filly Honoria in the Newmarket Town Plate of 14 October 1869. She was three, he was twelve and they finished last. To be fair, they were only in the race to make the running for the stable's Stromboli, who won, so Dawson had no cause for complaint. However, neither of Archer's first two successes came under Dawson's auspices. Before 1869 was out he'd won a Bangor steeplechase on Maid of Trent for Mrs Willans, a pony-racing acquaintance of his father, weighing out at 4st 11lb. It was a mite longer before the first of 2748 victories on the Flat was chalked up. That famous day was 28 September 1870; the place Chesterfield; the horse Athol Daisy, trained by John Peart at Malton; the race a 2-year-old nursery. In all Archer had 15 rides that season, winning two (the other was Lincoln Lass at Ayr) and being placed second no less than nine times. The following season's ratio was three wins from 40 rides. In 1872, however, the tally of wins rose to 27 and included his first important victory, the Cesarewitch on the Dawson-trained Salvanos. 'Little Archer,' stated a leading authority, 'rode Salvanos with the coolness and steadiness of a veteran and thus early made his mark as one of the rising lightweights.' Not everyone was deferential. 'Tha tell me he can ride,' the incorrigible Jem Snowden remarked prior to his initial encounter with Archer: 'Tha cassn't ride for nuts,' was Jem's verdict after he'd beaten Archer a head.

Archer did not remain a 'rising lightweight' for very long, on two counts. First, his metabolism rapidly invalidated the term lightweight and second, he profited from the sickness of Tom French to wind up the very next season with 107 winners, just three behind the champion, Harry Constable. He had ceased rising: he had arrived. French was a fine horseman and skilful race rider but he was unmerciful with whip and spur, and this attitude rubbed off on his Heath House disciple. The reputation for undue severity which Archer earned in his early years clung to him for the rest of his life, even though he modified his style toward the end. In 1884 he told an interviewer: 'It's a great mistake to knock a horse about and I know that a few years back I was a severe rider, but I've learnt better by experience. I rarely hit a horse more than twice in a finish now and I rarely or never have rowels to my spurs. You can hurt a horse almost as much without if you want to, but it's a bad policy to hurt them.' Archer, one might say, should have deduced something else from French, who was unusually tall for a jockey and wasted hard. In the summer of 1873 he died of consumption brought about by over-wasting. French had given his life to racing at the age of 29. The ultimate irony is that the career of his successor followed almost precisely the same course.

French's death presented Archer with an opportunity he eagerly accepted: in 1874 he won 147 races, including the 2000 Guineas on Atlantic, to be champion for the first time. It was the first of a dozen Classic wins for Archer in the magpie colours – black, white sleeves, red cap – of Evelyn Boscawen, 6th Viscount Falmouth, Dawson's principal patron from 1870 to 1883. Archer's triumphal season did not pass without one note of concern. The spindly youth was becoming a man. In the Cesarewitch he had to declare 3lb overweight when getting down to 6st 1lb to ride the Truth gelding. A tremendous gamble on the Dawson horse was foiled by a neck. Archer maintained the wasting had beaten him: his strength just ebbed away. It was a portent he would have been well advised to heed.

The Falmouth–Dawson–Archer triumvirate dominated the Classics over the next ten years. So completely, in fact, that it is said Lord Rosebery had a special form printed on which to send Falmouth his congratulations. 'Lord Falmouth's string grew to such proportions,' Dawson told a reporter, 'that it was difficult to know how or when to

Opposite: Archer with his most noted patron, Lord Falmouth, for whom he rode 12 Classic winners.

run them in the weight-for-age races and, be it known, he rarely stooped to handicaps.' Falmouth had no need of the latter for he seldom betted. The Classics were his target and right well was he served by his trainer and jockey. Atlantic's victory was followed by Spinaway (1875, 1000 Guineas and Oaks), Silvio (1877, Derby and St Leger), Jannette (1878, Oaks and St Leger), Charibert (1879, 2000 Guineas), Wheel of Fortune (1879, 1000 Guineas and Oaks), Dutch Oven (1882, St Leger) and Galliard (1883, 2000 Guineas). No doubts existed as to the identity of the best Falmouth standard bearer. When quizzed on the exceptional horses with which he had been associated Archer understandably held the likes of St Simon and Ormonde in the highest regard, yet he always ended the conversation by saying, 'Don't forget the mare. She was wonderfully good.' The mare in question was the diminutive Wheel of Fortune, who stood only 15.1 hands. In the words of the Duke of Portland, 'his long legs encircled her and she looked like a polo pony.' Together they won ten races out of ten before the 'Wheel' broke down at York in her last race prior to the St Leger.

'I know that a few years back I was a severe rider.' Were these the spurs that dug into St Simon?

Falmouth's withdrawal from racing in 1883 was prompted, rumour had it, by the suspicion that Archer had pulled Galliard in the Derby, in which the favourite was beaten a neck and half a length by St Blaise and Highland Chief. Archer, it was thought, had not exhibited the kind of demonic riding which had decided tight finishes in his favour aboard Bend Or and Iroquois. More significantly, Highland Chief was trained by Charles Archer, who stood to lose £1000 if the colt was beaten and to collect a king's ransom if it won. Adding two and two together equalled Archer stopping Galliard to let his brother's horse win. Although Archer loved his brother he had not previously been disposed to show him favours on the racecourse. During Charles's riding days he had put him over the rails for trying to take the inside. It is also inconceivable that Archer would consent to throw the Derby of all races. Nevertheless, speculation persisted and fuel was added to the fire when Falmouth chose this moment to announce he was selling all his horses. It was nothing to do with the riding of Galliard, he said; he was getting old and anyway, he'd made up his mind some months before the Derby. The fuse may have been lit the previous season by the furore surrounding Archer's riding of Dutch Oven. On the assumption she had been soundly beaten in the Great Yorkshire Stakes because she did not stay the distance of 1¾ miles, Dutch Oven's St Leger odds drifted out to 40–1. After she had comfortably won the Classic there could only be one conclusion: Archer had pulled her at York in order to get a longer price for himself at Doncaster. That Archer had tried all he knew to get off Dutch Oven to ride the favourite Geheimniss for John Porter, and that if he'd backed her the price would have shortened considerably, cut little ice with the scandal-mongers.

Tom Cannon and Robert the Devil, who got the better of Archer and Bend Or in both the St Leger and Champion Stakes of 1880.

The loss of Falmouth's support was alleviated by the emergence of St Simon and Ormonde. Each has advocates who claim it to have been the horse of the century. Neither met defeat. St Simon won nine and Ormonde all 16 of those he contested, including the Triple Crown. By contrast, St Simon missed all the Classics. His single entry had been the 2000 Guineas but this became void on the death of his original owner, Prince Batthyany. Several commentators such as Richard Marsh, Henry Custance and William Allison (Special Commissioner of *The Sportsman*) stated that St Simon never beat a really good horse. However, he destroyed the Classic winners of his generation – Harvester (Derby), Busybody (1000 Guineas and Oaks) and The Lambkin (St Leger) – on the gallops and trounced the 1883 St Leger winner Ossian by 20 lengths in the Goodwood Cup; but these victories hardly measured up to Ormonde's: Minting, The Bard, Melton, Bendigo. Objectivity could not be expected from either trainer – Mat Dawson and John Porter – but at least Archer rode both horses, and within a short period of time, so his opinion that St Simon was the better (in spite of describing Ormonde as 'a horse and a half') must be respected. Some time after Ormonde's Derby, Archer was asked by *The Sporting Times*: 'Which was absolutely the best horse you ever knew?' His answer was St Simon. 'As long as I live,' he said when St Simon had run away with him on the gallops in 1884, 'I will never touch that animal again with the spur; he's not a horse, he's a blooming steam engine.'

Archer's rides on St Simon were confined to the colt's five outings as a juvenile, the last of which was a match against Porter's Duke of Richmond. 'That's the best 2-year-old I have ever seen in my life,' was Dawson's only comment after St Simon had won with any amount in hand. Sadly, Archer could not manage the low weights allotted St Simon in the few decent races open to him as a 3-year-old viz the Epsom Gold Cup (7st 7lb), Ascot Gold Cup (7st 9lb), Gosforth Gold Cup (8st 6lb) and the Goodwood Cup (8 stone). A year after St Simon's retirement Archer began his association with Ormonde via three victories at Newmarket culminating in the Dewhurst. In the 1886 2000 Guineas, however, he deserted Ormonde for Sir John Blundell Maple's Saraband (and was handsomely paid for so doing) and thus missed achieving what would have been his only Triple Crown. Thereafter he won eight races on Ormonde, the 11th of their partnership being a walkover (one of a five-timer on the day of Archer's final winner) on Friday 29 October, just ten days before his death.

The 1880s unwound with Archer at the peak of his powers; his winning totals were 220, 210, 232, 241 and 246 – the last three actually improving his record. He could ride any sort of race. Said Porter: 'He developed a style of his own. Archer was an extremely "brainy" jockey . . . his body was short and his legs long and he used the latter as if they were a pair of tongs gripping a horse's body. As a rule he rode with a slack rein and sometimes at the finish of a race he was halfway up the horse's neck. His success was largely due to his wonderful energy, his determination and his pluck.' Not even Fordham could match Archer's clinical efficiency at the start or his nerve during a race. With no draw for places or even a gate, the start was a battleground where Archer reigned supreme. 'He used to cut his field up before he had gone a quarter of a mile, get 'em all sprawling, and that gave him an advantage which he rarely lost,' attested Tommy Heartfield. 'He used to dash his horse away from the start, take a position and hold it.' The fact that Archer and the senior starter Tom McGeorge were bosom pals did not go unnoticed in the popular press. Custance, who later became a starter himself (officiating at the Derby of 1885, won by Archer on Melton), believed Archer was the best man he'd ever seen at flagfall. Archer refuted any suggestions of impropriety. 'It isn't the getting away first so much as how you get away – how you set your horse going . . . I've always got my horse ready to go but not pulling at him, and then when we do start I'm off at full speed at once.'

Once away, Archer headed for the rails. In winning the 1881

FRED

Manchester Cup on Valour he rode so close to the rail his boot was ripped open from heel to toe. Woe betide anyone who attempted to deprive him of his favourite position. Riding Jannette in the Doncaster Cup of 1879 he very nearly put Tom Cannon and the 7–1 on favourite Isonomy through the rails. A combination of Cannon's skill and Isonomy's courage saw the favourite prevail by a head. When it was pointed out to Archer there was blood on Isonomy's shoulder from his spur he innocently replied that his feet were so flat and his ankles so weak that he could not always control them. For all the allegations of rough-housing, Archer only ever received one suspension – 14 days, back in 1874 for disobedience at the post.

Iroquois, America's first Derby winner in 1881, who needed all of Archer's renowned strength to overcome Peregrine by a neck.

Archer's steely resolve had no finer testing ground than Epsom, where he proved an unholy terror down Tattenham Hill. Although he won five Derbies, that total would undoubtedly have risen had he ridden freelance insteading of abiding by his retainer to Lord Falmouth, in whose colours he completed seven of his 13 Derbies, winning with just Silvio in 1877. His performance on Bend Or in 1880 has quite rightly entered Turf folklore. Twenty-five days before

the Derby, while riding work on the Heath, Archer was savaged by Muley Edris, a horse to whom he had administered some terrible thrashings in the hope of subduing the animal's vile temper and winning some races with him (which he did). The demented beast bit through the muscles of Archer's right arm so badly that the Derby would have been out of the question for any ordinary mortal. But Archer was extrordinary. His conversation with Sir James Paget, the eminent surgeon with whom Falmouth arranged a consultation, is another slice of legend.

Archer: How long will it take to heal?
Paget: Oh, I think in three or four weeks you will be all right.
Archer: But, shall I be fit for the Derby?
Paget: Yes, I think you may go to the Derby.
Archer: But, you don't quite understand me, Sir James, shall I be fit to ride?
Paget: Better drive – better drive.
Archer: I fear, sir, you scarcely realise who I am.
Paget: No, I see I have the honour of receiving Mr Archer but . . .
Archer: Well, Sir James, I suppose I may tell you, then, that what you are in your profession I am in mine.

Archer refused to concede defeat. He consulted a 'quack' bonesetter called Hutton; he recommended riding, but with the Derby a week away he had to shed a stone in weight. The dilemma now facing Bend Or's connections – owner the Duke of Westminster and trainer Robert Peck – was whether they should risk putting Archer up. Racing history will forever be in their debt for the decision they made. Archer went out to ride Bend Or with a pad in the palm of his hand and a piece of iron up the length of his arm. Physically and emotionally he was a wreck. His customary pauper's diet resembled a king's banquet compared to the morsels he had recently allowed to pass his lips. He visibly shook with tension. He was, by any definition, certifiable. Those jockeys foolish enough to get near him during the race heard him hissing through clenched teeth something like: 'Brr–brr–get out of the way, you–young scoundrels, brr–brr.' Archer came round Tattenham Corner so close to the rail that he had to lift his leg onto Bend Or's withers. 'I would not have given five shillings for my chance then,' he afterwards confessed. Be that as it may; he set about catching the clear leader, Robert the Devil. A hundred yards from the post Archer, forgetting his incapacity, went for his whip and dropped it. No matter. The gods were not about to desert, in his hour of need, one in whom they had invested so benevolently. Somehow Archer communicated his fanaticism to Bend Or. In the penultimate stride he seemingly hurled the colt at Robert the Devil and in the very last stride, to all intents and purposes, he lifted him past the post a head to the good.

FRED

The story of those 25 days in May 1880 would not have dawned on Messrs Gould, Runyon, Francis or any other writer of racing fiction. Only Archer could have written it. Nothing is ever lost in the retelling. It is quintessential Archer: setback, melancholy, an element of farce, a touch of madness. Even if Archer had not garnered titles and Classics like there was no tomorrow, this race alone would guarantee his entry to any hall of fame. After crossing the Channel to complete a Derby double on Beauminet in the Prix du Jockey-Club, he was forced to cease riding until the Goodwood meeting on 27 June.

Besides keeping on good terms with the starter, Archer attempted to curry favour with judges, albeit quite legitimately. As he explained to George Lambton: 'Most sit back when they finish and I sit forward, and you know, that may just catch the judge's eye.' Custance was less sure Archer's loose-reined finish was as effectual as he claimed. 'His mounts frequently changed their legs a time or two. Anyone who knows anything about riding at all must agree that every time a horse changes his legs he shortens his stride, and loses at least a neck, sometimes more.' However, when it came to race analysis or fishing for rides, Archer was without peer. Lambton spoke for many trainers: 'Nothing escaped his notice. Not only could he tell you all about his horse, which is more than most jockeys are capable of, but he knew what the others had been doing.' Armed with this information regarding a likely winner, Archer would then ask the owner for the mount next time out. Conversely, if he knew there was no possibility of ever getting the ride, he'd tell the owner the horse was no good and dissuade him from running it, all the while taking great care to be engaged for something that would win in its absence. Of course, Archer's desire for big winners occasionally prompted more venal methods. Before the 1881 Derby he approached Peck for the ride on the 2000 Guineas winner Peregrine and when told Webb had already been booked the reaction was pure Archer: 'Well, give Webb a thousand and put me up.' Peck demurred. After the events of the previous year he ought to have had more sense. Archer partnered Iroquois (second in the Guineas) and beat Peregrine by a neck.

Trumping Archer was no simple matter. 'I am so thoroughly wrapped up in racing, my mind is so entirely upon it, that I really never think of anything else, not even of where I am, and of what is going on around me as I travel from place to place.' In 1881, for instance, Sir John Astley owned a big chestnut called Peter with whom he intended solving his financial hardship by winning the Manchester Cup. Archer asked for the ride and in the same instant handed Astley a letter he'd received from Captain Machell. It read: 'If you will ride Valour in the Manchester Cup I will run him, if not I shall not send him to Manchester.' Astley was committed to his stable jockey Charlie Wood: sticking by him was about to cost Sir John

FRED

£12 000 in lost bets. Archer knew Valour would not stay a truly-run
1¾ miles, so he rode two races on the colt, driving him for the best
part of a mile and then easing him. In the straight he began riding a
second race on him, as it were, and collared Peter right on the post.
The following week Peter ran for the Gold Vase at Ascot. Astley's
friends implored him to replace Wood with Archer. Again he could
not bring himself to abandon his jockey. Peter, a 3–1 on favourite,
ran out. He would just not go for Charlie Wood. The next day Peter
was started for the Hunt Cup, carrying 9st 3lb. Archer was in the
saddle. After running a quarter of a mile the big horse tried to stop,
but with one pat down the neck Archer got him to grab hold of his
bit again and they went on to win. On Friday Archer rode him again
in the Hardwicke Stakes – with the same result.

Bend Or's Derby and Valour's Manchester Cup were, by general
consensus, two of the three most outstanding displays Archer ever
gave. The third was Melton's Derby of 1885. Archer had won the
2000 Guineas on Porter's Paradox but Mat Dawson now wanted him
for Melton. Archer had psychoanalysed Paradox: he was lazy and
disliked being left in front; he got bored and had to be brought with
a late flourish. So easily was Paradox travelling in the Derby that he
pulled himself to the front early in the straight. Archer watched him
for signs of disinterest. One hundred yards from victory up went the
leader's head. Archer pounced. Paradox fought back and with less
than 50 yards to go, seemed as if he might hold on. Archer produced
the wand. Two mighty swipes to Melton's rear achieved the desired
conjuring trick. He'd won by a head. 'Your horse had won
everywhere except at the winning post. One stride later he was a
neck in front,' Judge Clark told Porter. Melton's owners received a
congratulatory telegram from Oscar Wilde: 'I understand that
Milton's *Paradise Lost* is being revised and will be published under the
title of "Paradox Lost by Melton".' With Archer up, Paradox then
won the Grand Prix de Paris by five lengths. Apart from his debut
when he whipped round at the start, the Derby was the only race
Paradox lost.

Although the latter years of Victoria's reign were graced by a
plethora of excellent jockeys, the majority seemed distinctly run-of-
the-mill compared to Fordham and Archer. Certainly a great many
were in awe of the twin titans. One who would never bend the knee
was Jem Snowden. The first occasion Archer rode at Stockton,
Snowden beat him a short head. 'Noo, maw lad,' said Jem as they
returned to scale, 'thee can tell them i' the Sooth that there's mair
jockeys in the world than thee.' Archer always held Snowden in high
esteem. Fred Webb he acknowledged to be a strong rider, Charlie
Wood a good tactician. Tom Cannon, however, he considered the
most beautiful – 'too pretty at times' – and most finished of jockeys.
Cannon, in fact, was the one jockey who could be spoken of in the

Previous page: Kempton Cannon on St Amant. The pair ran through a tremendous thunderstorm to win the 1904 Derby by three lengths.

Above: The English style at its zenith. Jack Watts brings Persimmon home the neck winner of the 1896 Derby from St Frusquin.

Below: Tom Cannon, a shrewd businessman and a superb tutor of jockeys.

same breath as Archer and Fordham. 'There is no doubt he could outride anyone of his time,' said Charles Morton, 'and during the years that he, Archer and Fordham were in evidence we saw what I consider to be the three greatest jockeys the English Turf has ever known.'

Tom Cannon was born in 1846 at Eton, where his father kept The George Hotel. His first ride nearly ended in tragedy when his mount Mavoureen fell in a race at Plymouth, smashing the 3st 12lb thirteen-year-old into the turf. Undamaged and unruffled, Cannon won on another horse the following day. His formative years were spent at Danebury under the tutelage of John Day and George Fordham. Little wonder, then, that Cannon matured into a wonderful horseman possessing the lightest of hands, which made him particularly effective on 2-year-olds or temperamental females. Significantly, he gained his first Classic on a filly, Repulse in the 1866 1000 Guineas, and of the twelve which followed, nine came on fillies. It can be no coincidence that he twice won the 2000 Guineas on fillies (Pilgrimage and Shotover) and once the Derby (Shotover). Despite his shy and somewhat delicate visage, Cannon was an exceptionally shrewd businessman (his father at one stage had been a horse dealer): before Humewood won the 1887 Cesarewitch, Cannon sold the horse to

Mornington Cannon on the 1899 Triple Crown winner Flying Fox.

Lord Rodney. When asked by George Lambton why he had sold him so cheaply, Cannon replied, 'The horse was cheap but look at the advertisement. Everyone who wants a horse will now come and buy another cheap one from me.' In 1888 the immensely rich but woefully fickle Scottish industrialist George Baird wished to have first call on his services. Aware he might suffer instant dismissal with little or no salary, Cannon refused a one-year contract and instead demanded one for three seasons at £3000 each with the full £9000 to be paid in a lump sum at the outset. 'Nearly everybody in England wanted him,' wrote Baird's trainer Charles Morton, 'and ultimately, after considerable negotiation, Baird had to pay him.'

John Porter was another devotee; and after Archer's death it was to Cannon he turned for Ormonde's new jockey. As a result Cannon featured in one of Ascot's, and the Turf's, most exciting and memorable races, namely the titanic contest for the 1887 Hardwicke Stakes in which Ormonde defeated Minting and Bendigo. The latter pair led into the straight but the real battle was taking place behind them. George Barrett, the rider of the fourth competitor, Phil, was

Watts on Persimmon with trainer Richard Marsh at the horse's head.

incensed that he had not inherited the ride on Ormonde and coming round the bend he bored his horse onto the favourite, causing four-inch flaps of skin to be torn from Ormonde's near hind. Cannon and Ormonde managed to regain their poise, got to Minting at the distance and after a ding-dong tussle won by a neck. 'I have never seen such excitement on a course before or since. The most splendid finish ever seen on a racecourse,' enthused Lord Arthur Grosvenor.

Barrett's riding that day was one of the few things that ever caused Tom Cannon to lose his temper. His marvellous equanimity was never better illustrated than in his role as a patient teacher of jockeys. All his sons – Tom, Mornington, Kempton and Charles – became jockeys with varying degrees of success, while he also tutored Jack Watts, Arthur Coventry and George Lambton. His race-riding career extended over 32 seasons (and 1544 winners), which afforded him the dubious honour of riding against both Tom Junior and 'Morny' prior to his retirement in 1891. In the 1888 Eclipse Old Tom (on Orbit) enjoyed the paternal satisfaction of beating Young Tom (on Ossory) by a length. Young Tom's career was curtailed by weight problems

Neck and neck in the 1884 Champion Stakes, Fred Webb on Lucerne (far side) and Tom Cannon on Tristan. The judge could not separate them.

and although Kempton emulated his father in the Classics, it was Mornington (named after a horse his father had ridden to victory on the day he was born) who kept the family name truly in the spotlight – even though Mat Dawson contemptuously dismissed him as 'what I call a dilettante jockey'.

The most obvious manifestation of his father's teaching was Morny's almost pathological inclination to leave his challenge as late as possible and win by as little as possible. Says Lambton: 'It really was extraordinary, after apparently being out of a race, how he would sweep down on three or four struggling horses and beat them. There is no doubt that most of the jockeys were frightened to death of Morny with his tremendous rush at the finish.' Occasionally, this attribute became his achilles heel. In John Porter's view his delaying tactics cost William the Third the 1901 Derby, for example. However, Morny Cannon won six jockeys' championships in the 1890s to his father's one (1872); and six Classics, including a Triple Crown on Porter's Flying Fox in 1899.

Another sympathetic horseman cast in the same mould was Jack Watts, as quiet in the saddle as he was out of it. He got the last ounce out of a horse apparently doing nothing and, like the Cannons, would enter the winner's circle after a big victory, in the words of Lambton, 'looking as solemn as a judge who had just passed the death sentence.' Even after Watts had won the 1896 Derby on Persimmon for the

Prince of Wales, trainer Richard Marsh had to slap him on the thigh as he rode back and remind him of what he'd achieved in order for a faint smile to illuminate his glum face. In one respect Watts had due cause to look miserable. He had long been bothered by his weight and Marsh had needed to exercise all his powers of persuasion to stop him retiring the previous winter. As it was, two days before the Derby he still couldn't do the weight. Nevertheless, Watts continued riding for another five seasons but the years of deprivation finally took their toll. He had only been training two years when he was taken ill at Sandown Park in July 1902 and he died ten days later.

In addition to their style of riding, Watts and the Cannons were linked by the bond of impenetrable honesty. Likewise John Osborne, nicknamed 'The Bank of England' jockey on account of his integrity, who rode for 46 years and was the North's most popular jockey in the second half of the 19th century. He never smoked, drank little and bet even less. The same could not be said of Charles Wood, the man who rode St Simon during his 3-year-old career and was accused of

The 'Bank of England' jockey: John Osborne, aged 54.

In 1887 Charles Wood won both the 1000 Guineas and Oaks on Reve d'Or, became champion jockey for the only time, and was warned-off.

organising a Jockeys Ring. Wood survived this slur to become champion jockey in 1887 but he was subsequently warned off as a result of the irregular running of horses he was riding for Sir George Chetwynd, who was himself obliged to resign from the Jockey Club. Wood regained his licence in 1897 and celebrated by winning the Triple Crown on Galtee More. He left over £60 000 when he died in 1945 a few months before his 90th birthday. Wood was not the only Victorian jockey who lived to witness the numerous innovations in jockeyship propagated by a new century. Morny Cannon lived until 1962, long enough to see his great nephew Lester Piggott win three Derbies utilising a style he could never have imagined feasible.

The chances of Archer welcoming the 20th century, never more than slim, nosedived on the death of his wife Helen Rose, 'Nellie', (Dawson's niece) shortly after the birth of their daughter Nellie Rose in November 1884; their first born, a son, having died in January only a

Right: 'A powerful personality as well as a brilliantly successful jockey.' Archer in 1885 wearing the colours of Lord Hastings in which he had recently won the Derby and St Leger on Melton. Note the black armband – his wife Nellie had been dead for almost a year but Archer could not put her out of his mind.

Below: The weapon which finally ended Archer's increasingly troubled life.

few hours old. Archer's already chronically overloaded psyche became precariously so. 'Oh, if I could only love a woman half so well as I loved her. I would have gladly given up money, honours and everything else, even my life, in exchange for only one word from her dear lips.' His friends so feared for his sanity that one, Captain Bowling, frequently slept in his bedroom to guard against a suicide attempt. The chain of events which inextricably led to Archer's death two years later had been set in motion. He had lost the support of Lord Falmouth in 1883 and the Duke of Portland during 1884; now Mat Dawson announced he was to leave Heath House at the end of 1885 for a quieter life in Exning. The new season of 1886 started inauspiciously: he picked the wrong horse in the 2000 Guineas, riding Saraband instead of Ormonde. He began fretting about his own level of performance. Early in the season Charlie Wood actually led the table, the first time someone had shown him a clean pair of heels in 13 years. To cap it all, his betting was proving disastrous.

On October 19 Archer paid his first visit to The Curragh, in company with Custance, who was to act as starter. As he had not ridden for a few days he checked his weight and found it to be 9st 4lb. The situation was improved in the usual fashion and he got down to 8st 12lb to win on Cambusmore and Isidore 48 hours later. 'I never saw you look half so bad as you do now,' said Custance. 'Well, if I look bad now, how shall I look next Wednesday when I ride St Mirin at 8.6 in the Cambridgeshire,' laughed Archer. The Duchess of Montrose, St Mirin's owner, had plunged heavily on the outcome of the Cambridgeshire and she was anxious to ensure Archer's agreement to ride her colt would not be sabotaged by the likes of Custance. She sent a telegram to Archer's Dublin hotel: 'My horse runs in the Cambridgeshire. I count on you to ride it.' The noose around Archer's neck tightened.

All Archer's efforts to make the weight failed. He was one pound over and lost the race by a head. The moral of the Truth gelding's undoing in the 1874 Cesarewitch had not been absorbed. Rubbing salt into the wound was an accusation from the connections of the favourite that Archer had paid their jockey to lose the race. Since the accuser was Lord Edward Somerset, an old friend of Archer's, the jockey was entitled to feel aggrieved. However, his personal hell was not yet over. The unkindest cut of all was reserved for the last day of the meeting. He rode five winners but was beaten a head on the filly Queen Bee in a 2-year-old seller. Archer had advised Captain Machell to back the filly as if defeat was impossible and the Captain, in need of a coup, had done just that. Worse still, Archer had protected the 'tip' by actively discouraging anybody else who enquired about Queen Bee's chances. Unfortunately, one of this number was a lady friend of Machell's who rejoiced in passing on the fact that Archer had told her Queen Bee would not win. His judgement clouded by acute financial and personal embarrassment, the capricious Machell concluded he had been put away and when he met Archer in the paddock he turned his back on him. Having alienated Fordham, Machell had now helped to destroy another of his staunchest allies. 'Could you believe it possible that, after seeing a horse beaten a head in a desperate finish, I should think Archer was not trying and yet I allowed myself to think so,' he lamented once he had regained his senses. 'I am haunted by the look on his face when I refused to speak to him after the race.'

Archer's fifth winner on Friday 29 October 1886 came in the Houghton Stakes on Blanchland, a 2-year-old colt belonging, appropriately in the circumstances, to Lord Falmouth. It was the 2748th of Archer's career. There were to be no more. The fever contracted on Cambridgeshire day worsened. He rode at Brighton and Lewes the following week until his condition finally got the better of him after he rode Tommy Tittlemouse in the Castle Plate on Thursday 4 November. On returning to Falmouth House, the imposing residence built for him in the Fordham Road, typhoid fever was diagnosed. More importantly, however, he was deeply depressed and believed he was going to die.

'Are they coming?'

Nellie and his son to comfort him? Falmouth and Portland to patch things up? Machell to apologise? Or the burglars against whom the revolver in his bedside pedestal was intended as a precaution? Archer's last words leave us as confused as his own tormented soul. In some quarters it might be thought a trifle glib to wonder whether individuals like Fred Archer are ever destined for longevity, though Faustus might acknowledge a degree of truth in such a view. How much more could Archer's mind and body endure? It was best he died young. It had, after all, been foretold. In the autumn of 1878 Archer had gone to Chelmsford to ride a horse for his brother – and a fortune-teller crossed his palm with a piece of silver he had given her and foresaw his death by that very hand.

The day of the funeral, 12th November, was wet, cold and dismal. Newmarket closed down for the day, shops and businesses putting up their shutters and drawing blinds. Archer's epitaph was written in prose and verse. WB Portman, Audax of the *Horse and Hound*, wrote: 'As a jockey I never saw his superior and I have seen James Robinson, Sam Chifney, Frank Butler . . . and the immortal George Fordham show their brilliant skill in the pigskin.' While Edgar Lee's poetic tribute concluded:

> *Farewell, best jockey ever seen on course;*
> *Thy backers weep to think by Fate's decree*
> *The rider pale upon his great white horse*
> *Hath beaten thee.*

STEVE

STEVE

The Peter Pan of English racing.

Previous page: Captain Cuttle was not Donoghue's original hope for the 1922 Derby but he won on him just the same.

For over a quarter of a century Steve Donoghue was the Peter Pan of English racing, alternatively beguiling and infuriating everyone and anyone with whom he came into contact.

He never really grew up. His intuitive rapport with the thoroughbred earned him thousands of pounds; his incurable disregard for money just as easily squandered it all. The engaging air charmed many an employer and friend; the inveterate insouciance just as easily lost them. In Donoghue's language retainers were merely a basis for negotiation when it came to selecting a Derby ride, for example. Nonetheless, for sheer artistry and horsemanship Donoghue could not be outshone, even though his many challengers included rivals from America and Australia. One of the latter, Brownie Carslake, was once asked to pinpoint Donoghue's touchstone but he readily conceded that supernatural powers defy adequate description: 'Stephen can find out more about what is left in his horse with his little finger than most men with their legs and whip,' was all he would say. In point of fact Donoghue detested the whip: 'Nine times out of ten when the time comes to think of using the whip, the race is lost and no purpose is served by using it.' Then again, he didn't need a whip. Horses seemed to love him just as much as – or perhaps because – he adored them. From The Tetrarch to Humorist, from Diadem to Brown Jack, they gave their all for Steve. 'He is,' said Humorist's trainer Charles Morton, 'in a class by himself.'

Donoghue's period of ascendancy spanned a momentous period in British jockeyship. The dawn of the 20th century heralded a shrinking planet: ocean-devouring liners and continent-hopping aeroplanes brought an unprecedented internationalism to the Sport of Kings. In 1900 the American Lester Reiff became champion jockey, to be followed nine years later by the Australian boy wonder Frank Wootton. By 1923 racing's expanding horizon could even accommodate Donoghue and the Derby winner Papyrus crossing the Atlantic for the celebrated match-race with Zev in New York. Not surprisingly after a journey that still took a week, Papyrus was humbled.

At home, a similar fate was increasingly afflicting English jockeys. In 1900 as many as 17 of the 28 races at Royal Ascot went to American riders, who eventually occupied five of the leading ten places in the jockeys' championship. Six different American jockeys – Lester and John Reiff, 'Skeets' Martin, Danny Maher, Matt McGee and Frank O'Neill – rode a Derby winner in the century's first two decades. The colour and dash associated with these Americans (and Australians) resulted from the implementation of race tactics and a style of riding totally alien to the English Turf. Yet the man principally responsible for this breath of fresh air never won a Derby or a jockeys' title. And for that, James Forman 'Tod' Sloan had only himself to blame.

Above: *Tod Sloan, an abnormally short man with mere stumps for legs.*

Right: *Steve Donoghue: the master's hands do their work.*

Abnormally short with mere stumps for legs (a shape which in childhood gained him the name 'Toad', and thus 'Tod'), Sloan weighed no more than six stone. He was discovered by the notorious American gambler George Smith (aka 'Pittsburgh Phil') and he never managed to escape the shackles of various other like-minded gentlemen. Fat cigars, flash clothes and expensive champagne was an off-track lifestyle that promised only one outcome on the track. After barely four seasons in England, Sloan was told not to bother applying for a licence. He was finished at 26 years of age. In those four seasons, Sloan had won 254 races from 801 rides – a staggering winning percentage of 31.7 – and bequeathed a legacy that far outweighed his corruptibility (or his place in Cockney rhyming slang viz 'Tod Sloan – alone', hence 'On your Tod'), because it was this conceited, crooked little character who completely revolutionised English jockeyship as a result of his innovatory 'monkey-on-a-stick' seat and avant-garde race tactics.

The teenage Donoghue, for example, was one budding jockey mesmerised by Sloan: 'He was one of the finest jockeys and one of the most accomplished horsemen I have ever met. He could do anything with a horse; he was fond of them and he understood them. He had wonderful balance, beautiful hands and was a marvellous judge of pace. He used to crouch right up on a horse's neck, balanced like a bird, and he could get the last ounce out of his mount. There was never the least need for him to do anything but concentrate upon the interests of his master. But Sloan was a gambler, a born gambler and his mad gambling was the final cause of his ruin. Sloan's horsemanship, the effect his riding had had on English jockeyship and race-riding, should have earned him an honest fortune and caused him to be respected by everyone who loves horses.'

With the passing of each successive year it becomes more and more difficult to appreciate just how colossal an impact Sloan's arrival made on the English scene. Really and truly, only the elder Chifney exercised comparable influence. John Porter, who had not only seen but used all the great jockeys during a lengthy phase of native English excellence, maintained Sloan was a genius to rank alongside Fordham and Archer. 'From the long stirrup and long rein we passed to the other extreme – the short stirrup and the short rein. Here again we found a genius, who not only set a new fashion in riding races but showed us a new way in running them. Instead of the slow, muddling way of waiting, we had races run as they should be. In this Sloan showed his superiority by his knowledge of pace. He did not ride from pillar to post, as others are apt to do, but at a pace that would give his horse a chance to carry him to the end of the race.'

Sloan was not one to disagree with Porter's lofty estimation of his talents. 'I hope it does not seem that I am claiming for myself too much judgement at the expense of others,' he wrote of the 1898 Middle Park Stakes when he and Caiman caused the solitary career defeat of Porter's future Triple Crown winner Flying Fox, 'but without any brag or bounce I must say that there was such a hopeless ignorance of pace among the majority of those riding in the race that I suppose I managed to kid them.' On another occasion he confined himself to informing a newspaper: 'The riding is not so difficult as in America; here there is considerably less work.'

Positively angelic: just a word from Sloan and the most fractious animal was pacified.

Sloan crouched over the horse's neck, his hands within a few inches of the rings of the bridle, thereby reducing wind resistance and allowing the animal freer hind leverage. In achieving this, of course, he was greatly assisted – one might go so far as to say governed – by his short legs. He capitalised on this posture to encourage or pacify his mount by whispering in its ear. There were even some suggestions that his crouch masked the use of an electric battery. Whatever Sloan got up to, 'once he had been on the back of any horse he had an almost uncanny intuition into its pecularities and nature,' opined George Lambton after Sloan rode his mare Altmark in the Liverpool Autumn Cup of 1898. She was an impetuous animal and in the course of many false starts (the field were 40 minutes at the post) she three or four times took Sloan a furlong before he could restrain her. Amazingly, Lambton reports seeing Sloan lean over her neck and whisper in her ear. 'When they did go she was off like a rocket.

Morny Cannon refused to hitch up his leathers in the American manner.

Nothing ever got near her again.'

To ascertain just how much speed he had at his disposal, Sloan invariably let his horse sprint for a furlong on the way down. Then, out of the gate (introduced in 1897) like a shot, he allowed the animal to race the whole trip, albeit carefully preserving that burst of speed for the latter stages. The English jockeys were made to look silly. They continued to take the traditional 'pull' after leaving the gate, confident Sloan's horse would burn itself out long before they executed their version of the Chifney 'Rush'. 'When Tod Sloan arrived in England he found most of our jockeys fast asleep,' remarked Charles Morton. 'The Americans, especially Sloan, were openly contemptuous of our horsemen and it followed as a matter of course that if our jockeys wanted to cope with the invader, they had to adopt a similar style of riding.' Sam and Tom Loates hitched up their leathers; Kempton Cannon followed suit, though not Morny, who was certainly no lover of Sloan and one day at Doncaster took the uncharacteristic step of reporting him to the stewards for foul riding. It only remained for the outspoken Robert Sievier to sound the death knell: 'Monkeyship,' he wailed, 'has supplanted jockeyship.'

One direct result of the American influence was the dramatic improvement in race times. The average Derby time for the immediate post-Sloan period of 1899–1908 improved on the preceding ten years by 4.3 seconds, the average St Leger time by 8.2 seconds and the Ascot Gold Cup by 14.1 seconds. Some still needed persuasion. Richard Marsh conceded that 'this change in jockeyship has been the most revolutionary thing on the Turf that I can point to during 50 odd years of intimate association with it,' but as late as 1925 he continued to state that he never knew a jockey with the American seat get one pound more out of a horse than his own jockeys, Jack Watts and Herbert Jones. 'The genius of Sloan had nothing to do with his seat. He would have been just as great a genius . . . if he had been taught to ride in the English style. He was full of brains and a vitality which he shared with the horses he rode. His brains made him a wonderful judge of pace, while he had extraordinary hands. He inspired his horses and it was a thousand pities that off a horse he was devoid of those brains.' George Lambton, on the other hand was adamant: 'You cannot like it but it has come to stay and we must make the best of it.'

However much Sloan popularised the crouch and its tactical ramifications, it must be stressed that he neither originated them nor was he the first to unveil them in this country. The majority of his American contemporaries actually sat as upright as the English jockeys. The exceptions were the negro boys whom no one ever bothered to tutor. Their education merely consisted of being thrown up onto a horse equipped with just a rug instead of a saddle, and in consequence they were compelled to clutch the animal's mane to keep their balance. The first to gain prominence was actually named Verplanck, though he was generally referred to as 'Monkey Charlie'. After testing the 'monkey crouch' against the traditional upright seat, American trainers found it worth 3–7lb over five furlongs.

In the spring of 1895 one negro boy turned jockey came to Newmarket. Willie Simms had already won the Belmont Stakes twice and three times ridden five winners out of six of an afternoon. The sight of him taking Eau Gallie to the start of the Crawfurd Plate on April 16 induced ridicule and derision. Simms silenced the mockers in the time-honoured way: he won. In his slipstream toiled the cream of English jockeyship, including Morny Cannon, Sam and Tommy

Loates, Fred Allsopp and Walter Bradford – the five leading riders in the table. But prejudice was hard to overcome. In four months Simms secured only 19 rides (four wins, five places) and he recrossed the Atlantic to resume his Classic-winning habit in two Kentucky Derbies and a Preakness. Nevertheless, a beach-head was established. In 1896 Lester Reiff came over and rode 15 winners; the following October Sloan arrived to win on 20 of his 48 mounts.

Sloan was born at Bunker Hill near Kokomo, Indiana, in 1874. Bearing in mind his physique, adoption of the negro crouch seemed only natural, but one story attributes the decision to an experience in 1895 when a horse bolted with him at the Bay District track in San Francisco. To obtain a closer hold Sloan pulled up his knees and bent over its neck. The man probably responsible for bringing him to England in 1897 was James Keene, who hoped to repeat the Autumn Double success he had gained with Foxhall in 1881. The medium of the gamble was St Cloud II. Sloan had his first English ride on October 12 (Libra, unplaced in a Newmarket nursery) but the gamble came unstuck. St Cloud was unplaced in the Cesarewitch and beaten a head in the Cambridgeshire. Sloan was convinced he had won and told the judge so in no uncertain manner. He clearly wished to start as he meant to go on.

The pattern of phenomenal success was quickly established when Sloan returned to England in September 1898. He took Newmarket's First October Meeting by storm. On the Tuesday he won on his only two mounts; on Wednesday he won on two out of three and on Thursday three from four. On Friday came the *piece de resistance*: five wins and a second from seven rides. Back home Sloan had twice ridden five out of five but these four days were undoubtedly something special; twelve winners out of 16. By the time of his 98th and last ride of the season Sloan's score had risen to 43. 'If I were an owner,' stated Lambton's jockey Fred Rickaby, 'I should not run a horse unless Sloan rode it.' The floodgates opened: 1899 saw an American invasion. Lester Reiff (55 winners), 'Skeets' Martin (43) and John Reiff (27) all made their mark but it was Sloan (108 from 345 mounts) who stole the show, finishing fifth in the list behind Sam Loates's total of 160 gained from over twice as many rides. After this, bookmakers virtually throughout the country resorted to the cynical manoeuvre of charging five per cent on all his winning mounts. Sloan, however, remained the punters' pal. One of the London papers even ran a poetry competition in his honour. The first prize began:

> *Of Toddy Sloan now let us sing,*
> *Whose praises through the country ring,*
> *Undoubtedly the jockey king,*
> *Proclaimed by everybody.*

Much of Sloan's success resulted from the patronage of Lord William

Tod Sloan on the filly Sibola, whose 1000 Guineas victory of 1899 was his first and only Classic success.

Beresford, whose horses also benefited from the services of an American trainer in John Huggins at Heath House. For a brief period until Beresford's untimely death and Sloan's warning-off in 1900, the Beresford–Huggins–Sloan alliance threatened to register the kind of sweeping success enjoyed by the earlier Heath House triumvirate of Falmouth, Dawson and Archer. Beresford usually won around a dozen races a season but in Sloan's first full season of 1899 the figure soared to 69, three times the amount of the second owner in the list. Huggins also topped his table. Like Sloan, his methods were also a superb advertisement for things American. Huggins' stables were airy and cool with open doors, far different from their stuffy English counterparts. He swore by the lighter aluminium racing plates (made to order at Tiffanys) which he felt were the equivalent of four lengths over a mile, and he believed in the clock rather than weight on the trial grounds. Most of the Beresford horses, too, were American-bred.

Heath House did not have things all its own way in 1899. Flying

Fox, not Caiman, won the Triple Crown and although Sibola won the 1000 Guineas she ran second in the Oaks when she ought to have won comfortably. 'I shall always put it down to my own fault and temper,' said Sloan uncharacteristically. He had repeatedly tried to anticipate the start and having no doubt antagonised the starter he then found himself left when the field was allowed to go. 'I was mad with rage and in my furious temper I did what I had always told young boys never to attempt . . . I made up all the ground going up the hill.' Sibola still managed to dispute a close finish with Musa, whom she'd easily vanquished in the Guineas, and in fact Sloan reckoned he had got up. 'First the starter and then the judge,' he moaned. Nor did the following season's Classics bring greater fortune: second in the 1000, third in the Derby, Oaks and St Leger. Ironically, in 1901 Huggins won the Derby with Volodyovski, on whom Sloan would have worn the Beresford jacket had fate not intervened.

One particular half-hour typified Tod Sloan's approach to his profession. In the 1899 Great Jubilee he needed all his wiles to land a gamble on Knight of the Thistle, a huge, ungainly and slightly ungenerous beast. In the next race he was due to ride a 2-year-old called Bobette for Lambton. 'That was the meanest horse I've ever ridden. I'm tired to death and I can't ride any more,' he informed the trainer, and proceeded to lie down in the paddock. However, the instant he clapped eyes on Bobette looking a picture of health and ready to run for her life, he leapt to his feet ready, willing and, ultimately able to win the race. He was an unpardonable prima donna, besides being a spiv and a petty hoodlum. Beresford, the nicest of men, always stood by him. For instance, at the Ascot meeting of 1899 Sloan got himself into a fracas with a waiter which resulted in the latter receiving a cut lip from a champagne bottle. The scandal subsided when Lord William bought off the waiter. To his credit, once he knew this, Sloan insisted on repaying the money. At one time Sloan claimed to have over $1 million in the Bank of England, but a suite of rooms at the Hotel Cecil and nightly card-schools with wild American gamblers like Riley Grannan and John 'Betcha-a-million' Gates soon relieved him of that. As befitted someone who kept such company, Sloan was handy with a gun: in 1903 he won the Grand Prix du Littoral in Monte Carlo by killing 13 birds straight. But gambling was the bane of Sloan's life and it was this compulsion that brought about his downfall in the autumn of 1900.

As a jockey Sloan was not permitted to bet – but little things like rules were minor inconveniences. Accordingly, he and his cronies went for a big punt on Codoman in the Cambridgeshire. Nothing would be left to chance. In order to gauge the strength of key opponents, the cabal arranged for jockeys 'sympathetic' to their cause

Two innocent little boys: the Reiff brothers Lester (left) and John.

to ride them in gallops. Their influence even extended to allocating mounts in the race itself. The one stumbling block was the Irish-trained Berrill, to be partnered by the incorruptible Irish champion John Thompson. Try as they might, Sloan's accomplices could not nobble Thompson or the horse and, naturally, Sod's Law prevailed: Berrill beat Codoman by three lengths. Sloan was beside himself with fury. 'You Irish devil,' he shouted, throwing his cap at Thompson's feet, 'if I had won that race the stewards could have had that hat and this shirt for breakfast. I could have laughed at them.' Sloan finally got his comeuppance, for a steward was within earshot; the next day he was summoned. Was it true he had stood to win £66 000? 'Oh yes, I betted but I understand it is quite legal for a jockey to bet on his own horse,' he replied, showing an outrageous lack of either penitence or knowledge of the rules under which he'd been granted a licence. Sloan was dismissed with a serious reprimand but any thoughts he entertained of being let off lightly were soon dispelled when he was given to understand that applying for a licence in 1901 would be a waste of energy. The Jockey Club had seen enough; consequently, Sloan missed riding a Derby winner and forfeited, moreover, a £6000 retainer to ride for King Edward VII.

The last occasion an English crowd applauded the little man's unique talent was on 26 October and he rewarded the faithful with a double on De Ruby and Encombe. For the next 15 years he applied for his licence and 15 times his request was denied. The slippery slope was steep and descent total. Sloan rode a bit in France but was warned off in 1903 and kicked out of the country; in 1915 he received the same treatment from the British authorities for running a gaming-house in London. On his return to the United States he married the musical comedy star Julia Sanderson but she swiftly departed and he took to bumming around the South West. Writer and

Left: Lester Reiff in the saddle, the first American champion with 143 winners in 1900. Because of his height he never rode as short as his compatriots.

journalist Damon Runyon once discovered him working as a gateman at a racetrack on the Mexican border. Eventually he wound up behind a bar in Los Angeles, where, in 1933, he died in the charity ward of the city hospital. 'I really do think the life of Tod Sloan, the awful failure and waste of it, should be a lesson to any young jockey,' said Steve Donoghue, unaware that he, too, would fall into some of the same traps.

The Reiff brothers soon followed Sloan. Lester was champion jockey with 143 winners in 1900 and took Sloan's place on Volodyovski in the 1901 Derby. However, four months later, riding De Lacy in a small race at Manchester, he was beaten a head by his brother on Minnie Dee. The two Reiffs may have resembled innocent, pink-cheeked choirboys (especially in comparison to Sloan) but their involvement with the American gambling syndicates was as deep as Sloan's. The Stewards of the Jockey Club decided that Lester Reiff had not done his best to win, withdrew his licence and warned him off. De Lacy was a moody creature and some thought Reiff unjustly punished: indeed, the warning-off order was cancelled in 1904. But Reiff had walked a narrow line once too often.

The message was not lost on younger brother John who moved to France, where among the important races he won were both the Derby and Oaks. Although not as successful (or as obviously dishonest) as Lester, he could ride at a much lighter weight. On his arrival in England as a 14-year-old he stood four feet tall, weighed about 4½ stones and, dressed in Eton collar and knickerbockers, was fussed over like a pet poodle by women who should have known better. He was exactly the sort of brilliant lightweight to facilitate a handicap coup and in the space of two seasons he won the Great Met, Royal Hunt Cup, Stewards' Cup, Liverpool Summer Cup, Chesterfield Cup, Ebor and Cambridgeshire. Unlike his brother he did return to England for a number of important rides. In 1907 he won the Derby on Orby and in 1912 he was victorious again, leading from start to finish on Tagalie, the last filly to win an Epsom Derby. Twelve months later he was first past the post on the heavily backed Craganour only to suffer dubious disqualification for 'bumping and boring'. Somewhat ironically, he had won the 2000 Guineas by a head on Louvois when in the opinion of everyone at Newmarket bar the judge, Craganour had won.

American jockeys of less blemished character were John Henry 'Skeets' Martin and Daniel Aloysius Maher. New Yorker Martin made his English debut at the Liverpool Summer Meeting of 1899 winning the St George Stakes on Sweet Marjorie. When a fierce temper and a tendency to hit the bottle were not combining to undermine his confidence, 'Skeets' was as fine a rider as any. Sharp-witted at the barrier and the possessor of lovely hands, he was always in demand, for 2-year-olds in particular. His best year was 1902 when

'Skeets' Martin

John Reiff returned to England in 1912 to win the Derby on Tagalie, the last filly to win an Epsom renewal of the race.

80 successes included the Derby on Ard Patrick; a year later he won the 2000 Guineas on Rock Sand but gave way to Maher in the Derby and St Leger. The most popular horse Martin rode was unquestionably the gelding Hornet's Beauty, on whom he won 15 races in seasons 1911 and 1913 (from 18 starts), including four at Royal Ascot. Out of season Martin was a winter sports enthusiast who instantly decamped for St Moritz where skiing, curling and the Cresta Run revived his sense of well-being. Sadly, after he quit riding, unsuccessful property speculation reduced him to the position of hotel doorkeeper and he ended his days the inmate of an old people's home in Switzerland.

The career of Danny Maher was marked by constant comparison with two other great jockeys – his compatriot Sloan, against whom he had little opportunity to ride in England; and the brilliant young Australian prodigy Frank Wootton, an entirely different sort of character to himself, with whom he waged an occasionally bitter rivalry in the years prior to World War I. The son of Irish emigrants, Maher was born in Hartford, Connecticut, on 29 October 1881 and rode his first winner at fourteen. He came to England in the autumn of 1900 principally to ride for Mr Pierre Lorillard and won on his first two mounts, Paiute and Bad News, at Manchester on September 21. However, Lorillard died in 1901 and Maher established his reputation on two horses belonging to Sir James Miller: Aida in the

*Danny Maher, the
'aristocrat' of jockeys.*

1000 Guineas of 1901 and Rock Sand in the Derby and St Leger of
1903. George Blackwell also trained a useful colt called Flotsam for
Sir Daniel Cooper and the two knights reputedly tossed a coin for
Maher's services. Cooper called correctly and Maher rode Flotsam to
be second in the 2000 Guineas and thus missed the opportunity of
winning a Triple Crown. Nevertheless, Skyscraper's third place in the
1000 Guineas and Oaks meant he'd been placed in all five Classics,
something rarely achieved before or since. George Barrett did so in
1890 without winning one Classic and Walter Swinburn did it in
1986, winning the Derby. In its own way Maher's impact was as
sensational as Sloan's. Furthermore, he lacked Sloan's brattishness and
jealously guarded his good name. It was said he had left America
because one afternoon his riding was, unjustly he felt, called into

question. After he had been beaten at Leicester on a horse called Sallust, the local stewards asked him to explain his riding and referred the matter to the Jockey Club. Maher was exonerated but he refused to ride at Leicester again.

Even though Maher inevitably mixed with his fair share of seamy characters, a blend of intelligence and charm opened innumerable doors to him; in truth, something of the snob lived within Danny Maher. In October 1909 he rode Edward VII's Minoru to victory in the Free Handicap and was overwhelmed when the King went to the weighing room to shake his hand and express his gratitude. 'I have at last achieved my ambition,' mumbled the stupefied jockey. Maher was perfectly happy to be accepted into the establishment fold on its terms rather than his own. He married the actress Doreen Frazier, darling of the Lyceum, and for a time lived at Cropwell Hall, near Nottingham, and was regularly to be spotted out with the Hunt. In short, Maher quickly appreciated the significance of forelock-tugging in affecting social advancement. Right well could *The Sporting Life*'s Meyrick Good write of him: 'Danny was the 'aristocrat' of all the jockeys I have known.' He was ever eager to dispense largesse in the direction of old friends and acquaintances, such as the famous card-seller 'Old Kate', but he seldom, if ever, sought their company. A genuine affection did develop between Maher and the 5th Earl of Rosebery who invited him to cruise on his yacht and to stay at Dalmeny, his Scottish country seat. Maher reciprocated by riding Cicero to victory in the 1905 Derby and Neil Gow in the 1910 2000 Guineas. A measure of Maher's lofty status on and off the track may be gleaned from the size and source of his retainers for 1910 – £4000 from his first retainer Lord Rosebery, £2000 from the Australian millionaire Mr AW Cox, while for the same amount Mr Leopold de Rothschild was content to exercise third claim. He also rode frequently for Lord Derby. Boasting that calibre of patronage Maher could hardly fail and he rarely did: on six occasions between 1906 and 1913 his winning percentage exceeded 26 and in 1906 was as high as 29.17. 'He was the most stylish finisher,' said Good. 'I have seen him ride races that almost made one's hair stand on end.'

Maher made much more of a conscious effort than either Sloan or the Reiffs to adapt the Yankee style of riding to English tracks, though in fairness to his fellow countrymen, he did benefit from more time in which to experiment. He realised that a method honed on the dead-level American race bowls demanded refinement if it was to cope with undulating switchback courses on which maintaining a horse's balance became a considerably tougher proposition. Maher also had to overcome sterner opposition from the English jockeys, who were by now beginning to put into practice the gospel according to Sloan. To consistently outride them, averred trainers like Lambton, Morton and Sam Darling, proved Maher was by far and away the

STEVE

American jockey *par excellence*. 'He was the true artist. Sloan was the relentless revolutionary,' wrote Sydney Galtrey, the much respected Hotspur of the *Daily Telegraph*.

Despite professing a dislike for Epsom (especially on a wet day, when he considered Tattenham Corner dangerous) Maher won a third Derby on Major Loder's Spearmint in 1906 and two days later completed the Classic double on Lord Derby's Keystone in the Oaks. Some said Maher lost his nerve after fracturing his skull in a motor car smash in 1903 but this failed to stop him from once riding over hurdles. As a novice under National Hunt Rules, Maher was entitled to claim 5lb and his mount Dafila easily justified favouritism at Kempton in December 1908. 'His seat was the perfect mixture of the old and the new style,' said Keystone's trainer George Lambton, another bastion of the Turf who warmed to Maher. 'His patience was wonderful and nothing would induce him to ride a horse hard unless he had him going as he wanted. When Danny took a fancy to a horse, he wanted to be on his back every day if possible, and when a jockey does this it is wonderful how much he can improve a horse. I know that Danny, when he rode for me, made one or two quite ordinary horses into good ones.'

Accordingly, if a jockey like Maher was thought to have got it wrong, the error received all the more attention. He was widely blamed for giving Pretty Polly too much to do in the Prix du Conseil Municipal of 1904, thus bringing about her first defeat in 16 races. Maher believed she was not a true stayer. 'If I meet her in a two mile race with a good horse I shall beat her,' he insisted; in the 1906 Ascot Gold Cup he did just that on Bachelor's Button. Lemberg's defeat in the 1910 St Leger may also have resulted from want of stamina but Maher still took plenty of stick. Earlier that summer Lemberg's elder half-brother Bayardo got Maher into even hotter water. He had won all but two of his 24 races prior to the Goodwood Cup of 1910, among them the St Leger and Ascot Gold Cup with Maher up. Only two others thought it worth opposing him and he started 20–1 on. However, Maher overdid the waiting tactics, allowing the 3-year-old Magic (receiving 36lb) to set a strong gallop and, at one point, lead Bayardo by a furlong. Consequently Bayardo's final race resulted in ignominious defeat and provoked his trainer, Alec Taylor, the 'Wizard of Manton' and a man not noted for blaming jockeys when things went wrong, to say bluntly: 'Maher let Magic get a furlong in front and never attempted to close the tremendous gap until reaching the comparatively short straight. And he was giving away all that weight too. I always told Maher the day would come when something awful would happening through overdoing the waiting and waiting.'

Every jockey has his weaknesses and Taylor had put his finger on one of Maher's. Another was his fiery Irish temper. Generally this was kept under control, unlike his weight – and thus his health –

Previous page: Danny Maher on Rock Sand – but for the toss of a coin the American would have partnered the colt to the 1903 Triple Crown.

which Maher experienced difficulty holding below 8st 8lb after 1910. He was always a delicate man, inclined to be consumptive and often after a strenuous ride almost speechless from want of breath. Heavy smoking had not helped and he was a very sick man by 20 November 1913 when he rode his last winner, Declaration, in a Liverpool seller. The flushed cheeks, abnormally bright eyes, rasping cough and shortness of breath were symptomatic of tuberculosis.

During the winter of 1913–14 Maher, now a naturalised British subject, went to South Africa as the guest of Sir Abe Bailey in the hope that the dry, warm climate might improve his condition. He returned bronzed on the outside but still ravaged on the inside. Every night he slept in a tent on his lawn so that fresh air could have full play in his defective lungs. The comeback mooted for 1915 failed to get off the ground, though Maher did take one ride. On Thursday 16 September Mr JB Joel's Sun Yat, who had 10st 1lb to carry, looked a good thing for the Eriswell Plate at Newmarket. Against his doctor's advice, Maher could not resist the temptation. The crowd gave him a rousing cheer as he cantered the 6–5 on favourite down the Rowley Mile but the partnership got away badly and could finish no nearer than sixth. Maher was back alongside the Rowley Mile for the Cambridgeshire of 1916, propped up in the seat of a motor car. He was ready for death, and eight days later, on 8 November, he died at the age of 35. Maher's funeral at Paddington Cemetery vividly illustrated the diverse circles in which he moved. All the arrangements were made by Lord Rosebery, who accompanied the coffin from the cemetery gates to the graveside where Old Kate was among the mourners; floral tributes included one from Bob Sievier bearing the card, 'Weighed in, old friend, farewell'. Another came from Maher's natural successor, Steve Donoghue, who felt his loss greatly. 'He was the most brilliant jockey I have ever known and one of the finest characters I have ever known.'

Declaration was the 115th winner of Maher's second championship season (and the 1421st of his English career for a winning percentage of 25.26) which came five years after the first. The four intervening titles had all fallen to his arch adversary Frank Wootton. In just eight English seasons Wootton rode 882 winners for a success rate of 22.8%, a truly remarkable feat when one remembers he was only a 12-year-old boy at the outset. His first two seasons mustered 55 victories but in 1908 he finished a mere ten behind Maher's 139, initiating the sequence of championship duels which enthralled racegoers. In 1909 (aged 15) and in 1910 Wootton took the title with scores of 165 and 137 to Maher's 116 and 127; in 1911 the American could only total 99 (third place) to the Australian's 187 and the following year the champion retained his crown with 118 to Maher's 109. Wootton's 91 of 1913 (24 behind Maher's winning total) signified the onset of the weight problems which prompted a switch to jump racing after the war. Even so, this consummate horseman could not be excluded from the limelight: in 1921 he topped the jumping table with 61 successes to become the only man ever to head both lists. 'He and Danny Maher were great rivals and there was not much love lost between them,' George Lambton was to write of his two former jockeys, 'but I am bound to say that it was chiefly Maher's fault, for Frank Wootton was always a good-natured, easy-going boy when off a horse; but in a race, like all good jockeys, he was quick to take advantage of anybody or anything. I think he had a cooler head than Danny, who had a very quick temper, and in a big field of horses he was perhaps a little better at overcoming difficulties.'

But was he, all in all, a better jockey than Maher? Jack Jarvis, who as Lord Rosebery's trainer was open to a charge of bias, declared: 'Frank Wootton could be very effective, but to compare him with Danny Maher was like comparing a T-model Ford with a Rolls-Royce; they both got you there in the end, but you had a far better ride in the Rolls.'

Wootton achieved twice as many championships as Maher but only succeeded in two Classics to the American's nine. However, in one of those two, the 1910 St Leger, he enjoyed the gratification of upsetting Maher who was riding the 5–4 on favourite, Lemberg. Wootton rode Swynford, who represented Maher's old accomplices Lord Derby and George Lambton. Lemberg had beaten him in the Derby and the St James's Palace Stakes, but after Ascot Swynford began to improve by leaps and bounds and he won the Liverpool Summer Cup in a canter. Believing the favourite to be a non-stayer, Lambton instructed Wootton to make the pace a hot one. Wootton did as he was told but, still only a 16-year-old boy weighing 7st 4lb, the effort of doing so on a big, powerful horse like Swynford reduced him to near exhaustion inside the final furlong and, hanging away from the rail, he was almost caught by Bronzino. 'The jockey was far more beat than the horse,' joked Lambton. Lemberg finished third; that night young Wootton was heard shouting in his sleep, 'I won't let you up, Danny, you shan't get up.' Lambton recognized the physical and mental enormity of Wootton's achievement in getting Swynford home with the spectre of Maher at his shoulder. 'He was a great jockey: all horses or courses were alike to him. I have never known a jockey with fewer fads and dislikes, and he seldom came back with an excuse after a race. When he was beat it was because the horse was not good enough.'

The animosity between Wootton and Maher never flagged, not even toward the end of their weight-restricted careers. In the 1913 Nassau Stakes at Goodwood, Wootton, riding the 1000 Guineas winner Jest for Charles Morton, was beaten by Arda, partnered by Maher, who had refused to let him through on the rails. Jest's

Frank Wootton, the Boy Wonder, Classic winner and champion at the age of 15.

connections duly lodged an objection. Maher contended Wootton had no business to be there. 'I would have done the same if I had been riding for you,' he told Morton. 'What would you have done? Would you have let him through?' After 45 minutes' deliberation the stewards announced that although Maher had undoubtedly stopped Jest from coming up the inside, they felt Wootton had no right to try and force his way through. Arda kept the race.

Wootton's obsession with the rails was to bring him as much trouble as Maher's penchant for waiting. In this regard he could lay some blame at his father's door. Australian trainer Richard Wootton had set up shop at Treadwell House, Epsom in 1906 accompanied by Frank (then aged 12) and his other son Stanley (nine). As the boys could not ride in Australia until they were 14, Wootton had taken them to South Africa where Frank rode his first winner in the Germiston Handicap at Turffontein when he was 9 years and 10 months old. Like all Wootton's apprentices the brothers were taught to go the shortest route and heaven help them if they were espied doing otherwise. Stanley became a tidy enough jockey to pull off the Chester Cup–Northumberland Plate double on Elizabetta in 1910, and although he eventually found fame as an outstanding tutor of apprentices in the manner of his father, his own skills in the saddle were markedly inferior to his elder brother's. Then again, most jockeys were inferior to Frank Wootton. His first English winner, it goes without saying, was for his father – Retrieve, at Folkestone on 23 August 1906 – and 14 months later he landed some hefty Australian bets when Demure won the Cesarewitch at 4–1. Landing gambles for his father become more of a regular feature than riding Classic winners – for that, he had to wait until his first championship season of 1909. After riding Perola into third place in the 1000 Guineas he beat the King's filly Princesse de Galles to win the Oaks by two lengths. A Classic and a championship at the age of 15 – accomplishments surmised beyond any other jockey in the history of the English Turf. John Parsons is thought to have been 16 when he won the 1862 Derby, while Archer was 17 when he won a Classic and became champion in 1874.

Had it not been for his railing instinct Wootton might conceivably have won the Derby of 1913 on Shogun, because he was hopelessly shut-in when the barging match between Craganour and Aboyeur caused them to roll down the camber towards the inside rail. Richard Wootton, the colt's trainer, was on the verge of tears. 'Did you ever see anything like that in your life?' he said to Charles Morton. 'I thought he was an absolute certainty.' Morton could only remind him of the pitfalls awaiting his boys if they stuck to the fence. 'They undoubtedly won innumerable races by this method and also lost many, so it is probably six of one and half a dozen of the other.' On this all-important occasion Wootton had fallen on his sword.

Frank Wootton survived war service in Mesopotamia, which encompassed a victory in no less than the Baghdad Grand National, and also his one attempt at the genuine article which ended in a fall from Any Time in 1921. He trained for a while before returning to Australia in 1933. He was unquestionably one of the all-time greats. That winning percentage of 22.8 achieved as a teenager says as much: by comparison, Gordon Richards's was 22.3 and Lester Piggott's (up to his 1985 retirement) was 22.0. Maher's was 25.3!

Wootton was in the vanguard of the Australian wave which followed in the wake of its American cousin. Reared on similar tracks and public training regimes geared to the clock, the Australians were also excellent judges of pace. 'Many people, I am fully aware, strongly disapprove of trainers engaging imported jockeys,' said Morton, who frequently used Wootton, 'but every trainer knows that the supply of competent horsemen is so limited nowadays that it becomes practically imperative to engage the best man you can get, irrespective of his birthplace. Anyhow, Empire preference is good, sound business.' Other Australians to impose their presence were Frank Bullock and Bernard 'Brownie' Carslake, though neither confined their riding exclusively to England.

Frank Bullock in the colours of Lord Astor for whom he won the 1925 1000 Guineas and Oaks on Saucy Sue.

With the notable exception of his 1905 Melbourne Cup victory on Blue Spec, many of Bullock's finest hours occurred on the European mainland rather than in England. From 1908–13 he rode in Germany as first jockey to the Graditz Stud, the Kaiser's stable, and won the 1912 German Derby on Gulliver II. In 1920 he won the Grand Prix de Paris and Prix de l'Arc de Triomphe on the English-trained Comrade; the following year he achieved the Chantilly Classic double of Prix de Diane (Oaks) on Doniazade and Prix du Jockey-Club (Derby) on Ksar; and in 1922 he partnered Ksar to an Arc victory. The French *turfistes* considered him superior to both Steve Donoghue and Joe Childs. In addition he twice won the Irish Oaks and out in India he won the prestigious King Emperor's Cup in Calcutta. His second place on Clarissimus in the 1916 St Leger proved the forerunner of several near misses in the English Classics, however, and he only won two, the 1000 Guineas and Oaks of 1925 on Lord Astor's Saucy Sue. Bullock was a superlative all-round jockey who was an absolute wizard in match races and no rider more upheld the highest standards of fair play and rectitude.

He could have ridden Pogrom when she won the 1922 Oaks but honoured his obligation to Laughter, owned by JB Joel and trained by Morton, even though both were prepared to release him. 'He was an admirable type of man, one of the straightest jockeys I have ever known and scrupulously fair in all his dealings,' said the trainer. Flying and cigarettes were the only crosses Bullock had to bear: the prospect of the former reduced him to jelly while he couldn't exist without the latter and was one of the ringleaders in a jockeys' revolt

Brownie Carslake, who for years lived on 'a cup of tea and hope'.

Beetle-browed Joe Childs.

of 1922 against an edict that forbade smoking during racing hours. 'A cigarette between races is just what a jockey needs,' he told the Newmarket stewards, 'it calms the nerves after a strenuous race and takes the mind off things. It would be impossible to do without a cigarette after hard wasting . . . I would rather go without a meal.'

Bullock's retirement in 1925 was hastened by several nasty falls but the perils of 'hard wasting' had no sharper definition than the face of fellow Aussie Bernard Carslake, whose nickname 'Brownie' derived from his sallow, health-drained complexion. He was quite a tall, big-boned man who often existed on no more than 'a cup of tea and hope', as he put it. If that were insufficient to make him actually feel like death, he still managed to convey that impression. The aquiline nose dividing a pair of piercing black eyes set beneath severely brushed-back black hair yielded an uncompromisingly saturnine air which was reinforced by a finely-tuned sardonic wit. 'Don't believe anything you hear and only believe half of what you see,' was one of his stock replies. Sometimes without even opening his mouth Carslake, according to journalist Quintin Gilbey, 'could make you feel you were something the cat had brought in which would have been better left outside.'

However, whilst the duration of his European career – 1906 to 1940 – easily outstripped Bullock's, Carslake's probity did not attain the immunity of his compatriot. Ugly rumour surrounded his victory on Salmon Trout in the 1924 St Leger, for instance. Victory in the Princess of Wales's Stakes gave the Aga Khan's colt a chance in the final Classic, yet the bookmakers, particularly Mo Tarsh, a friend of Carslake's, began to lay him heavily in the weeks before the race. The stewards smelled a rat and told Carslake his riding would be closely scrutinised. On the day, Salmon Trout came with a wet sail inside the last 100 yards to beat Santorb by two lengths. The conviction that Carslake had originally intended to stop Salmon Trout from winning but had changed his mind was supported by the market, in which the horse was a solid 6–1 second favourite. Years later Carslake admitted to Quintin Gilbey that he had thought Salmon Trout would not stay the trip and so he instructed Tarsh on his behalf to lay the horse to lose. 'But I was determined to give him the best ride possible.' To chance his arm like this Carslake must have been beleaguered financially, since betting alone constituted a warning-off offence. Instead of wearing the broad grins they usually wear when a favourite is beaten in a Classic, the bookmakers looked flabbergasted. 'They gave the idea of having been betrayed,' observed Sydney Galtrey, before adding cryptically, 'The possibilities of boomerang damage had clearly never been entertained.'

Carslake's earliest experiences came in Australian 'Bush' meetings. As a 12-year-old he won three races on the same horse in two days. His first English winner (aptly named The Swagman) was achieved at

Childs with Coronach, on whom he won the 1926 Derby.

Birmingham during a brief visit in 1906. Most of the next ten years Carslake spent plying his trade round Europe. He became champion jockey in Austria–Hungary (winning the Hungarian St Leger and the German Derby) and Russia, before the 1917 Revolution prompted his return to England and the advantage of plentiful opportunities from George Lambton and Atty Persse. For the former he won the 1918 1000 Guineas on Ferry and the 1919 St Leger on Keysoe; for Persse he won the 2000 Guineas of 1920 on Tetratema and the 1000 Guineas of 1922 on Silver Urn. Tetratema failed to stay in a strongly-run race for the Derby; some Jeremiahs were critical of Carslake's riding round Epsom, but while it is true he was three times placed in a Derby without winning, he rode an enchanting race to win the 1934 Oaks on Light Brocade.

The most distinctive facet of Carslake's race-riding was his finish, for he liked to come late and, spartan diet or no, he was immensely strong. Although only able to use the whip effectively (and then only sparingly) in his left hand, Carslake kept his mounts balanced and dead straight with the tremendous strength of his long legs. Foxlaw's Ascot Gold Cup of 1927 and Epigram's Doncaster Cup of 1938 are often cited as quintessential Carslake, but in Lambton's opinion he

Brown Betty, who gave Joe Childs the last of his 15 Classic victories in the 1933 1000 Guineas.

never surpassed his effort on Diadem in the 1918 Salford Borough Handicap at Manchester. Carrying 9st 8lb they got up to pip Golly-Eyes (receiving two stone) and the July Cup winner Irish Elegance (receiving nearly three stone) in the dying moments. 'She was a tired mare a hundred yards from home and Carslake fairly lifted her past the post. Although he had never hit her, she had given every ounce.'

Off a horse there was nothing Carslake enjoyed more – like all true sons of Australia – than a game of cricket and, a useful right-hand bat and tricky slow left-arm bowler, he was the scourge of the Press team in their annual encounters with the Jockeys. At least Carslake had no weight problems on the cricket field. In 1928 his plight was so acute as to bring about his retirement in favour of training but when the change of occupation failed to increase his weight he resumed riding. However, a further ten years living on 'a cup of tea and hope' could have but one outcome for a man in his fifties: on 20 April 1940, in the aftermath of a short-head victory, Carslake collapsed in the Alexandra Park weighing room. The serious heart disease diagnosed ensured his immediate retirement. He did not take readily to his new existence, and death the following July was in some respects a merciful release. 'The monotony is dreadful, having nothing to do except read the paper and dream of great times in the past.' By permission of the stewards, Carslake's ashes were scattered over the Rowley Mile at Newmarket, which had always been his favourite course.

When it came to a beetle-browed glare and withering ripostes there was one jockey who could out-Carslake Carslake at the drop of a hat. Joe Childs was as tall as Carslake, and accordingly experienced similar anxiety on the scales, but with his dark, bushy eyebrows giving broody, bellicose expression to a hair-trigger temper, he made Carslake seem positively cheerful. Sensitive to criticism and quick to take offence, he would argue with anyone, be they his NCOs in the Army ('What I do not know about grooming a horse you certainly could not teach me'), an employer (a blazing row with Lord Astor's racing manager cost him that job) or a steward ('You were not at the gate and could not have seen the incident as you stated you did'). Although senior jockeys knew these rages soon abated, young apprentices cowered at his very approach. Childs also stood accused of only being adept at riding one kind of race – to wait and come from behind. Justified or not, this tag gave rise to one of racing's peerless one-liners after Childs' mount Coronach had made virtually every yard to win the 1926 Derby. One can almost touch the sense of betrayal in Childs' voice as he muttered the immortal victory quote: 'The bastard ran away with me.'

Coronach's martinet of a trainer, Fred Darling, was one of the select few possessing the necessary clout to handle Childs. Other trainers to whom Childs bent the knee were Alec Taylor, Willie Jarvis and Cecil Boyd-Rochfort, for whom he rode the last of his 15 Classic winners, Brown Betty in the 1000 Guineas of 1933. The best of the quintet he partnered for Taylor was Gainsborough, a wartime Triple Crown winner in 1918, but the Classic which meant most to him was the single one he rode for Jarvis, since the colours he wore on Scuttle in the 1929 1000 Guineas were those of his sovereign George V. Jarvis was a good friend and Childs was a fervent royalist. Whenever he won a race for the King during his decade as royal jockey, he would immediately send his valet out for champagne so he might toast the man he referred to as 'My Governor'. As a token of gratitude for Scuttle's victory, the King presented his jockey with a cane which became Childs' most treasured possession. 'Scuttle was His Majesty's only Classic success and that I should have been fortunate enough to win this race for him will always live in my memory.'

All Childs' patriotism was required at the start of the Guineas when Scuttle began to act the fool. Childs rewarded for patience, declared the *Daily Express* headline at this display of self-control. Perhaps old Joe was angling for a knighthood. On the other hand, Childs might just have recalled his experiences on Fifinella at the same gate in 1916: she, too, played up, Childs lost his temper and hit her. As a result the 11–10 favourite sulked away her chance. Because the colts of 1916 were so mediocre (with the exception of Hurry On, who was not entered) Fifinella then lined up for the Derby. On the morning of the race she behaved like a right little madam, greeting her trainer Dick Dawson with a kick and a bite and refusing to be dressed over or have her mane plaited. In the race she took no interest in proceedings until well inside the last furlong. Suddenly she consented to gallop with a vengeance and Childs shot her through a narrow gap to win by a neck. Two days later, behaving now like a lady instead of a cook, she added the Oaks in a canter by five lengths, the fourth (and last) filly ever to complete such a double. Childs rode his final winner at Derby in November 1935 some 35 years after his first on Lincoln's Carholme. He was never champion jockey but he was associated with several oustanding racehorses both in England and throughout Europe, where he won the Grand Prix de Paris (twice) and the French Derby. His career ended on the note he would have wished: on 17 December the King invited him to an audience at Buckingham Palace.

The youthful Steve Donoghue modelled himself on Tod Sloan but it was the more polished and urbane Danny Maher whom he eventually resembled most. Indeed, Maher was so impressed by the young jockey that he put him in for rides, and as the great American's career wound down it was to Donoghue that many of his owners were to turn. Ever since the day Donoghue tamed a bucking donkey during a visit of Ohmy's Circus to his home town of Warrington, he

Donoghue up on Diadem – the filly he described as the 'sweetest' horse he ever rode.

STEVE

had been consumed by a passion for horses. After placing his feet on the bottom rung of the ladder with John Porter (he lasted four months – the first horse he 'did' threw him and scattered Porter's string, earning the boy a thrashing), Dobson Peacock and Alfred Sadler, he developed his technique with spells under Edward Johnson in France (his first winner came on Hanoi at Hyeres, a tiny Mediterranean track, on 24 April 1905) and Michael Dawson on The Curragh. In 1908 Donoghue became Irish champion and rode the first of his 11 Irish Classic winners, Queen of Peace in the Oaks. That same season he had his first mount in England (finishing third) and three years later accepted a retainer from Atty Persse. The process of capturing the hearts and imaginations of the English public had begun.

As far as horses were concerned Steve Donoghue was the nearest thing to Doctor Doolittle: he really did seem able to communicate with the thoroughbred like no other. 'My sympathy with them,' he called it. Brown Jack, he said, was his favourite; Humorist the gamest; Gay Crusader the best; The Tetrarch the fastest; Tishy the slowest; Ramus, the French nutcase on whom he gave a 25-minute rodeo display in order to reach the start of the 1923 Goodwood Cup, the most bad-tempered; Diadem the sweetest – he won 13 out of 22 races on Lambton's filly. 'I've seen her after a hard race, as he unsaddled her, turn round and rub her nose against his hands more like a dog than a horse,' said the trainer. One day in 1919 Donoghue rode her with one hand useless owing to a broken wrist. 'She seemed to know that I was injured for she helped me in every way. She was carrying a great weight and it was a fast-run race, but she did everything and I won a grand race by a short head. She wanted nothing more than a kind word whispered in her ear at the crucial moment and she would strain every nerve in her body. She always seemed to understand every word I said to her.' Donoghue's divine rapport with horses summed up in four sentences.

And then there was the telepathic understanding he shared with the incomparable Brown Jack – 'I loved the old fellow like a brother' – which gave rise to the historic six consecutive wins in the Queen Alexandra Stakes, not to mention the Ascot Stakes, Goodwood Cup and Ebor Handicap, in the grand total of 14 they enjoyed together. As a photographer prepared to take Brown Jack's retirement portrait in 1934, the gelding pushed his head forward and licked Donoghue's face from ear to ear and chin to forehead. On the night of a dinner for Donoghue's own retirement in 1937, the old horse's owner Sir Harold Wernher arranged for a radio receiver to be placed in Brown Jack's box so that the jockey could send his old pal a message. When Donoghue signed off with the words, 'Goodnight, Brown Jack, I hope to see you again soon,' the attendant groom swore Brown Jack recognised the voice.

Opposite: 'I love horses with all that is in me.'

STEVE

GREAT JOCKEYS OF THE FLAT

133

STEVE

At the zenith of his powers in the 1920s when the cry 'Come on, Steve' was heard everywhere, Donoghue and his genius were put under the microscope in a newspaper article written by the renowned hurdle race jockey George Duller, no mean stylist himself. 'There is not one secret of astonishing success: there are many,' he argued. Daring, assurance, speed at the gate, balance, judgement of pace, tactical acumen; Duller was unstinting in his praise. Donoghue attributed his alertness at the barrier and knowledge of pace to his grounding at Chantilly, where gallops were timed furlong by furlong. 'This taught us to be keenly on the alert to get away the instant the flag fell; then, knowing that our times would be clocked, each rider learnt to pay great attention to the speed shown by every other animal in the gallop as well as his own.' Duller concluded his piece with some observations of Donoghue on the way to post where, in slower motion, his sorcery might be better appreciated. 'If the horse tried to fight for his head, Donoghue will lean over and give him a reassuring pat on the neck, or, dropping his hands, will take his ear. The effect is magical. The mount becomes calm and tractable immediately.' Underpinning the entire Donoghue method were those exquisite, God-given 'hands' with which he could instil such confidence into the most timorous animal, or master the most fractious beast, that one was given the impression the reins might as well be made of gossamer. Indeed, doctors actually X-rayed them in the forlorn hope of discovering some quality not possessed by other mortals. The gods refused to reveal their secrets that easily.

Donoghue was in his element round Epsom where he won four of the five Derbies between 1921 and 1925. 'On the switchback Epsom track he had no superior in the world,' said Charles Morton, for whom he partnered Humorist in 1921. 'His immense dash and courage was worth 7lb to a horse in a race like the Derby.' Donoghue once more gave a vote of thanks to his education on the tiny French tracks of the Midi which were frequently less than ¾ mile round, all sharp elbows and bends with next to no running rails. 'Unless a jockey was entirely without fear he was useless on these courses.' Consequently, Donoghue was wanted by almost every owner and trainer in the land when the Blue Riband came around and he, in turn, almost always wanted to take his pick of the leading fancies. This situation invariably led to a number of acrimonious exchanges and shattered relationships.

The first two of Donoghue's six Derby victories were in wartime substitutes at Newmarket, on Pommern (1915) and Gay Crusader (1917): on both he went on to complete the Triple Crown, the only jockey to achieve the feat twice. In 1921 Lord Derby had first claim on Donoghue and expected him to ride Glorioso at Epsom. Donoghue had other ideas and despite a £3000 retainer he was released. Nevertheless, Lord Derby made it plain this would be the

Donoghue's least controversial Epsom Derby: no arguments about his choice of mount and Manna wins by eight lengths.

only time he'd waive his claim. Humorist and Donoghue hung on to win by a neck. 'I would rather have cut off my right arm than ever show him the whip. I sat still as a bird on a bush. I think that was the greatest race I have ever ridden.' After weighing-in Donoghue went to Humorist's box where he stayed talking to him. Less than a month later the gallant Humorist was found in a pool of blood, dead from a lung haemorrhage. 'I loved him like a child. It was his love for me which caused him to make that brave effort and win the greatest race in the world with only one lung to feed his dauntless heart.'

The following year saw Donoghue at the centre of a similar contretemps. On the Friday before the race, Lord Woolavington offered him the ride on Captain Cuttle, trained by Fred Darling. The next day, Donoghue turned up at Beckhampton to ride the horse in his final piece of fast work only to find a bemused Darling totally ignorant of any such arrangement. Captain Cuttle bolted home in the Derby by four lengths. Donoghue's machinations continued in 1923. Woolavington now had first call on his services (for a reputed £4000) and wanted him for Knockando, trained by Peter Gilpin. Knockando could not be fancied and as soon as Donoghue was approached to ride Papyrus he quickly protested that he understood his retainer only related to those of Woolavington's horses trained by Darling. Donoghue abandoned Knockando and the third consecutive Derby victory was a formality. At least Manna's success in 1925 was relatively free of controversy. Donoghue had won the 2000 Guineas on him and though there was some talk of him switching to a French challenger he and Manna added the Derby by eight lengths, a margin unsurpassed till 1981.

Donoghue did not reach the frame in another Derby (he rejected what turned out to be a winning ride on April the Fifth in 1932) yet he still managed to make his presence felt. In 1934 he thought he ought to have been riding the unbeaten 11–8 favourite Colombo. Coming down the Hill, Colombo and his new jockey Rae Johnstone were pocketed behind the 25–1 outsider Medieval Knight, had to be pulled wide and failed to catch either Windsor Lad or Easton. Medieval Knight's rider was S Donoghue. 'Had I ridden Colombo he would have won on the bit by lengths,' was the implacable assertion. 'Johnstone just did not know the course well enough and tried to follow me,' he added with a twist of the knife.

Donoghue did depart in a blaze of glory, however. In his last season of 1937 he won the 1000 Guineas and Oaks on Exhibitionnist and the Irish 2000 Guineas and Derby on Phideas. Even if he did Johnstone no favours in 1934 (the Australian bore no grudge) one is tempted to forgive anything of a jockey who so palpably meant every word when he wrote: 'I love horses with all that is in me. Some people think of them as animals – I think of them as my friends, my greatest friends.'

GORDON

GORDON

From the tips of his riding boots to the peak of his cap, all 4ft 11½in of Gordon Richards was imbued with the will to win. No less authorities than the Aga Khan and the Duke of Norfolk said so, and the point was proved 4870 times between 1921 and 1954. For 26 of those 34 seasons Richards reigned supreme as champion jockey (1926 and 1941 were lost due to tuberculosis and a broken leg respectively), a period of domination not exercised before or since – or likely to be in the future. On 12 occasions he rode more than 200 winners, breaking Archer's record in 1933 with a total of 259 which he subsequently raised to 269 in 1947. 'I was lucky because I could stay at eight stone without having to waste. I did not have to have a frugal diet, I could eat almost anything, and so kept my strength up. I was also lucky in having good horses to ride a lot of the time. No matter how talented you are, you can't do it without the horse.'

There is no denying that Richards' riding weight and Fred Darling's retainer, for example, were of the utmost importance, but so was the quality identified by another Turf sage, Lord Rosebery: he lost fewer races he ought to have won than any other jockey. Richards also made few mistakes out of the saddle and the knighthood bestowed on him in 1953 was as much a recognition of the manner in which he had conducted himself as an ambassador for his sport as a reward for his prowess on a horse. 'I am delighted to receive the honour,' he said, 'but I am more delighted at the honour it brings my profession.' Loyalty and integrity meant everything to Richards. In 1946 he rejected a huge retainer of £7000 from the Aga Khan in order to remain with Darling and later refused an offer of £100 000 for the film rights to his life story. No shadow, not even one the faintest of grey, ever hung over Gordon Richards. As a jockey and a man he was a true champion, a view reinforced in 1970 when he was elected an honorary member of the Jockey Club, an absolutely unique distinction for a former professional jockey.

The formula for unparalleled success was not discernible from either Richards' seat or his style of riding, which were not calculated to wow the purists. The rudiments of his totally individual method were fashioned on Steve Donoghue, stable jockey at Martin Hartigan's Foxhill yard when the 15-year-old Shropshire lad from Potato Row, Oakengates, alighted from the motor car which had brought him from Swindon station. 'I never took my eyes off him. I was watching everything Steve did, trying to do the same . . . and Steve began to take an interest in me. It was a marvellous bit of luck for a kid who didn't know the first thing about riding.' The slightly upright body position which Donoghue had increasingly been obliged to adopt as the result of a shoulder injury became the Richards stance. So did the long rein; guidance and control would come from the short, stocky legs built like the proverbial tree-trunks. Light hands yet absolute control.

Previous page: Gordon Richards on Sun Chariot. A memorable combination.

GREAT JOCKEYS OF THE FLAT

The young champion.

Richards prospered and rode his first winner (at his third attempt) on Gay Lord in an apprentices' plate at Leicester on 31 March 1921. Upon returning after a six-length victory, Richards was asked by Hartigan's travelling head-lad Lang Ward why he had taken the horse round the wide outside. 'Well, sir, you said he wanted it farther, so I went farther.' His education continued slowly and methodically. One of the reasons cited for the flowering of English jockeyship between the wars was the time given young jockeys to find their feet. Richards did not lose his allowance until 1923. By the opening of the 1925 season he had won 120 races; by November he had accumulated another 118 to become champion for the first time. Some scoffed at his peculiar style. Others were more circumspect. 'If I did one of half a dozen things this kid does I should fall off,' said Brownie Carslake, 'but they seem to work for him. They can laugh at him but I seem to remember they laughed at Tod Sloan.'

Three furlongs from home in the 1939 Princess of Wales Stakes at Newmarket. Gordon Richards (right) on Comptroller cannot catch Heliopolis and Dick Perryman. Nevertheless, a typical Richards finish: note the loose rein, swinging whip and body position.

Carslake was no mean student of jockeyship and his impressions of the young Richards are worth quoting more fully. 'I attribute his success to one word – balance. He might have been equally successful as a disciple of Blondin. Do you remember the little figure that you cannot knock over? Every time that you push him over he bobs back again. That is Richards. It is all a question of balance. Richards, because of his perfect balance, is really carrying less weight than would another jockey of the same weight. At least that is the effect that it would have upon the horse. Gordon has the knack of doing the right thing every time. His perfect balance helps him to stick close to the rails on a round course and when he throws the reins at a horse in a driving finish his balance keeps the horse straight. Make no mistake about it. No other jockey could copy Gordon Richards. He is a law unto himself. If any of us tried throwing the reins at a horse the way Gordon does the horse would swerve all over the place.'

Carslake's words were echoed by trainers, jockeys and commentators alike over the ensuing 25 years. Noel Murless inherited Beckhampton and Richards from Darling in 1948. He, too, believed balance was the key. 'Gordon had this immense strength in his legs and in his knees. He could hold on to an animal and keep it balanced whatever he did on top, riding with a loose rein, half turning round to drive it home. Whatever he did, his horse was always perfectly balanced and running for him.' Doug Smith, seven times runner-up to Richards after the war and champion five times himself after Richards' retirement, was quick to say: 'His ability to keep a horse running dead straight in a desperate finish with the reins loose on its neck was sheer genius, resulting from his faculty for communicating his own determination to win. No one could copy Gordon's style without courting disaster. I tried and soon found I didn't have a hope, so I modelled myself on Harry Wragg instead. But in other respects, Gordon's methods were absolutely sound and merited close study. He never tried to do clever things by coming through on the fence if there was the slightest danger of being shut off. He was always prepared to sacrifice a length by switching to the outside if he could make sure of a clear run by doing so. Then, having switched his position, he had the patience to wait for a few strides to get his horse perfectly balanced before picking him up and making his effort. Then, when you'd go alongside him to challenge and think maybe you were going to get past, he'd pull a little extra out and keep his horse going until the post.'

In 1947 Smith achieved a personal record of 173 winners, a total good enough to secure many championships yet some 96 behind Richards' record 269. Another who chased the champion's shadow immediately after the war was the Australian Edgar Britt, second in 1948. 'When he sent his horse into the lead, he was terribly hard to run down. He had a habit of urging his mount to the front just before the turn, probably getting two or three lengths' break which in many cases won him the race. I also noticed that if Gordon were following the leaders and his mount gave the slightest indication that it was going to tire, he would use up a bit of speed he was holding in reserve and send his horse to the front. I asked him why he did this and he told me that once a horse "died" in a jockey's hands he had no hope of improving his position. Having felt that his mount was going to tire he had sent it to the front while it still had enough pace to get there. Then, often while unable to muster more speed it kept plodding along in front and hung on to win. Gordon had everything which went to make a good jockey – beautiful hands on a horse, a quick thinker, smart out of the gate and exceptionally strong in a whip finish. While Gordon was no stylist, I believe that had he served his apprenticeship in my country he would have looked just as pretty as the average Australian rider who crouches as low as he can and really looks part of the horse. Gordon himself was the first to acknowledge that he did not look as polished as some riders, but his style was most effective and he soundly reasoned that he would be silly to try to alter it.'

Riders in the stand soon learned to recognise the new champion's

updated version of the Fordham 'kid'. If Gordon was sitting
motionless two furlongs out, he was in trouble; if he appeared uneasy,
you could start counting the money. 'He would usually start to make
his final effort sooner than most jockeys,' John Hislop informed
readers of *The Observer*, 'getting his whip out with a characteristic
flourish and swinging it with the horse's stride in a high, long arc,
moving his legs in unison, the whole action carried out with
exceptional vigour. He had a trick of turning his body half sideways,
according to the hand in which he was swinging his whip, which may
have been due to the vehemence and scope of his swing.' Hislop,
himself a champion amateur rider and a notable theorist, conceded
that Richards had his faults – he could be impatient on a horse which
had to be held up, for instance – but concluded by saying, 'His
qualities triumphed over his shortcomings.' Sydney Galtrey drew the
attention of his followers in the *Daily Telegraph* to the fact that
Richards rarely struck his mounts. 'If you watch closely and note the
whirl of the whip you will see that there are two flourishes per stride.
Now you cannot possibly hit a horse down the quarter more than
once in a stride. The jockey's arms must move with the stride, if
balance is to be maintained. Richards is using his left arm on a loose
rein as an urge and sitting low, but slightly askew, in doing that
double flourish and seldom actually hitting, because he knows the
horse is doing his best and cannot do more.' Galtrey also made a
point of describing the Richards routine at the gate: 'See him alert

*Richards on Myrobella, a
grey granddaughter of The
Tetrarch who topped the
Free Handicap of 1932.
'Gordon had this immense
strength in his legs and in
his knees.'*

Tommy Weston, winner of the 1933 Derby on Lord Derby's Hyperion.

and eager, with elbows uplifted and reins held high. He throws quick glances ahead, from left to right, to decide for himself if the moment is at hand but scarcely ever does he take an eye off the starter or his raised platform. He is watching the hand which is on the lever which releases the barrier. If the hand is hidden by a shield he must keep his eyes on the shoulder, for he knows when that is depressed that the signal is given. His horse, which he has been keeping on the move, turning perhaps this way and that, is straightened and away.' So sharp was Richards at the gate that many jockeys were convinced the official never released the tapes unless Gordon had given his consent, while at the conclusion of a race he swung his whip to the bitter end (winning cleverly made no appeal to him), leading the occasional disgruntled opponent to complain this was not only intended as an incentive to his own mount but also as a deterrent to any other in the vicinity.

'Gordon always tries' became the watchword of seemingly every punter. Donoghue once told an admirer who asked his advice on betting, 'If you must back a horse and do not know anything, back Gordon Richards. You will always get a good run for your money.' Small punters backing his mounts in crossed doubles began winning so much money that bookmakers refused to pay more than 3–1

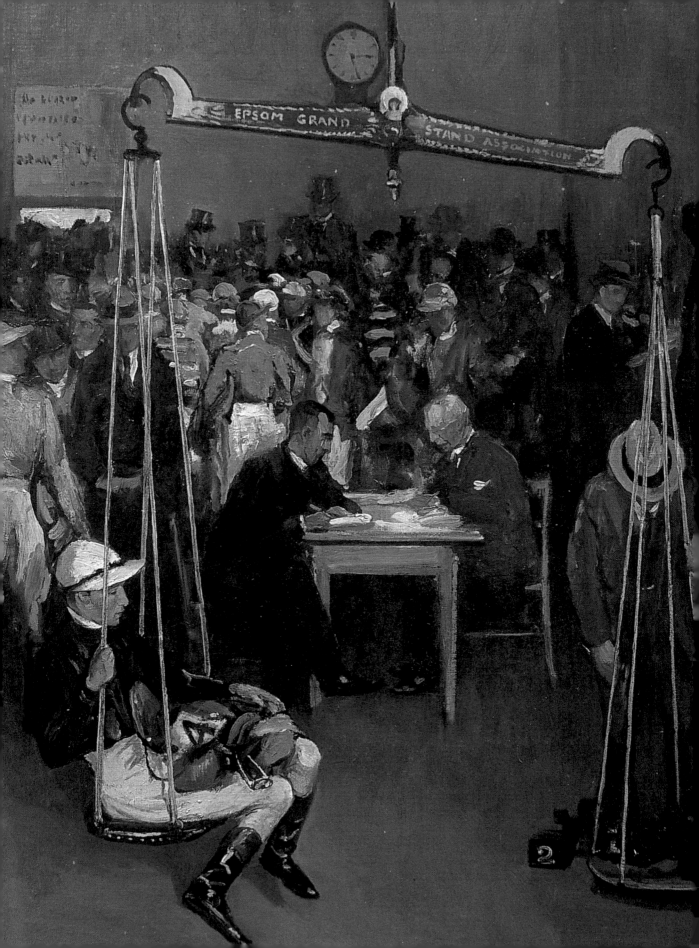

against any horse he rode. Only twice before had this ever happened – once with Archer and once with Sloan. However, the role of punters' pal had its drawbacks. Being so light meant Richards could pick from almost the full range of weights in a handicap. Seldom would he ride in fewer than five races of an afternoon. In seven of his championship seasons he had over 900 mounts and in 1936 he actually registered 1000. The most Archer rode was 667 and Lester Piggott, even with the advent of widespread night meetings, never more than 703 (although his totals were extensively augmented by numerous rides all round the world).

Richards had a price to pay. 'I used to book all my rides – no agents in those days – so I'd be on the phone as much as I'd be on a horse. By the weekend I was ready for Sunday; by the end of the season, when it was becoming a grind, I'd be ready for my holiday in Barbados or St Moritz.' The pressure told. Richards' convivial, level-headed demeanour concealed a highly-strung personality who lived on his nerves. If things went wrong he worried and in the winter of 1944, for example, he was not far short of a nervous breakdown. The strain of race-riding, the strain of travelling, the strain of trying to do all he could for the war effort. All this accumulated strain had got right on top of him. He refused to answer the telephone. He refused to read or write any letters. He refused to see anyone.

'Looking back, it seems to me that I nearly went mental. My nerves were bang on top of me and I was ludicrously tense. I could not eat, I could not sleep and I dare not think. Finally, I took to my bed permanently and I simply refused to get out of it.' Only those closest to him were aware of these bouts of depression: not even Fred Darling knew in 1944, nor Noel Murless when a worse attack struck Richards in the summer of 1949. To the outside world the champion's absence between 8 July and 26 July was due to 'a touch of sunstroke'. He resumed in time for the Goodwood festival and rode 11 winners. At the end of the season his total had soared to 261, just eight short of his record. There was no stopping Gordon.

Perhaps Richards fell victim to a career that came to be dominated by, and preoccupied with, quantity rather than quality, particularly if the latter is equated with Classic success. Richards had been champion jockey four times before he won his first Classic (the 1930 Oaks on Rose of England) nine years after his first winner. In all he would ride 14, the same number as one contemporary, Charlie Elliott (two titles and a seasonal best of 106), and only one more than another, Harry Wragg (one championship and a seasonal best of 110); while both Tommy Weston (one championship; 95) and Charlie Smirke (none; 98), two other cavaliers from the inter-war years, each partnered 11 Classic winners. Though in no way trying to belittle the many quantitative peaks scaled by Gordon Richards, one can't help wondering how many he might have been persuaded to sacrifice for a

Weston weighs in after Sansovino's Derby win in 1924, one of his 11 Classic successes.

Charlie Elliott: champion jockey while still an apprentice. A natural, according to his guv'nor Jack Jarvis.

few more Classic successes. The answer would probably have been none. Would he have swapped his world record of 12 consecutive winners in October 1933 for another Derby?

On Tuesday 3rd, he won the last race at Nottingham, the Elvaston Plate, on the 11–2 shot Barnby; on the Wednesday, Manner (6–4 on), Brush Past (evens), Miss B (7–4 favourite), Arcona (6–4 on), Red Horizon (7–4 favourite) and Delicia (5–4 favourite) took him through the card at Chepstow, a feat duplicated in Britain by just Alec Russell, at Bogside on 19 July 1957. 'I thought I'd only win one race. I'd been trying to get off three or four of them to ride something else.' To the crowd who had gathered outside the weighing room to cheer him, he sang, 'Little man, you've had a busy day.' On Thursday 5th, he continued remorselessly with The Covenanter (evens), Kirriemuir (6–4 on), June Rose (9–4), Montrose (7–4 on) and Lady Swift (evens). 'Then in the last I started 3–1 on on a horse called Eagle Ray. I did not think I could possibly be beaten, as in my view this was the best bet of the whole meeting. I was, however. After a great race home, I finished third, beaten a head and a neck.'

No, a man who so loved the scent of victory would not wish to forsake an achievement of that magnitude. The 'Magnificent Dozen' proved the highlight of a year in which Richards beat Archer's record of 246 winners in a season. The 247th came on Golden King at Liverpool on 8 November, the 47th anniversary of Archer's suicide. Richards added another twelve to the score but with customary modesty refuted all suggestions that his was a superior performance. 'Oh no! Fred Archer's performance easily outstripped mine and let nobody doubt that. I make this statement with absolute sincerity and honesty. Think of poor Fred Archer, never able to eat normally, wasting away all the time. And don't forget that at eight stone I had far more opportunities than Archer at 8st 8lb. His achievement in 1885 is the greatest feat a jockey will ever achieve.'

While Gordon Richards racked up winners like an automaton, others were forging reputations in the Classics. Charlie Elliott was the same age as Richards but collected four Classics before the latter had won his first – and he'd won two jockeys' championships (1923–24), the first when no more than a 19-year-old apprentice. According to his guv'nor Jack Jarvis, he was a natural: 'I don't think he knew what he was doing half the time but as it was the right thing I never enquired what went on in his young head. He was learning all the time and by the age of 19 he was the equal of any jockey in the world.' Jarvis decided Elliott was ready to assume the responsibilities of stable jockey, which involved riding Lord Rosebery's horses in the Classics on level terms against the likes of Donoghue, Childs and Carslake. Any burden seemed to rest easily on Elliott's shoulders, however. He won Rosebery the 1923 2000 Guineas on Ellangowan by a head and the 1924 1000 Guineas on Plack, who upset the non-staying hot-pot Mumtaz Mahal by half a length. Unlike many so-called prodigies, Elliott could already ride any kind of race on any kind of horse. In 1922, for instance, he rode Golden Myth to victory in the Ascot Gold Cup over 2½ miles and a month later won the Eclipse on him over half the distance.

Elliott was no shrinking violet. 'You have to be convinced that you are as good as the next man and maybe better. I think it's true to a large extent that great jockeys are born, not made, that the ability to communicate with a horse so that he'll run for you, give you his maximum, is some kind of natural gift. But you've got to work to develop it and you've got to have a lot of self-confidence to make the most of it on the big occasion. What it is that makes one jockey so much better than another at getting a racehorse to do its best, I defy anyone to define . . . at the end of the day there's a lot of mystery. There's something strange and marvellous happens between the horse and certain men who get on his back and you can't explain it, you can only demonstrate it by getting up on the animal.'

Elliott took great delight in demonstrating he was one of those 'certain men'. He rode in 29 Derbies between 1922 and 1953 (one more than Richards), winning three and coming second twice and third four times compared to Richards' single victory, three seconds and two thirds. By peculiar coincidence Elliott's three successes signalled technological landmarks in Derby history. Call Boy's race of 1927 was the first to be broadcast on radio; Bois Roussel's in 1938 was the first covered by television; and in 1949 Nimbus required the revolutionary evidence of the photo-finish camera to confirm he'd held off Amour Drake by a head. On both Call Boy and Nimbus Elliott made virtually all his own running. 'The majority of horses in the race are above the ordinary, so where's the sense in giving them lengths of a start?' he reasoned in defence of the catch-me-if-you-can tactics popularised by Donoghue. 'Mind you, it was a different course in those days, bare and almost always hard with scarcely a blade of grass. And Tattenham Corner was far more of a corner, not the curve it has become, so I'm sure our way of riding the Derby was right.'

Elliott's self-confidence was not confined to race-riding. He acquired a taste for the high life which necessitated betting in large sums in order to pay for it. After so much muckraking concerning betting among jockeys, the stewards were determined to stamp it out once and for all. Elliott sensed they were gunning for him: in 1929, therefore, he accepted a lucrative offer from Marcel Boussac to ride in France. With such a powerful string of horses behind him, Elliott was enormously successful. He won the French Derby for Boussac on four occasions during the 1930s, most notably on the unbeaten Pharis II (1939) whom he considered the best horse he ever rode; three times he wore the orange Boussac jacket to victory in the Prix de l'Arc de Triomphe, twice on the grand mare Corrida and once on

Caracalla, another unbeaten colt, whose eight victories included the 1946 Ascot Gold Cup: indeed, the Boussac-Elliott tandem plundered English prizes at will in the immediate postwar years with horses such as Ardan, Goyama, Djeddah, Arbar and Dynamiter winning the likes of the Coronation Cup, Eclipse, Gold Cup and Champion Stakes.

Right up to his retirement in 1953 Elliott exhibited the standards of elegance and proficiency redolent of that golden era of English jockeyship spawned in the 1920s. In 1951 he won the inaugural King George VI & Queen Elizabeth Stakes (known as the Festival of Britain Stakes) on Supreme Court and his final season saw victories on Argur in the Eclipse and Souepi in the Ascot Gold Cup. Elliott had tilted with the best. 'Whether you're talking about the men who were established when I got to the fore or those who were working their way through as apprentices along with me, the string of names would take your breath away.' Not least among those names was that of Charlie Smirke.

No jockey can ever have fancied himself as much as this son of a Lambeth costermonger, surely the definitive 'Cheeky Chappie'. There had been no smoother self-publicist since the elder Chifney. Unfortunately, Smirke never knew when to stop talking and rapidly became his own worst enemy. In Smirke's world, according to Quintin Gilbey, 'a man was either a grand fellow or a bastard – it was as simple as that.' Elliott, trainer Marcus Marsh, the Aga Khan and the members of the Crazy Gang most definitely represented the former category; bearers of the second label had best remain anonymous. Gordon Richards, Edgar Britt and Doug Smith had little reason to love Smirke, who was as quick with his fists (he was a trained boxer) as he was with his tongue. The weighing room was always a lively place when Smirke was around. He and Britt almost came to blows on numerous occasions. Smirke liked to indulge in a primitive form of psychological warfare whereby he attempted to unsettle the riders of anything he feared in a race. 'Had his riding been on a par with his gamesmanship he would have been the greatest rider the world has ever had,' said Britt. 'Everybody knew Charlie was good – and so did Charlie.' Smirke's ingratiation with firstly the Maharajah of Baroda and later the Aga Khan cost Britt valuable retainers and at least two, possibly four, Classic winners. Doug Smith was another to lose mounts as a result of Charlie buttering up an owner: 'He could bring strong influence to bear when he felt so inclined.' Even Richards himself was not completely immune and many a time his easy-going temperament was stretched to breaking point by Smirke's antics. The chalice of poisonous rivalry never emptied. In the summer of 1952, for example, Smirke needed to do 8st 4lb to ride his Derby winner Tulyar in the King George VI & Queen Elizabeth Stakes – otherwise the mount went to Richards. Smirke more or less lived in the Turkish baths for six days to sweat

Left: Charlie Smirke, 'Cheeky Chappie' par excellence.

Windsor Lad, quite probably the finest horse Charlie Smirke ever sat on, is led in after their 1934 Derby success.

the necessary poundage from his already emaciated frame (and he still put up 2lb overweight) rather than hand the ride to Richards. Smirke just could not accept the degree of adulation heaped upon a jockey he believed was only the second best around.

The Aga Khan's trainers Dick Dawson, Alec Head and, especially, Frank Butters made no secret of their loathing for Cheeky Charlie. Dawson and Butters were fully paid-up members of the autocratic school who regarded jockeys as not entirely trustworthy. They frequently put up exercise riders in gallops to reduce the risk of information passing into the wrong hands. Smirke often rose at 5am, left his London flat for the Jermyn Street Turkish baths and then motored up to Newmarket to ride work, only to be left cooling his heels at the side of the Limekilns. The fraught relationship between Smirke and Butters has no finer definition than a conversation said to have occurred on the Heath while Smirke was away in the Army during the war.

GORDON

Gallop watcher: Have you heard the news, Mr Butters? Charlie
  Smirke's been awarded the VC in Sicily.
Butters: Really, what for?
Gallop watcher: For stopping a German tank.
Butters: I'm not surprised. When he was riding for me he would stop
  anything.

Smirke rode for the Aga Khan – on and off – for 30 years and his
association with the last of the Aga's trainers, Alec Head, was no
more harmonious than with the first, Dick Dawson. They won the
1957 1000 Guineas with Rose Royale II but there were no
celebrations: Smirke wore an expression that said he'd lost a fiver and
found sixpence while Head preferred to attend his other runner who
had finished second. Jockey and trainer did see eye to eye on one
thing: they wanted nothing further to do with each other.

Charlie Smirke being caught on the hop was a rare event. The
Crazy Gang always contrived to get the better of him and liked
nothing more than dragging him on stage after some big win – then
while he was soaking up the applause one of their number would
sneak round behind him and pull down his trousers. However, on the
momentous occasion when his entire career depended on his
renowned eloquence, Smirke was embarrassingly tongue-tied and his
silence was interpreted by the Stewards of the Jockey Club as an
admission of guilt. In consequence they took away his licence.

Under the watchful eye of Stanley Wootton he had developed into
an accomplished and much sought-after young rider. 'Confidence,
obedience, cleanliness, get the rails and stick there' was the
philosophy of the jockeys' academy over which Wootton presided in
the professional manner of his father. Smirke learnt a bagful of tricks,
which may or may not have included this one on how to overcome a
poor outside draw: 'I would deliberately jump my horse off sideways,
shuttling the four or five next to me, so that their riders would have
to snatch at their heads. I would then be careful to call out "Sorry,
sorry" in a loud voice, so that the starter would hear and give
evidence later, if required, that he had heard me apologise and that I
had therefore jumped off sideways by mistake. The beauty of this
manoeuvre was that after a furlong or so I could, quite legitimately,
move over to a more favoured berth near the inside.' On 31 August
1928 when he went to post on Welcome Gift, the 11–4 on favourite
for the Home Bred 2YO Plate, overcoming a poor draw was going to
be the least of his worries: when the tapes rose, Welcome Gift
refused to budge.

At the subsequent stewards' enquiry the starter, Captain Hubert
Allison, alleged that Smirke had made no attempt to start. The case
was referred to Cavendish Square and on 6 September the habitually
loose-lipped Smirke was so overawed in the presence of Lords

"HARD RIDDEN"
C. SMIRKE.

Top: Michael Beary, 'a hard rider with Hitler-like tendencies'.

Above: Freddy Fox, vulpine by name and facial resemblance.

Previous page: Hard Ridden, a fourth Derby winner for Smirke at the age of 51.

Rosebery, Ellesmere and Hamilton that for the first and, apparently, only time in his life, he was struck dumb. The harshest possible sentence was imposed – warning off *sine die*. Every February for the next five years Smirke applied for his licence, to no avail. Welcome Gift was sold to race in India where his trait of refusing to start got more pronounced, and he eventually became so spooky he tried to jump some running rails, injured himself and had to be destroyed. He had also very nearly destroyed Smirke's career.

Smirke occupied his time selling vacuum cleaners and sparring with professional boxers. However, news of Welcome Gift's Indian 'adventures' began to filter back to England and in October 1933 he was allowed to resume his tempestuous career. True to type he proved irrepressible: within eight months he'd ridden a Derby winner, Windsor Lad, quite probably the finest horse he ever sat on. The next 20 years comprised a regular rollercoaster of bust-ups and big pay-days. Further Classic glory on Bahram, Mahmoud, My Babu, Palestine, Tulyar ('What did I Tul-yar' was the inevitable crack after his Derby victory), Never Say Die and Hard Ridden. Smirke was rising 52 when Mick Rogers asked him to partner Hard Ridden in the 1958 Irish 2000 Guineas. They won that Classic by four lengths and the Derby by five.

Smirke secured just one other victory from the 198 rides he had in this, his penultimate season. 'He rode with the judgement and confidence which has made him the best Derby rider since Donoghue,' wrote John Hislop in *The Observer*. 'Smirke's artistry is undiminished.' And Smirke's message to the press corps? 'Tell 'em to send a cable to Aly Khan and Alec Head saying that Charlie Smirke is still no dunce as a jockey.' Yes, quite a lad, our Charlie.

A third stormy petrel of the period was Michael Beary, 'not the dove of peace and tranquillity when waters are ruffled on the Turf', in the opinion of Sydney Galtrey. This volatile son of Tipperary came to England in 1912 to be apprenticed to Atty Persse. In consequence Beary learnt a lot from Steve Donghue, including how to rub some people up the wrong way. However, he was a born horseman and an exceptional jockey, 'a hard rider with Hitler-like tendencies' as Galtrey memorably put it. He won the Derby and the Oaks and the St Leger twice, the second time at the age of 53 on Ridge Wood in 1949, but he also had his licence withdrawn three times and was made bankrupt three times. By December 1954 a parlous financial situation reduced the 59-year-old Beary to riding over hurdles and he was only 60 when he died.

The antithesis of Elliott, Smirke and Beary – Three Musketeers in anyone's language – were Freddy Fox and Harry Wragg, both of whom managed to deprive Richards of a jockeys' championship. Although Fox celebrated his first Classic success in 1911 (the 1000 Guineas on Atmah) his sweetest moments were delayed until the evening of his career. The last seven seasons of Fox's 30 were heightened by five Classics (which would have been six and included a Triple Crown on Bahram had he not suffered a terrible fall the day before the St Leger) and the 1930 jockeys' title when he pipped Richards, 129 to 128, by riding two winners to the reigning champion's one on the final afternoon. Richards did not begrudge Fox – a natural lightweight like himself – his success, for the 42-year-old, who curiously bore a remarkable facial resemblance to his red-haired and wide-eyed vulpine namesake, was one of the most popular and amusing men in the weighing room. 'Be quiet, respect your elders, don't get cocky,' was his perennial advice to young apprentices. 'Remember, however good you are, there's always someone better.' When Fox called it a day in 1936 he abandoned plans to train in favour of living the life of a country gentleman at Letcombe Regis, near Wantage. He rode to hounds, was made a JP and became known affectionately to the racing fraternity as the 'Mayor of Wantage'.

Harry Wragg was the thinking man's jockey. Blessed with considerable intelligence, he constantly sought to apply it to the science of race-riding, so much so that many of his colleagues called him 'Brains'. 'To keep riding winners you must have confidence, determination and last, but not least, brains,' he insisted. 'The moment you sit on a horse's back, that horse knows all about you. He knows immediately if you have confidence in yourself. So that horse will produce more for you than anybody on him grafting and niggling at him.' A jockey needed to be as sharp as a tin-tack to outwit Richards at the gate but Wragg did just that at Leicester in 1939. The starter was performing his duties for the first time and was determined that the champion, on the favourite, should get a perfect break. Richards' horse, however, was acting up, wheeling round and forever delaying matters. 'Are you ready, Gordon?' the obsequious official enquired. Quick as lightning Wragg yelled, 'Yes, sir, I'm ready,' the tapes shot up and Wragg shot away to win the race comfortably.

As this instance demonstrated, Wragg was a superb opportunist. He was also a formidable tactician: he could win from the front but more often than not he chose to employ stealth. 'I had a certain talent for coming from behind at the last minute. You mustn't press a horse too much. Give them a break. Step off fast and then just ease a little – don't pull him back but drop in on somebody's heels. You can do it in athletics, you can do it in racing. Slipstreaming is the name of the game, and at the last minute . . . boof.' As a boy, Wragg had been taken to the local running track by his father and educated in the art of timing and its value. He never forgot those lessons. His amazing judgement of pace won him a hatful of races – and the soubriquet 'Head Waiter'. Two disconsolate punters pooled their resources for the 'getting-out stakes' in the last race of a Salisbury fixture. One

Harry Wragg on Felstead: the swoop of the 'Head Waiter' landed the 1928 Derby.

Previous page: Freddy Fox and trainer Frank Butters admire the 1935 Triple Crown winner Bahram.

wanted to back Wragg; the other didn't because Wragg had given him so many near heart-attacks, by leaving it until the last split second to pounce, that he couldn't stand the strain. His companion's silver tongue won the argument and Wragg duly won the race in a last-gasp thriller. As Wragg's number went up in the frame one half of the triumphant duo was heard to say: 'That bugger should be Head Waiter at the Café Royal.' The name stuck, for it captured to a tee Wragg's inclination to hover in the background judging the moment to swoop. 'Brains' also knew that with no camera to aid his verdict the judge tended to favour the horse gaining ground at the finish. Richards, for one, maintained Wragg gave him 'a crick in the neck whenever he pulled in behind me and I was always anxious until the winning post had been reached.'

Wragg successfully employed these tactics in three Derbies. The victorious trailblazing strategy of Steve Donoghue had made a profound impression on his young disciples, and a ghosted newspaper article of his which appeared in 1926, to the effect that you needed to be in the first three at the top of the Hill to stand any chance of winning, seemed to receive further credence a few weeks later when even the most fanatical exponent of waiting, namely Joe Childs, to all intents and purposes followed Donoghue's advice on Coronach. In 1928 Richards and Elliott were so consumed by their idol's literary pearls of wisdom that they set off like the clappers on Sunny Trace and Flamingo, hell-bent on hammering the opposition into submission. Wragg sat back on Felstead and waited: 'Keep it up, lads, one of you has got to die,' he told himself. A furlong from home Sunny Trace dropped away and Wragg pounced before Flamingo could get his second wind. Two years later Wragg rode Blenheim in a similar manner to catch Iliad in the shadow of the post and in a 1942 substitute Derby at Newmarket, he and Watling Street collared Hyperides 50 yards from the line to win by a neck.

The swoop of the Head Waiter became a familiar sight in the other Classics. Garden Path took the 1944 2000 Guineas by a head (the first filly to win since Sceptre in 1901, and the last), Herringbone the 1943 1000 Guineas by a neck and the St Leger by a short head, and Sun Stream the 1945 Oaks, also by the minimum distance. One Wragg Classic that scarcely required the magic lantern rubbing was the Oaks of 1938 in which he made all on Rockfel to win by four lengths in a time two seconds faster than Bois Roussel had clocked in the Derby. In October this wonderful filly humbled Pasch, winner of the 2000 Guineas and the Eclipse, by five lengths in the Champion Stakes and she was allotted 9st 7lb in the Free Handicap alongside Bois Roussel.

Wragg signed off on Manchester November Handicap day 1946 with a hat-trick that included the big race winner Las Vegas at 20–1. By now Richards had won all the Classics except the Derby. The Blue

Sun Stream does not look as though she has had a race but Wragg has just got her home by a short head in the 1945 Oaks.

A portrait of Harry Wragg on the second of his three Derby winners, the Aga Khan's Blenheim in 1930.

Riband at last seemed his for the taking after Tudor Minstrel slaughtered his field in the 1947 2000 Guineas to the tune of a record eight-length victory. Tudor Minstrel would be his 22nd conveyance in the quest initiated by the complete no-hoper Skyflight in 1924. While plenty of the others were also rank outsiders, Richards had been up on two unbeaten favourites, Pasch (third at 9–4 on in 1938) and Big Game (sixth at 6–4 on in 1942). He'd been second three times – on Easton (1934), Taj Akbar (1936) and Fox Cub II (1939) – and also filled third spot on Nasrullah (1943), beaten a head and half a length, the closest he had got, in one sense, to actually winning. On three occasions Richards fell into the unwelcome trap of siding with the wrong horse. He preferred Taj Akbar to Mahmoud and Pasch to Bois Roussel. Nor did Lady Luck shine her torch on Richards. Fred

Darling won the 1940 Derby with his own horse, Pont l'Eveque, but had insisted it would be improper of him to monopolise the stable jockey; so Richards rode Tant Mieux, who finished fourth. When Darling collected another wartime substitute a year afterwards with Owen Tudor, poor Richards was laid up with a broken leg. Like Pasch and Big Game, Tudor Minstrel came to the Derby boasting perfection – six starts, six wins. Would it be a case of third time lucky for Richards? The auguries were not propitious. Steve Donoghue's boots, presented to Richards by his colleagues for the occasion, did not fit, and the horse's ability to stay the trip was not the only factor weighing heavily on the jockey's mind as the hottest favourite (7–4 on) since Flying Fox in 1899 crossed the Downs to the 1½ mile gate. The handsome, powerfully-built brown colt was a very free runner who had never ever been headed: would he settle? Furthermore, when preparing Tudor Minstrel on Beckhampton's replica Epsom gallop, Darling and Richards found him to be all at sea running on a left lead. 'I did not know how to ride him,' Richards later confessed. 'Whether to let him go and risk the left turns or whether to take him right up and give him every chance at the finish. He might fight me all the way and kill his chance. I have never, in the whole of my life, had such an uncomfortable ride at Epsom. Every time I held him up, he fought me. Every time I let him down to go, he shot off to the right – if I'd let him go he'd have ended up at Epsom station. The whole race was a nightmare but he still finished fourth.' Tudor Ministrel reverted to a mile in the St James's Palace Stakes and coped splendidly with the right-handed turn to win in a canter. However, over an extra quarter-mile at Sandown he was defeated in the Eclipse by the future Prix de l'Arc de Triomphe winner Migoli.

As Richards entered his fourth decade in the saddle, the odds on him winning the Derby lengthened by the year. Records he had in abundance (he'd passed Fred Archer's record aggregate in April 1943) but hopes of that elusive first Derby were fast receding. Even so, he could reflect on a career in which his name had been linked with several racehorses of exceptional merit, even if the list did not include a Derby winner. Before the war he had ridden the electrically-fast filly Tiffin to win all five of her juvenile races in 1928. In 1946–47 he was to be associated with another unbeaten animal in the shape of Combat, a colt who won all his nine races culminating in the Sussex Stakes. Had Combat not been foaled in the same year as Tudor Minstrel he might have achieved even greater things. The following season Richards sat on a horse who would develop into Tudor Minstrel's equal – albeit as a sprinter. Abernant was a grey by the Derby winner Richards missed – Owen Tudor – out of a daughter of Mumtaz Mahal, the legendary 'Flying Filly' of the 1920s. After losing on his debut, Abernant showed he could 'fly' with the best of them.

GORDON

Sun Chariot: 'Probably the greatest racehorse I've ever been across,' according to Richards.

His solitary reverse during the next two years occurred in the 2000 Guineas when he did not quite see out the trip and Nimbus beat him by a short head in the first photo finish for an English Classic. His other defeat in 17 races came in the 1950 King's Stand Stakes in which he failed by half a length to concede 23lb to Tangle on soft ground. Abernant's haul of prestigious sprints included the Champagne, Middle Park, King's Stand and doubles in the July Cup, King George Stakes and Nunthorpe Stakes. Richards thought the world of Abernant and the grey fittingly provided him with his 4000th winner, in Sandown's Lubbock Sprint on 4 May 1950 – the day before his 46th birthday. 'A character quite unlike any other sprinter I have ever ridden. He would canter quietly down to the start and then when he got to the other side of the gate he would give a great big sigh, prop himself lazily on three legs and have a look round . . . When you faced the gate, however, it was an entirely different matter. I could feel him tense up and he was away in a flash.'

And there was Sun Chariot. Richards needed all his wits about him when he made her acquaintance in the spring of 1942. 'She was a machine and what a character. I've a few grey hairs and she gave them to me. She was probably the greatest racehorse I've ever been across. You never knew what she would do. In the Oaks she let them go a furlong at the start; then decided to go after them and won in a canter. In the St Leger she made a hack of the Derby winner.' If Big Game had not been such a raging favourite for the race it's not inconceivable that the irascible filly would have lined up for the Derby and ended the champion jockey's agonising wait. 'She would have won that just as easily.' In the St Leger she murdered the first two in the Derby, Watling Street and Hyperides, by three lengths and five lengths. 'They never really saw the way she went. What a memorable year. His Majesty, Mr Darling and myself had won four out of the five Classics. And if Sun Chariot had run in the Derby . . . oh well, she did not.'

The year to rival 1942 in Richards' affections was still a good way off. In the wake of Tudor Ministrel's anticlimactic performance, Richards endured a further five years of disappointment comprising a non-stayer, long-shots and another thwarted favourite (the 9–2 Royal Forest, fourth in 1949) before Pinza worked the oracle at his 28th and, as it transpired, final attempt in the Coronation Derby of 1953. It had been a long while coming but the timing and circumstances surrounding its ultimate arrival were perfect. Pinza was bred by Fred Darling from a half sister to Pasch, on whom Richards had won the 1938 2000 Guineas, and was trained by Norman Bertie, formerly Darling's travelling head-lad. Then, shortly before Epsom, the Queen conferred a knighthood on Richards. 'Gordon is the first man to be knighted for his equestrian performances since the Middle Ages,' joked Lord Derby at the Press Club lunch preceding the race. 'I only hope he is not so much moved that he turns out to ride Pinza in a suit of armour and a lance.' Pinza's impressive victory in the Newmarket Stakes had seen his odds tumble and he started 5–1 joint favourite. The big colt proceeded to win in so straightforward and authoritative a fashion that Richards might have wondered why winning the Derby had constituted such an onerous task. Taking it up at the two furlong pole, Pinza won by four lengths from the Queen's Aureole. With Fleet Street's accustomed gusto, the *News of the World*'s headline declared: 'Yes Sir! Gordon's FIRST Derby, ½ million groaned for Elizabeth the SECOND.' Richards was knighted 24 days later on 30 June and rode his first winner as Sir Gordon on Blue Fire at Newmarket on 1 July.

Richards had already decided to retire at the close of the 1954 season when the moment was hastened by Abergeldie, his mount in the Star Stakes for 2-year-old fillies at Sandown on Saturday 10 July, who reared over backwards on leaving the paddock and rolled on him, breaking his pelvis and cracking four ribs. With 54 winners to his name (the last on Princely Gift the previous afternoon) he had been on target for a 27th jockeys' title. Ahead of him now lay moments of triumph as a trainer and as a racehorse manager; and thousands of words spoken and written in tribute to this country's most famous jockey. His final guv'nor, Noel Murless, retired in 1976 and received a knighthood in recognition of a glorious career during which he handled any number of outstanding horses, won 19 Classics and was leading trainer on nine occasions. Sir Noel was emphatic: 'I have had four greats in my life: Abernant, Crepello, Petite Etoile – and Gordon. The greatest jockey of my time and off the racecourse one of the greatest men.'

Perhaps Murless's final observation identifies the true secret of Richards' success. He was a consummate professional in every sense. Fame and adulation failed to turn his head; mingling with the high and the mighty could not sever his roots. Richards remained a man of the people in whom every person found a quality they admired and respected. Peers or paupers – it made no difference to Richards. To all he extended courtesy and a kind heart. Shortly before Sir Gordon's death in 1986 he received a letter from an aspiring writer (of whom he would have had no knowledge whatsoever) requesting a few minutes of his time to reminisce about Sun Chariot for a forthcoming book. Within hours Sir Gordon was on the telephone and, though obviously feeling none too well and pleading poor memory, he relived those far-off days as best he could.

I was extremely grateful and totally awestruck. He could so easily have ignored the request or written back in the negative. But Sir Gordon Richards was not like that: he took the trouble, the same kind of trouble that had contributed to his winning more races in his homeland than any other jockey.

LESTER

LESTER

Lester: not many sportsmen, and certainly precious few jockeys, are ever readily identifiable by christian name alone. Exactly what is responsible for this public acclamation defies adequate definition. Boy Wonder? There have been plenty of those. Punters' Pal? Ditto. The eternal Nice Guy? Hardly. The Anti-Hero? Getting warmer, perhaps. Piggott cut a mysterious figure, a man of few words who let his actions speak for him. He'd pinch mounts from other jockeys, pinch races from under their noses and, on one infamous occasion, even pinch a rival's whip ('I only borrowed it') in order to ride a finish after he'd lost his own. Old-fashioned heroes don't do these things. Lancelot, Beau Geste or Biggles would rather die than stoop to such subterfuge. But Piggott acted out his equestrian version of 'My Way': he made his own rules – usually as he went along. That way they can always be broken whenever it is expedient. Piggott was the archetypal maverick who could have strode across the opening frame of a James Bond movie or ridden out from the screen of a Western. The man who does 'what a man's gotta do' and then rides off alone into the sunset. He might have auditioned for the role of Shane or The Pale Rider, written the script for A Fistful of Dollars. Essentially good but with hints of a ruthlessness we'd rather not know too much about, a man not to everyone's liking but revered nonetheless, a character above the traditional nomenclature of christian name and surname: Lester will do just fine, mighty fine.

Wherever Lester Piggott fits into the pantheon of great jockeys, the assertion that his genius ranged across the entire spectrum of horsemanship is beyond dispute. From the 11 machine-gunned strokes of his whip during the last furlong of the 1972 Derby which won the race for Roberto, to that blend of sensitivity and glacial resolve which nursed the temperamental, tiring and sore-mouthed Ribero to victory in the 1968 St Leger, the racing public has been treated to a veritable cornucopia of skills. Piggott's destiny was preordained. His father Keith rode 500 winners over jumps before training Ayala to win the 1963 Grand National; grandfather Ernest had won three. His mother Iris was also no mean jockey, having twice won the Newmarket Town Plate. She was a Rickaby, daughter of Frederick who won three Classics and sister of Frederick Lester (after whom her son was named) who rode five. Great-great-grandfather Rickaby trained Wild Dayrell to win the 1855 Derby. Keith Piggott's antecedence revealed further evidence that 'jockeys are born not made'. His mother was Margaret Cannon, sister to Morny and Kempton and daughter of Tom, whose own wife Kate represented the Day dynasty of Stockbridge. Wherever you look in Lester Piggott's family tree you find jockeys, and outstanding ones at that. In those earlier Classic-winning champion jockeys Tom and Morny Cannon one can even discover the origins of the face that came to be described as resembling a 'well-kept grave'. Said Keith Piggott: 'He had to be a

Previous page: Lester keeps the pretenders at bay – he and Storm Warning win the 1985 Scarbrough Stakes at Doncaster from Pat Eddery and Steve Cauthen.

GREAT JOCKEYS OF THE FLAT

166

jockey and before he was able to run around I can remember him saying, "I'm going to be a jockey, I'm going to be a jockey".'

Lester was taught to ride on a hare-brained pony called Brandy leased from Fulke Walwyn for £5. 'I used to ride at gymkhanas – I wasn't exceptional because I could never get up on the pony. They used to have these obstacle races and I could never get back on again.' Nevertheless, by the age of ten he was riding racehorses and on 7 April 1948, six months after his 12th birthday, he made his debut on The Chase in an apprentices' race at Salisbury. The filly came nowhere, but four rides later he imbibed the heady wine of success when The Chase won the Wigan Lane Selling Plate at Haydock on 18 August by a cheeky 1½ lengths at odds of 10–1. In its report *The Times* noted: 'Most intelligently ridden by young apprentice L Piggott.' The prodigy's own account? 'It was terrific. I rode the last five furlongs hard and managed to pull ahead.' Keith Piggott's immediate reaction now seems a wonderful example of calculated understatement: 'There is no reason why he should not become a good jockey.'

The Piggott Perch (1): an early version. Note the length of Lester's whip – not permissible nowadays.

The Boy Wonder was on his way and never again would he rejoice in a private life. The chubby-faced, 4ft 6in boy weighing 5st 4lb, who adored ice-cream and differed not one jot from the thousands of Just Williams terrorising the playgrounds of England's schools, gradually became a persona firmly rooted in the past. When Never Say Die launched his Classic-winning career in 1954 he had grown into a 5ft 7½in man with a riding weight of 8st 5lb. The endless tyranny of wasting had begun. 'It is not something you dip into, like a cold shower, or flirt with like the morning jog,' explains Jimmy Lindley, a fellow slave to the scales. 'It is perpetual. It becomes part of you; let go and you're lost.' Piggott's diet became the object of bizarre interest. A cough and a copy of *The Sporting Life*, some jocularly suggested. If he was riding at 8st 6lb he could afford the luxury of a boiled egg; 8st 5lb and he gave up the egg, contenting himself with 'a cigar and a dry retch. But I have a sandwich in the jockeys' room after I've finished riding and I always have a meal at night. You lose the habit of eating. The less you have, the less you want. But I don't starve and I don't live on cigars. And I don't drive to every meeting in a rubber suit.' This constant self-control unerringly chiselled away at Piggott's soul. The affable youth grew into a remote and aloof man whose partial deafness and speech impediment – seemingly less insurmountable barriers to communication when younger – were converted into potent defence mechanisms later on. Hunger and reticence make likely bedfellows. 'Sometimes you read that I've told people to push off but that's never because I'm hungry; it's because I'm angry,' he countered. 'I live and work in a tough world. I can be a decent human at 8st 4lb but I can't be a saint even at 9st 7lb.' However, in Lindley's opinion, 'With glory you can live on an egg . . . he knows what he has to do and he knows what the rewards will be if he does it. When Lester was riding winners as an apprentice he was still at school in Upper Lambourn and he had to bike there. And I always remember when he came back he wasn't riding a bike, he was racing, and he would do anything to win, even put a stick in another kid's wheel. It wasn't just determination, it was an obsession and that has never left him.' This ruthless streak which sharpened one appetite at the expense of another was a quality bound to bring Piggott into conflict with the racing establishment. 'Old jockeys riding for old trainers and old stewards,' is Piggott's own theory for the troubles that dogged him throughout the early 1950s.

For Boy Wonder read Enfant Terrible. 'Your filly needs a longer trip, Mr Persse,' the 14-year-old Piggott informed the 80-year-old trainer after one unsuccessful ride in 1949. 'Just because she's by a sprinter it doesn't mean she won't stay and she gives me the feel of a stayer.' Persse turned to his owner Lord Sefton (a mere stripling of 51) and with a twinkle in his eye said: 'D'you hear that, Hugh? He's all of 14 and he's teaching me how to train my horses.' Within a

In the beginning . . . An 18-year-old Piggott pulls off a sensational win in the 1954 Derby on Never Say Die at 33–1, riding noticeably long in his early years.

month of becoming a fully-fledged jockey he had fallen foul of the authorities once too often. After riding Barnacle to victory over Royal Oak IV at Newbury on 20 October 1950 he lost the race on an objection from the latter's pilot, Scobie Breasley, and was reported to the Stewards of the Jockey Club for 'boring and crossing'. The Stewards suspended him for three weeks. They were doubtless mindful of the young firebrand's burgeoning reputation for recklessness. Already that season he had received four suspensions of one or two days' duration. In the words of officialdom, he was riding with 'disregard for the safety of other jockeys'; in the eyes of Joe Public, however, he was nothing more than a kid always trying to win who was rapidly being cast as villain and handy scapegoat for any fracas in which he was involved. Establishment justice seldom veers from the feudal and it appeared Piggott was marked down for a lesson in subservience. The elder statesmen of the Turf – stewards and jockeys – were determined to bring the whippersnapper to heel. So ran public opinion.

The running sore burst open after the King Edward VII Stakes at Royal Ascot on 17 June 1954. Only a fortnight earlier Piggott had won the Derby on Never Say Die at the age of 18; in 1952 he'd been second on Gay Time and he was adamant the wilful Zucchero would have won in 1951 had he not conceded yards at the gate. Never Say Die's sensational victory at odds of 33–1 had handsomely rewarded Lester's growing band of devotees but the outcome of the King Edward VII Stakes, for which the colt started 7–4 favourite, proved shocking for all the wrong reasons. Not since Colombo's Derby did a race undergo such public scrutiny. By general consent it was an exceedingly rough race. The short Ascot straight was no place for faint hearts, with horses either swerving or bumping into each other as Gordon Richards came by on the outside to win on Rashleigh. Never Say Die finished fourth. Some racegoers swore they heard Piggott call out, 'Move over, Grandad, I'm coming through,' but this was hotly denied by both parties. 'As soon as we got back,' said Piggott, 'the stewards objected to Gordon but when they heard the evidence of the other jockeys they withdrew their objection and turned their attention to me.' Of all the riders involved in the schemozzle – Richards, Gosling, Rickaby, Carr, Poincelet and Doug Smith (average age 39) – only Piggott (18 years 8 months) incurred the displeasure of Lord Derby, Lord Allendale and the Duke of Norfolk. They suspended him for the remainder of the meeting and reported him to the Stewards of the Jockey Club. After hearing the case the Stewards announced that they 'had taken notice of his dangerous and erratic riding both this season and in previous seasons and that in spite of continuous warnings, he had continued to show complete disregard for the Rules of Racing and the safety of other jockeys.' They withdrew his licence and stated that no consideration would be given to its renewal until he had served six months with a trainer other than his father. 'I'm not saying I wasn't partly to blame for what happened but I've always felt Gordon was equally at fault. If there had been a camera patrol in those days it must have been that the stewards must have put down Gordon as well. I felt that everyone was against me.'

This was to be the last occasion Piggott and Richards rode against each other. The same Racing Calendar that carried the official notice of Piggott's sentence also reported that Manny Mercer had been fined £50 for striking another jockey during a race. Comparable justice? Piggott's was no open-and-shut case but you can watch the film of the 1954 King Edward VII Stakes time after time and you'll still come to the conclusion he got a raw deal. Quintin Gilbey, for one, pointed out that while Lester might have been a naughty boy he had not, so far as he knew, committed a murder. From ecstasy to agony in the space of 15 days: the patent for a bitter-sweet career in the saddle, complete with its burning resentment of authority, had been well and truly registered.

However regular they were, subsequent brushes with authority – and there would be plenty of them – failed to dim the flame of brilliance increasingly lit by a jockey whose inimitable style and flair for the unorthodox came to be universally recognised and acknowledged as pure genius. The portfolio of superhuman feats of arms expanded. Classics on Crepello, Carrozza, Petite Etoile; Ascot Gold Cups on Zarathustra and Gladness; big sprints on Right Boy; a century of winners in a season at the age of 19. The Old Guard broke ranks: fulsome praise began to outweigh carping criticism.

Edgar Britt: 'In his early apprenticeship days he was a menace to the older jockeys in a race. He would stay on the fence, sending his mount through where there was insufficient room. Lester is smart at the barrier, uses his brains throughout a race and can ride patiently . . . he relies a lot on his whip to get the best out of his mount and can really make a lazy horse move.'

Harry Carr: 'There are occasions when his riding has the sharp, cold, sparkling brilliance of a diamond . . . I have yet to see his superior in speed out of the gate, correct positioning of his mount in all stages of a race and strength in a finish. Probably Lester Piggott will never go through a season without running into trouble, for by nature he has never been, nor will be, the type to accept reverses and frustrations quietly and meekly; but he has star quality, that curious indefinable something which raises a man, whatever his profession or calling, high above his fellows. He has done a great deal for racing. His personality has come through to the man and woman in the street. He is talked about in the factories, the mines, shipyards and in pubs every day and there is no doubt at all that he is the pin-up boy of housewives all over the country. He pulls in the crowd and the public get a great run for their money on every horse he rides.'

Gordon Richards: 'Even in those first days you could tell that Lester had a touch of the devil and a touch of genius. Of course he ran into trouble with stewards. It was inevitable, I suppose. If he saw a gap, he would go through. If he didn't see a gap and he couldn't go inside, outside, over or under he would just go through. He didn't seem to understand the notion of being a loser. There's no doubt about it. From the moment he came into racing it was very clear that he'd got that certain something the others hadn't. The secret of his success is his confidence in his own genius.

'For he is a genius, as Steve Donoghue was before him. From the very beginning he has instinctively known what to do and when to do it. Take Epsom, the trickiest course of them all. Lester never worries about the bends or the crowding or the changing ground or what the other jockeys are doing. Like Steve, he gets in exactly the right position and then at the psychological moment he goes. That was how he won the Oaks on Carrozza. This was the best race I have ever seen him ride. I swear that mare never knew she'd had a race. It was one of the most perfect pieces of riding I've ever seen and when it seemed that it was not enough, well, right away he produced something more. Believe me, Lester Piggott stole that race. There is no rational explanation of how he got Carrozza home. We come back to the word genius – a man's ability to communicate something to a horse.'

Few were now prepared to quarrel with Sir Gordon's opinion of his successor as stable jockey to Noel Murless, least of all the trainer himself. He knew his powerful yard had lost nothing by the replacement of one established champion with another potentially greater. 'Lester is improving each year. He gets a little tougher, a little shrewder. His eyes are open all the time. He doesn't miss a thing.' Piggott knew he was now the number one rider for the country's number one trainer. 'He trained with one thought in mind – to win the Classics.' In a collaboration which began in 1955 and lasted till Piggott chose to go freelance in 1967, trainer and jockey combined to win seven Classics – and it would have been eight had Piggott not chosen the wrong one in the 1959 1000 Guineas. The filly he rejected was Petite Etoile.

Lester Piggott and the 'Little Star' were positively made for each other. 'Petite Etoile was an awful monkey,' according to Murless, an affectionate view that could equally have applied to her jockey. Most of Petite Etoile's family – that of Mumtaz Mahal – could be counted upon for pyrotechnics and she proved no exception. On more than one occasion she got loose before a race; she insisted on having other greys in front and behind her in the string going to the gallops; and she hated strangers. One day Cyril Hall, stud manager to her owner Aly Khan, visited Warren Place and viewed Petite Etoile in her box. 'You're getting a bit fat, old girl,' he said, prodding a finger into her neck. In a flash the mare turned on him and picked him up by the lapels of his coat. 'Hers is a woman's face and a woman's character,' said Murless. 'She has a very nice, well-bred nature but if anything upsets her, well then, all hell breaks loose.'

Piggott's avowed belief in Petite Etoile's ability to 'paralyse anything in a burst of 100 yards' very nearly caused the duo to come unstuck in the Champion Stakes of 1959. By this stage Murless and Hall were becoming perceptibly edgy at Piggott's regular tight-rope act on the filly. 'Lester, let us go easy on anxiety today, please,' begged the trainer. No words could have more assuredly invited the opposite. In a three-horse field he somehow engineered a scenario where they were shut-in with less than a furlong to go. The riders of Barclay and Javelot were not about to provide a gap through which Piggott could unleash Petite Etoile's devastating speed. Seconds ticked

Doug Smith, pictured in 1967 at his most successful hunting ground, Newmarket; the scene of all four of his Classic wins.

away and he switched the filly to the rails where only the narrowest chink of daylight existed between Javelot and the fence. The shooting star did the rest. The judge's verdict was half a length; the medication prescribed Messrs Hall and Murless is unrecorded, as were their words to Piggott, who merely commented drily, 'I could still have run round the other side and won.'

Some spoke of Petite Etoile as a better filly than Sun Chariot and the best since the 'peerless' Pretty Polly, so the shattering of her much-touted invincibility by Aggressor in Ascot's 1960 King George VI & Queen Elizabeth Stakes constituted a major upset. Excuses were two a penny. Softer ground than she liked . . . the strong gallop . . . a bump . . . she'd been coughing . . . Lester had given her too much to do. A more machiavellian explanation later surfaced when Scobie Breasley confessed to deliberately impeding Petite Etoile's progress as a means of repaying Piggott for having done the same to him earlier in the season. Piggott and Breasley had their initial set-to, of course, back at Newbury in October 1950, and upon Richards' retirement the venerable Australian was Doug Smith's chief ally in repelling the advances of the young pretender.

Smith struck first, exerting a stranglehold on the jockeys'

*The Grandad from Wagga-Wagga (**right**) employing a noticeably shorter rein in the early sixties than Piggott . . . And also noticeably quieter in a finish (**above**).*

championship during the second half of the 1950s. The success was richly deserved. Every year between 1946 and 1953 (bar 1948 when illness kept him out of action until July) only Richards had stood between Smith and the top of the tree. In 1947 he rode 173 winners, five more than he ever achieved as champion. He was also as straight as a die and completely untouched by any breath of scandal. In short, the stable jockey *par excellence*, which is why his services were so valued by trainers like Butters and Boyd-Rochfort and owners like Lord Derby. Yet, for a jockey who was five times champion, Smith did not enjoy comparable success in the Classics. He won only four, two of those (Pall Mall and Petite Etoile) on 'spare' rides, but Smith did achieve the rare distinction of riding a Classic winner for two different monarchs, having won the 1946 1000 Guineas on Hypericum for George VI prior to collecting the 1958 2000 Guineas on Pall Mall for his daughter. Significantly, all four of Smith's Classics came at Newmarket. He also excelled in staying races. In 1949 he won the stayers' triple crown on Alycidon, whom he rated the best horse he ever rode; altogether he won the Doncaster Cup seven times, the Goodwood Cup three times and the Ascot Gold Cup twice. Accordingly, his phone was the first to ring as soon as the weights for the Cesarewitch were published. Out of 31 rides in the Newmarket marathon he won six, was second and third four times each and fourth twice. Four of his successful mounts carried 7st 8lb, one 7st 5lb and the sixth only 8st 3lb; few experienced jockeys could make those weights and no apprentice possessed either Smith's intimate knowledge of the track or the strength to ride a dynamic finish at the end of 2¼ miles.

Doug Smith was an unspectacular, albeit dependable, rider who retired in 1967 having ridden 3111 winners, a career total then second only to that of Richards. Arguably his brother Eph (2313 winners) possessed greater talent, though not tact. Dangerously forthright in his utterances, he frequently returned to the weighing room after losing a race on a 'good thing' to be met with a chorus of 'Here's another one for the farmyard' from his colleagues who knew Smith was wont to call any such flop a cow or a pig. Arthur Edward Breasley was anything but unspectacular. 'Scobie' refused to win by centimetres if millimetres were possible. Indeed, he once admitted to frightening the life out of himself with some of these eleventh-hour challenges.

Like all Australian apprentices, Breasley was weaned on riding against the clock and taught to hug the rails. 'We boys would get a hell of a blowing up or even a kick on the tail for being a couple of seconds off the pace either way when we were riding work.' In consequence he was a superb judge of pace. The second characteristic derived from all tuition occurring on the racetrack itself, where sharp bends and restricted confines ensured that every apprentice was

Right: *Scobie Breasley and Ron Hutchinson are still the best of pals despite Scobie depriving Ron of a Derby-winning ride on Charlottown.*

imbued with the necessity of keeping a tight hold of their animals via a short rein and sticking to the rail like glue. Breasley was obliged to adopt a slightly longer rein in England but otherwise his quiet, bobbing seat and last-gasp race-stealing remained true to his Australian roots. Such patience (tactical naivety some called it) often invited disaster. When Sayonara slipped up at Alexandra Park in May 1954, Breasley's head struck a concrete post supporting the running rail and he fractured his skull. Doctors told him his riding days were over and that he might never again walk unaided. Despite the severity of this prognosis Breasley was back riding within 12 weeks.

Thankfully, the most common outcome of Breasley's railing instinct was the odd race lost through his mount being boxed-in or baulked when making its run: the fate of Dart Board in the 1967 St Leger for example. 'But you cannot steer half a ton of horseflesh by computer,' argued Breasley. 'You simply make your choice and go – hoping that it will pan out. I can look back on any number of races and think "if only . . ." but there's not a lot of point in doing that.' If a run failed to materialise Breasley just sat still, which caused many an irate English punter not conversant (or sympathetic) with the Australian's method to jump to the conclusion that he had either ridden a stinker or not been trying. However, racing's cognoscenti were impressed. 'For me he was marvellous,' says Vincent O'Brien. 'The best Australian jockey could win a race by a neck or half a length for you with 7lb or more in hand and, of course, they were very good judges of pace. He would wait and wait. Your horse had the easiest possible race. He'd just put him in front on the post. He was so gentle with horses.'

Further evidence of Breasley's calibre can be gleaned from the

Left: *A feud? Piggott: 'I was closer to him than anyone else.' Breasley: 'The press boys hardly gave us a moment.'*

names of the two trainers who tried to retain him once he'd settled
to an English career in 1953. Noel Murless approached him to replace
Gordon Richards; Breasley declined that offer but in 1956 accepted
one from Sir Gordon himself which was to endure for the last 12
years of his career. 'He is right up in the class of Brownie Carslake
and Frank Bullock,' stated Richards. 'His horsemanship was equal to
anyone's and when I began to train it never even crossed my mind to
want another man as my stable jockey. He's riding with his head the
whole time and he's a natural horseman. Me, I was a more thrustful
rider. Scobie is persuasive. Like all Australians he's got all the guts in
the world. On those sharp tracks out there they've got to be quick
out of the gate, get a good position, keep it and go the nearest way.
Sometimes they get into trouble with these tactics but if they make a
success out there, then they are natural riders with cool heads and
guts. I could trust him completely and never gave him any
instructions. He knew what he was doing, and in any case he would
not have taken any notice of them if I had.'

Piggott's verdict? 'I think he was the best of all the Australians I've
seen.' His duels with Breasley illuminated the 1960s largely because
the two men appeared total opposites. Breasley was 21 years Piggott's
senior, which, according to popular mythology, prompted the
younger man to revive the 'Move over Grandad' line (Breasley had
actually got married the day Piggott was born). He was genial as
opposed to withdrawn and he rode in a manner calculated to make a
hibernating tortoise seen hyperactive. In his entire English career
Breasley was only suspended once – for starting too fast, in the days
when horses had to line up standing still. Back in Australia, however,
the young Breasley had carved quite a reputation as a tough, no-
nonsense rider, an attitude which incurred any number of 'holidays',
including one of two months in 1930. A fierce will-to-win burned
beneath that tranquil exterior. The racing press did all it could to
portray these differences as raw material for a tangible feud between
the pair, particularly during 1961 and 1963 when the destiny of the
jockeys' championship was only resolved at the very last. There had
been nothing like this since the Richards–Fox battle of 1930, but they
were bosom pals; this showdown smacked more of the Maher–
Wootton rivalry half a century earlier. In reality it was nothing of the
sort. 'I like him,' said Piggott. 'We rode together every day for
probably 20 years. I was closer to him than to anyone else. He was a
good jockey, very tough.' But in spicing their copy, journalists had
produced so much smoke it was felt there had to be a fire. 'The press
boys hardly gave us a moment,' observed Breasley. 'All the attention
was on Breasley versus Piggott and every day the pressure grew – and
so did the misquotes in the newspapers.'

The first of Breasley's 1000-plus Australian winners had been as
long ago as 1928 and the first of his four English jockeys'

Piggott and Nijinsky leave the stalls en route to victory in the 1970 St Leger and the realisation of the Triple Crown. To their right is Bill Williamson on Melody Rock.

championships in 1957, seven years after his debut at Liverpool. He was runner-up to Piggott in 1960 but regained the title the following season. This was the first of the two spellbinding championship battles he had with Lester and it bore all the hallmarks of a typical piece of Breasley race-riding. Piggott had 20 winners on the board before Breasley even got started: a fall on the third day of the season kept him out of the saddle for a month with a broken collar bone and a broken toe. But as Piggott landed the big prizes, such as the Ascot Gold Cup, Eclipse and St Leger, Breasley made steady inroads into the reigning champion's lead. By the end of September the gap was reduced to two – 150–148 – and 14 winners over the next month saw Breasley finally nose ahead 162–161 with less than a fortnight of the season remaining. Going into the penultimate day's racing at Lingfield, Breasley led by four. In the first, Piggott's mount Tenebre put her foot in a hole and came down, fortunately throwing the jockey under the rails and away from flying hooves. Scobie proceeded to ride a treble and establish an unassailable advantage. Quipped Piggott: 'You couldn't get me evens Breasley for the championship could you?'

A lengthy suspension of two months arising from the infamous Ione 'affair' put paid to Piggott's chances of recovering his crown in 1962, but 1963 culminated in a nailbiting finish in which Breasley prevailed by a single winner. As the final day started at Manchester on 9 November, the state of play evoked memories of 1930. Breasley led by two. He and his constant foe each had four rides, but Piggott could only win the last – incidentally the very last race ever run at Manchester. When it came to the prestigious races, however, the lion's share had again been snaffled by Piggott. In 1964 the roles would be reversed. Piggott took the jockeys' title but Breasley at long last won the English race he'd always coveted – the Derby.

Despite what seemed innumerable attempts (16 to be precise) Breasley had never succeeded in winning the Australian event cherished above all others, namely the Melbourne Cup. The head which separated him and Shadow King from victory in 1933 was the closest he came to realising every Australian jockey's greatest ambition. Although getting off to a bright start in the English Classics with Guineas victories on Ki Ming in the 1951 2000 and Festoon in the 1954 1000, Breasley's fortunes in the Derby began to yield every indication they were about to go the same way as his Melbourne Cup aspirations. Telegram II, fourth in 1950, seemed a fair opening throw but thereafter disappointment followed disappointment. Of his 11 subsequent mounts Alcaeus was beaten three lengths by St Paddy (1960), Pipe of Peace was third to Crepello and Ballymoss (1957), while Baroco II (1958) and St Crespin III (1959) both finished fourth.

Breasley's tactics in the Derby were no different from normal: 'I wanted the rails – I always wanted the rails – and in order to secure that position it was necessary to stay back in the early stages.' Such plans had a history of coming unstuck in the Derby, which frequently deteriorated into a barging match at some stage. On Pipe of Peace, Baroco and Alcaeus the nightmare scenario struck Breasley with a vengeance. He got boxed, chopped or messed about descending Tattenham Hill only to make up ground hand over fist in the straight when it was all too late. Consequently, it showed tremendous strength of character and self-belief on the part of the now 50-year-old grandfather to go out on the 15–8 favourite for the 1964 Derby with the deliberate intention of sticking to a strategy which had regularly met such an inglorious fate.

Breasley was asked to ride Santa Claus, appropriately, around Christmas time by his Irish trainer Mick Roger. Stable commitments prevented Breasley from partnering the colt to victory in the Irish 2000 Guineas but luckily for him Sir Gordon Richards possessed no Derby contender so he was free to accept the mount at Epsom.

Above: The Piggott Perch (2): look at the short leathers Lester employs on Alleged in the 1977 Arc.

Right: The 1978 version with his point of balance still right through the horse's shoulder.

Breasley reasoned that because Santa Claus was a tall colt he might not be suited by the track's undulations. 'He was not blessed with the soundest legs. It was vital to balance him down the Hill even if it meant leaving us with a lot of ground to make up in the straight.' Scobie never spoke truer words. At halfway he had only three of the other 13 runners behind him; five furlongs out he was still only tenth and rounding Tattenham Corner there were eight in front of him. Santa Claus had at least a dozen lengths to recover on the leaders.

Passing the two furlong marker he had moved into fourth place yet it was not until well inside the last 100 yards that he swept by Indiana to win by a length. Breasley was vindicated, but the fact that he was not asked to ride Santa Claus again gave rise to the assumption that the colt's connections were somehow dissatisfied with his nerve-jangling performance at Epsom. 'It must be a record – I'm the only jockey who was ever fired for winning the Derby. All I had done was to go out and ride to win the race, which I did in all races. I was never concerned whether they won by ten lengths or a short head.'

Some grandstand critics may have cavilled at the ride Breasley gave Santa Claus (Paddy Prendergast, on the other hand, thought it one of the best rides he'd ever seen round Epsom); few found complaint at the way he handled Charlottown to win in 1966. Nevertheless, his second Derby did not pass without incident. By rights Breasley should not have been aboard Charlottown. Trained by Gordon Smyth for Lady Zia Wernher, the colt was usually ridden by fellow Aussie Ron Hutchinson. However, after Charlottown had lost his unbeaten record in the Lingfield Derby Trial due, it was claimed, to an ill-judged ride from Hutchinson, the axe fell. Then, two days before the race, Breasley suffered a crashing fall on Caspian at Windsor which seemed sure to put him in hospital. Yet again Breasley demonstrated what a tough old bird he was. Twenty-four hours later he declared himself as fit as a flea and rode a double on Epsom's first afternoon to prove it. Finally, just as Breasley was preparing to mount, Charlottown trod on his off-fore and spread a plate. While the remaining 24 runners circled the paddock in teeming rain for fully ten minutes, Smyth's own farrier, George Windless, skilfully reshod Charlottown. The colt possessed thin-soled feet and even a tiny slip by the blacksmith could have resulted in his withdrawal. In fact, Windless accomplished his job so expertly that the new plate stayed securely in place for three weeks.

Breasley saw no reason to ditch the tactics that had at last won him a Derby. Settling Charlottown in rear and hugging the rails as usual, he was content to bide his time. Gradually and miraculously he began to steal his way up the inner past tiring horses until, a quarter of a mile from home, he pulled Charlottown out to overtake Right Noble and St Puckle only to find further progress blocked by the leading pair – Black Prince and Pretendre – who were directly in front of him. The very idea of pulling even wider in order to continue his challenge, a safer but ground-forfeiting option, never for a second entered Breasley's mind. He steered Charlottown back toward the fence and pushed him through the tiny gap – 'Not much room but just enough' – on the inside of Black Prince. Scobie got his horse balanced again, gave him a couple of taps with the whip and then sat down to ride one of his strongest finishes. Charlottown had half a length to find on Pretendre inside the final furlong, but responding gamely to the sorcerer on his back he won a thrilling race by a neck.

The 1966 Derby was a red-letter day for Breasley and constituted the finest of many fine hours on English racetracks. It was an exhibition of pace-judgement and wily jockeyship to be savoured. Breasley went on for two more seasons when the best horse he rode was Reform, the top European miler of 1967. However, there can be no question of the greatest horse with whom Breasley was associated in Europe – Ballymoss. Breasley partnered the O'Brien 4-year-old to successive triumphs in the Coronation Cup, Eclipse Stakes, King George VI & Queen Elizabeth Stakes and the Prix de l'Arc de Triomphe of 1958. Torrential rain in Paris prompted O'Brien to contemplate withdrawing the horse, but neither the prospect of soft ground nor a losing streak currently standing at 36 perturbed Breasley. 'Never an anxious moment,' he informed O'Brien afterwards, a neat four-word precis if ever there was of the Australian maestro's supremely confident attitude toward race-riding in general.

Breasley's retirement effectively coincided with Piggott's decision to leave Noel Murless and ride as a freelance. This move, deemed retrograde – even reckless – in 1966, made no appreciable inroads into Piggott's domination of his peers since he topped the jockeys' table for the next five years, seeing off challenges from Ron Hutchinson, Sandy Barclay, Geoff Lewis and the up-and-coming Willie Carson. Even so, a winning total of 117 (from only 557 rides) in the first year of freelancing proved to be the lowest of his 11 championships and illustrates how difficult it is to become champion without the regular supply of winners from a large retaining stable. In 1966 Piggott had ridden as many as 682 races and achieved his best ever score of 191; however, only 35 of them were supplied by Murless. Nor had he provided Piggott with a Classic winner since Aurelius took the 1961 St Leger. Piggott's first Classic for five years – Valoris in the Oaks – came courtesy of Vincent O'Brien. This victory sparked off a prolific period in Piggott's career during which his name was invariably linked with virtually every top-class animal to set foot on a racecourse. That he never actually rode them all is incidental; retained jockeys throughout the land lived in fear of being jocked-off. Although he now ceased to be champion, this crusade for quality instead of quantity heralded a new era in which the words Lester and telephone became synonymous. A racing legend was about to be born.

From 1967 to 1980 (before he embraced the retainer system once more with Henry Cecil) the sequence of great horses partnered by Piggott comprises a lengthy and mouthwatering cavalcade of equine heroes and heroines. Sir Ivor, a picture of the perfect thoroughbred: 'He had that terrific turn of foot. He must have been one of the best Derby winners ever.' The magnificent Park Top: 'She was a great mare. Great character. She knew what she was supposed to do and

Above: Jimmy Lindley, a noted stylist who kept his weight in check for the best part of 25 years.

did it. She goes into the gate as if she was going into church and comes out as if hell were after her. She knows more about racing than I do.' Nijinsky, as highly strung as his namesake: 'Flamboyant. Probably better than any horse I had ridden.' The Minstrel, small but all guts: 'One of the gamest horses of the whole lot.' Dual Arc winner Alleged: 'The easiest to ride.' The enigmatic Roberto: 'I felt he could go faster, if only he would.' His first Arc winner Rheingold: 'I honestly do not think I ever sat on a horse that would have held him that day at Longchamp.' Triple Gold Cup hero Sagaro: 'He could have gone round again.' Humble Duty, the easiest winner of the 1000 Guineas this century: 'Her acceleration was just terrific.' The globetrotting Dahlia: 'Tremendous. She really cleaned up.' And then there were Ribocco, Ribero, Athens Wood, Boucher, Thatch, Juliette Marny, Empery, Artaius, Godswalk, Solinus . . . Between 1967 and 1980 Piggott rode 14 English Classic winners provided by six different trainers, namely Vincent O'Brien (eight), Fulke Johnson-Houghton (two), Maurice Zilber, Peter Walwyn, Tom Jones and Jeremy Tree. Had he remained with Murless he would have partnered nine, no mean tally by most jockeys' standards, but not by Lester Piggott's.

Piggott's unrivalled status triggered repercussions beyond redefinition of Classic success. When he began pulling up his stirrup leathers further and further his brother jockeys followed suit. 'Although I may not look very comfortable, I feel more comfortable . . . everybody has to ride the way he feels most comfortable. One of the disadvantages of being tall is style. Style is the way you look. If you are small it doesn't matter so much how you look because there isn't much of you to be seen and your legs don't take up so much room. If you're big you can be seen better and there's less horse showing. I smile when people ask me why I ride with my bottom in the air. I've got to put it somewhere, haven't I?'

Left: The forces of orthodoxy, in the guise of Messrs Lewis and Mercer, prepare to combat Piggott's wizardry at Royal Ascot.

Right: The quintessential jockey of the traditional English school. Joe Mercer in perfect concert with Le Moss in the Ascot Gold Cup of 1980.

The Piggott Perch was here to stay. Initially the purists were aghast. Too much pressure was being put on the horse's mouth, they argued. In 1969 Peter Willett went so far as to assert in the *Sporting Chronicle* that Piggott was technically limited. 'His inability to use his whip in his left hand and his lack of control over the lateral movements of his mounts through his legs allows them to deviate more often than they should.' On this particular point Willett drew support from Doug Smith. 'I never made my effort on his left if I could avoid it because his mounts tended to veer over in that direction. Lester, like Gordon, has a streak of genius and it would be equally fatal for any young jockey to copy his methods. His riding became even more unorthodox when, after one of his visits to America, he pulled up his leathers so short that he was practically kneeling on the saddle. By doing so he must have sacrificed all control with his legs and the ability to kick out a horse with his heels in a finish. In this respect he differs from Gordon and other English jockeys, including myself, for whom the use of the legs is an essential part of jockeyship. For this reason he can be deceptive; he may be sitting stock still with his mount apparently going easily but often there is very little more to come if Lester has to move.'

Noel Murless also expressed reservations about the increasing obsession with short stirrups, though not with the status of his erstwhile stable jockey. 'There is none finer than Lester. I think the short stirrups have done a lot of harm. Lester and Yves Saint-Martin are artists and can do it but none of the others who try to ape them can. Balance is the essential thing for a jockey.' Vincent O'Brien turned the spotlight onto another aspect of the Piggott genius. 'Lester revolutionised race-riding. Before, if there was no pace, if no one wanted to take up the running, no jockey would go on, and the horses would crawl. But Lester finished all that because if nothing went, he went, and you never see slow-run races any more.' Piggott administered the most lethal antidote to any criticism: he booted home winner after winner in the top races, be they in England, Ireland, France or the USA. As John Hislop, that most respected theorist on the art of jockeyship phrased it, 'He gives the impression that if he rode facing backwards he would still win the races that count.'

The 'Perch' was really no more than the expected outcome of racing's growing internationalism on a rider of Piggott's physique. Recalls Jimmy Lindley: 'If you look at the pictures of Lester winning his first Derby, he is riding long even by jumping standards. It was not until about St Paddy's time that Lester began to really pull his leathers up. He was the first to bring this style over to Europe. He had been riding in invitation races abroad with starting stalls and American-style jockeys, and he realised he had to adapt. And he also did it because he was embarrassed about his size. He was never built

Signs of the shorter leathers which would lead to the more exaggerated Perch as St Paddy is led in after winning the 1960 Derby.

to be a jockey and wanted to tuck himself away a bit. Of course, his backside is high in the air but his point of balance is right through the horse's shoulder which is the easiest place for him to carry weight.'

Piggott preferred to dwell on the positive aspects of his height and weight. 'A horse responds to a good weight on its back – live weight not dead weight, lead under the saddle. When a biggish jockey gets up, the chances are that the horse feels the authority. If you've got a good length of leg you can communicate more with the horse, squeeze him with your knees, control him generally – show him you are there. . . . If all the weight the horse is carrying is live and the jockey can put it in the right place at every stride, the horse runs freer than he would if part of the weight is in a fixed place in a bag on his back. If you're as tall as I am you've got to work out your own method. Most jockeys are small. There weren't any models for tall jockeys like me in my time.'

This explanation of his unique style came in the famous *Observer* interview of June 1970 wherein he was equally forthcoming on numerous other elements of his profession, most notably the source of his phenomenal strength in a finish. 'I don't say it's the strength that bends iron bars. It's the strength of an acrobat on a tightrope. Or of a juggler. Getting a horse balanced means keeping your balance, every stride, every second to suit his. In the finish of a race, as well as keeping your horse balanced you've got to be doing things with him. You've got to be encouraging the horse – moving your hands forward when his head goes forward, squeezing him with your knees, urging him on with your heels, flourishing your whip, maybe giving him a crack, and all this without throwing him off balance which means doing all these things and not letting yourself be thrown around in the saddle. Keeping the horse balanced in the last 100 yards and making him put it all in can take a lot out of a jockey. Where strength comes in is that to keep doing this needs a lot of muscle control – you've got to be holding yourself as still as you can while you're making the right movements. The more control you have of your body, the fewer movements you have to make but the more muscular effort you need: you need more strength to stand still on one leg than to walk down the street.'

And the role of the whip in a whirlwind Piggott drive? In 1963 the RSPCA had voiced the opinion that Piggott was cruel on his horses. Piggott demurred: 'In the natural state [the horse] lives in a herd and even when he's running away from danger he doesn't like to be first; he likes to be in the middle. The whip doesn't hurt a horse unless you hit him in a certain place – and instead of extending his stride he'd shorten it. A thoroughbred has got a pretty tough hide. Old ladies tell me that I'm cruel to horses because I hit them too hard. Because I flourish the whip a lot and look to be going to use it people get the wrong impression. I'm sure Scobie Breasley hits them as hard as I do

Top: Edward Hide: 2591 winners in all, including six Classics, but never champion.

Above: 'Weary Willie', one of several top riders to be jocked off in favour of Lester Keith Piggott.

but he does it in a quiet fashion. No one who loves horses as much as I do would deliberately hurt them. It's just that some are lazy and won't do their best without a crack or two.'

The forces of orthodoxy bidding to combat Piggott's wizardry were led by men like Edward Hide, Jimmy Lindley, Joe Mercer and Geoff Lewis. If Hide never seemed to attain the same degree of prominence as Lindley, Mercer and Lewis it was only because he spent the overwhelming majority of his 35-year career based in the North where he was the leading rider on numerous occasions. Winning big handicaps became his stock in trade, commencing with the 1956 Ayr Gold Cup on Precious Heather. That same season he won the Cesarewitch, and four years later he added the Cambridgeshire. The Lincoln (thrice), Portland (thrice), Manchester November Handicap and Northumberland Plate were other prestigious Northern handicaps that fell to this eloquent spokesman of the unostentatious school who methodically accumulated 2591 winners, the greatest aggregate for a jockey with no championships to his name. Second place in 1957 was as close as he came. Yet he did ride six Classic winners, including Morston in the 1973 Derby, though the best horse – pound for pound – he ever partnered was most probably the North's crack sprinter Lochnager on whom he collected the King's Stand Stakes, July Cup and William Hill Sprint Championship of 1976.

Lindley and Mercer were beautiful horsemen boasting styles seemingly lifted straight from the purists' manual. Both were taught by masters: Lindley by Tom Masson and Mercer by the redoubtable Major Frederick Sneyd who had also tutored Eph and Doug Smith. Unfortunately Lindley experienced as much (if not more) of a struggle controlling his weight as Piggott and at one stage switched to hurdles. In 1957, for example, he finished third in the Champion Hurdle itself on Retour de Flamme. However, by sheer bloody-mindedness he got his weight back down to 8st 7lb and kept it there long enough to win the St Leger on Indiana and the 2000 Guineas on Only For Life and Kashmir II, in addition to being Aggressor's ally in that famous Ascot coup of 1960 at the expense of Piggott and Petite Etoile. Mercer was hampered by no such problem and the hissing-swishing melody of his breathing and whip action operating in perfect harmony composed a symphony which came to be admired and feared by his colleagues for the best part of 40 years. In the twilight of his career, three years after his puzzling, to many people, sacking in 1976 from Dick Hern's West Ilsley stable, he won his single jockeys' championship with a total of 164.

The necessary firepower was brought about by a new job with Henry Cecil. However, the prince of thoroughbreds ridden by Mercer was Hern's Brigadier Gerard, quite possibly the best horse trained in England since the war: 17 wins from 18 races, which included ten in races currently holding Group I status, is a record which speaks for itself. Geoff Lewis also experienced the pleasure of being associated with a truly great horse, in his case the Brigadier's arch-rival Mill Reef. The Brigadier won their only confrontation, the 1971 2000 Guineas, by three lengths. Mill Reef was not beaten again. To the Dewhurst he had won as a juvenile he added the Derby, Eclipse, King George, Arc, Ganay and Coronation Cup. These were halcyon days for the former Waldorf pageboy who had come up through the ranks to be appointed Noel Murless's stable jockey in 1970. Mill Reef's Derby proved only the first leg of a unique Epsom treble in 1971 as Lewis then won the Coronation Cup on Lupe and the Oaks on Altesse Royale. Lewis holds another distinction unlikely to be emulated in the near future: he rode winners for both his sovereign and a prime minister, having won numerous races for the Queen and the 1959 Steward's Cup on Tudor Monarch for Sir Winston Churchill.

With his purposeful, rolling gait and upright, loose-reined technique, Lewis closely resembled Gordon Richards both on and off a horse – in spite of words of wisdom from Stanley Wootton. ' "Toes down, knees down, elbows down," Stan Wootton told me one day, but all I could do was stand up like PC49. "I'm afraid, my boy, it didn't work," he said after the race. "Stick to your own style." I thought, if it's good enough for Gordon it's good enough for me.' Lewis also acquired for himself the reputation of being a dab-hand at delivering comic one-liners. 'It was difficult to get out more than one line because of my stutter,' he says by way of explanation and neat example rolled into one.

Lewis could never quite wrest the jockeys' title from Piggott, who was prepared to pull every trick in the book if necessary. Two days before Lewis was due to ride two favourites for Cecil at Hamilton in September 1969, the trainer received a call from Piggott. 'I'll ride

*The last of five Classics for Geoff Lewis (**below**) as Mysterious wins the 1973 Oaks (**right**) by 4 lengths.*

No longer the Waldorf pageboy: Geoff Lewis wears the colours of Jim Joel as Noel Murless' stable jockey.

your two at Hamilton. Geoff will be at Nottingham.' When Lewis spotted the change of jockey in the press he rang Cecil to ask what had happened. 'Lester said you would be at Nottingham,' explained Cecil. 'But that's a bloody jumping meeting!' exclaimed Lewis. Needless to say, Piggott duly won on both horses. Lewis was not a man to harbour a grudge. 'He was the inspiration. He did it for a whole generation of jockeys, you know. He gave us our ambitions and our hopes. He showed us what could be done.'

Geoff Lewis kept distinguished company when it came to jockeys who had the very horse stolen from between their legs: Messrs Carson, Williamson, Saint-Martin, Murray, Swinburn and McHargue all knew the feeling. Says Carson: 'That was Lester, wasn't it? Nobody else can do it. He's such a legend people allowed him to do it, people were pleased for him to do it. He saw the right horse, he knows the right horse he wants to ride; he's used the telephone a lot. He might have a speech impediment but, by Christ, when he's on that telephone you wouldn't think so. If the trainer won't let him ride he'll ring the owner up two or three times before they'll say yes. He's ridden some helluva good horses that way.' A lot of the time Piggott didn't have to reach for the phone. As Carson readily admitted: 'There is a fair possibility that someone will be jocked off in the Derby. He has the best record and that's why no one is safe when he goes hunting for a ride. It's a fact of life. The owners pay the bills and they are entitled to have who they want.'

The most notorious instance of the man who pays the bills exercising his rights was John Galbreath, the owner of Roberto. Ten days before the 1972 Derby, Roberto's intended jockey Bill Williamson bruised a shoulder in a fall at Kempton. A week's rest was prescribed at the end of which Williamson was passed fit. Galbreath, who also owned the Pittsburgh Pirates baseball team and reckoned he knew a bit about sports injuries, was less sure. Williamson failed to ride out the day before the race; Piggott was already booked for the other O'Brien runner, Manitoulin – why not switch him to Roberto? O'Brien agreed. 'Weary Willie', as he was known to the public, once described by Piggott himself as 'the best big-race jockey in the world', was off the favourite. 'I would like to stress that the owner's decision is nothing to do with me,' Piggott informed the press. 'If someone asks you to ride a good horse you don't say, "No, let so-and-so ride it". You say, "Yes, all right".'

The Piggott-propelled Roberto touched off Rheingold by a short head. The victor's return to unsaddle was greeted by stony silence; one irate female yelled abuse at O'Brien, another attacked him with her umbrella. 'Lester would have been foolish not to accept the ride on Roberto when it was offered,' was as much as the dour Williamson was prepared to say on the matter. O'Brien probably summed up the situation best: 'I suppose Lester gave so much thought to the riding of

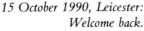

15 October 1990, Leicester:
Welcome back.

each horse that he rode in the Derby that he had no equal round Epsom. I don't remember Steve Donoghue but he was a great jockey round Epsom too; but for me in my time Lester was worth 7lb on your horse.'

Fifteen months later Piggott compered another session of jockeys' musical chairs and once more Roberto was part of the furniture. He was due to be Piggott's conveyance in the Benson & Hedges Gold Cup at York but he was withdrawn at 7.30am on the day of the race because of the soft ground. At 10am Piggott rang Harry Wragg for the ride on Moulton in place of Geoff Lewis, who, to be fair, had only been booked on the understanding that he would give way to Piggott should Roberto not run. By 1.25pm Piggott had been approached by the owners of Rheingold to ride their horse instead of Yves Saint-Martin. Piggott said yes; Lewis was back on Moulton; Saint-Martin, who had already won four races on Rheingold in 1973, arrived at the Knavesmire to discover his journey from France had been for nothing. Saint-Martin was to receive 10% of the prizemoney (the same deal Williamson got) should Rheingold win. The French champion complained to the York stewards who took the remarkable step of issuing a statement saying they 'deplored the fact that riding arrangements were changed at the last moment'. The Rheingold syndicate were unmoved. 'We had a contract with Piggott to ride Rheingold in the Arc,' said Charles St George. 'We also had an understanding that he would ride him whenever he was available. Saint-Martin was already booked to ride Allez France in the Arc so it was common sense to let Lester have his first ride on him.' Chuckles abounded as Rheingold trailed in six lengths behind Moulton, a 33–1 shot. Lester, as usual, had the last laugh. In October he and Rheingold beat Allez France and Saint-Martin to win the Arc by 2½ lengths. Said St George: 'I remember Vincent O'Brien saying once that the real charm of having Lester ride for you was that it got him off the other fellow's horse.'

The last of Lester's Classic winners? Shadeed provides number 29 in the 2000 Guineas of 1985.

Saint-Martin was never liable to be the last victim of the Piggott factor. Tony Murray won the 1972 Oaks for St George but he too was forced to bite the bullet when he was jocked-off the same owner's Giacometti for the 1974 St Leger. In the summer of 1981 it was the turn of Walter Swinburn Senior, champion jockey of Ireland

but never the winner of an English Classic, as Piggott replaced him on Blue Wind to win the Oaks by seven lengths. This victory remains the only English Classic won by the filly's trainer, Dermot Weld, and her owners, the Firestones. Clearly, no margin for error was acceptable in what might be a once-in-a-lifetime situation.

Piggott's engagement for Commanche Run in the 1984 St Leger was shrouded in similar controversy. By now Lester's Classic total stood at 27, the equal of Buckle's. He was 48 years old and there might not be too many opportunities remaining. He had ridden Commanche Run to victory in the Gordon Stakes when the colt's regular rider, the American Darrel McHargue, was under suspension. McHargue had once ridden 405 winners in a racing year in North America, had won an American Classic – the Preakness on Master Derby – and in 1980 assisted the immortal gelding John Henry to six consecutive victories. However, neither trainer Luca Cumani nor Singapore-based owner Ivan Allan had experienced Classic glory. 'I've never known Lester ring me out in Singapore about a dozen times,' confided Allan. 'He really put the pressure on. He called on friendship, he called on everything he could think of. His exact words to me were, "I want to break that record and I won't be riding for much longer." So I really had no choice but to put Lester on. From my point of view I wanted Lester. I felt Lester went very well for the horse and over the St Leger distance and course there's nobody better than Lester.' Old Stoneface drove Commanche Run into the lead at the top of the straight and having steadily worked the pace up to an exhausting crescendo still had a mite in reserve to thwart Baynoun by a neck. The record belonged to Piggott alone; just for good measure he added the 1985 2000 Guineas on Shadeed, trained by Michael Stoute – the 14th trainer for whom he had won an English Classic.

Old Stoneface, the Long Fella, A Face Like a Well-Kept Grave: terms of endearment, each and every one. Before formulating their own plans, trainers now consulted Piggott to first learn of his. 'Has there been any word from God yet?' a journalist enquired of Bernard van Cutsem around Classic time. 'No, there has been no word from Mount Sinai,' came the deadpan reply. To Vincent O'Brien, his counsel was incalculable. 'His advice mattered so much; he really thought about the horses, their temperament, liking for different kinds of ground and their idiosyncrasies. Maybe on the day after riding a horse he wouldn't say anything, but perhaps a week or two later when I met him again he'd comment about that particular horse. He really thought about horses, especially, of course, the good ones. Bringing The Minstrel to Epsom was down to him. He talked me into it. We had some doubts – some very serious doubts – but when a man like Lester Piggott speaks you had better listen.'

Sometimes the advice craved was of a more personal nature. One day Old Etonian trainer Jeremy Tree asked: 'I've got to speak to my old school, Lester, all the boys at Eton, and tell them all I know about racing. What shall I say?' A short pause. 'Tell 'em you've got flu.' Piggott's gift with throwaway lines even managed to transcend the language barrier. 'Le baton, s'il vous plait,' he requested of Alain Lequeux during the closing stages of the 1979 Grand Prix de Deauville after his own had been accidentally knocked from his grasp. 'Well, he didn't seem to mind at the time and he'd got no chance but I must admit it looked bad on the telly.' Piggott handed the whip back; the stewards handed him a 20-day suspension; the whip later fetched £8400 at an auction for the Invalid Children's Aid Society.

At the time of writing the Piggott legend shows every sign of rolling along like Ol' Man River. The sensational decision to make a riding comeback in October 1990, just days away from his 55th birthday, was immediately vindicated by a breathtaking performance on O'Brien's Royal Academy to win the Breeders' Cup Mile which can only be described as out of this world. It was the first Breeders' Cup win for an English jockey in the seven-year history of the series. The racing canvas was once again being enriched by the broad, glorious strokes of a master, *the* master. At the outset of the 1991 season bookmakers quoted him at 33–1 to regain the jockeys' championship he had last held in 1982. Only the hopeless sentimentalist or mug punter would accept that carrot but 6–1 Piggott to ride an English Classic winner or 16–1 to ride his tenth Derby winner was altogether more tempting. After all, Frank Buckle was 60 when he won both Guineas in 1827. Who knows when the book will finally close on the saga of Lester Keith Piggott? Buckle rode till he was 65 and even as Piggott dusted off his boots, 63-year-old 'Geep' Ryan was making a comeback in the States and 68-year-old Willie Clark was still kicking home the odd winner at Charles Town racetrack in West Virginia. Which jockey would first dare utter 'Move over Grandad' in Lester's hearing? 'Riding, for me, is 80% skill and experience and if you are physically fit there shouldn't be any problems. It's only really a question of two or three minutes' work at a time. It's not as though I've got to run around a football pitch for 40 minutes.'

How will posterity even attempt to sum him up? 'Do you know,' one of his professional comrades once said, 'they say he's mean. That's not true. He's twice as mean as they say. They say he's difficult to get on with. That's not true either. He's impossible to make real friends with. And they say he's great. That's certainly not true. He's the greatest jockey the world will ever see. Great will never describe him, he's too good for that.'

Perhaps the person best qualified to comment on the qualities which have guaranteed Lester Piggott an elite pedestal in racing's hall of fame is his wife Susan. She once said of him: 'He's as close to being a centaur as any man can be.'

Opposite: The Maestro.

PAT

PAT

Occupying the role of perpetual understudy can be a thankless task. The final straw comes when you get the star part only to find yourself rudely upstaged by some ageing thespian hamming it up among the spear carriers. How would Scofield's Macbeth have fared with Olivier investing the Ghost of Banquo with a magnetism beyond the call of duty? The spotlight tended to follow Lester Piggott all over the stage, which left many a fine rider kicking his heels in the depressingly darkened wings. From Smith and Breasley via Mercer and Lewis to Carson, Cauthen and Eddery, jockeys have tried to steal centre stage from racing's Olivier and failed. Pat Eddery is no Piggott – who could be? – yet he is no less a leading man for that. Even if there were not countless other reasons to support this claim, his achievement of riding over 200 English winners in 1990 seals the issue. Eddery, riding at only 2lb less, had conquered a peak which regularly defeated Piggott for 30 years. Apart from Archer and Richards only Tommy Loates (222 in 1893) had achieved the double century. Eddery had joined exalted company. At 38, in a sense, he had finally come of age: the brooding presence of Lester Piggott had been exorcised at last. 'While Lester was around he always attracted most of the attention and quite rightly. I have personally noticed a big difference. I can't really go anywhere in England now without being recognised.'

Pat Eddery's ascension to the throne occupied for so long by Lester Piggott begs several points of comparison. A natural gift with horses born of family heritage and a fierce missionary zeal to succeed which inevitably resulted in a spate of teenage suspensions epitomise the most salient common denominators. In some respects, however, Eddery's elevation to master jockey was faster than Piggott's and, the realisation of the magical 200 being a prime example, his career actually outstripped Piggott's. Six seasons and 487 winners after breaking his duck Eddery was champion jockey at the age of 22, the youngest holder of the title since Gordon Richards in 1925; Piggott's score at the equivalent stage of his career stood at 230 and he did not win a championship until past his 25th birthday – at the 11th attempt. It took Piggott seven years before he notched his first century; Eddery needed only five.

Like his illustrious predecessor Eddery was bred to be champion jockey. Both his father Jimmy and his maternal grandfather, Jack Moylan, had been Irish champion and won their country's Classics. They actually dead-heated for the 1944 Irish 2000 Guineas. This side of the 'Water', James Eddery had finished second in the Derby on Panaslipper and the Oaks on Silken Glider (the filly who unfortunately encountered Piggott's alchemy on Carrozza) and Moylan, though never making the frame in a Classic, finished second in the 1924 Grand National on Fly Mask. James Eddery spent most of his career attached to one of Ireland's legendary racing families, the

Car Insurance FAQs

💜 Q. WHAT IS AN EXCESS?

A. There are two types of excess (compulsory and voluntary) and both may need to be paid by you when making a claim. Voluntary excess can be tailored by you when you get a quote, and depending on the level of excess you choose, this could either increase or lower your premium. You may be able to claim back any excess you have paid if you had to make a claim because of an accident that wasn't your fault.

💜 Q. AM I ENTITLED TO ANY CUSTOMER DISCOUNTS?

A. As an LV= customer you're entitled to a range of discounts on our other insurance products. You'll automatically receive your exclusive customer discounts when you call our UK based call centre for a quote and take out a policy. You'll also continue to receive your customer discounts year after year for as long as you hold your LV= car insurance policy.

💜 Q. WHAT HAPPENS TO MY DISCOUNTS IF I NEED TO MAKE A CLAIM?

A. Don't worry – if you need to make a claim, your customer discounts won't be affected. If you have any no claim discount (NCD), this may be affected depending on the type of claim. You may have the option to protect your NCD, so it might be worth considering if you'd like to add this optional extra for peace of mind.

💜 Q. WHAT ARE OPTIONAL EXTRAS?

A. Optional extras are add-ons that enhance your level of cover. You may choose to add breakdown cover, courtesy car or legal protection to your car policy to make sure you can stay on the move. You can also tailor your cover to suit your needs at any time before or during the life of your policy.

💜 Q. HOW CAN I MAKE CHANGES TO MY POLICY?

A. You can make changes at any time during the life of your policy, just call us on 0845 640 5266 if you need to update your details or add any optional extras, but please note that your premium may change. If you need to cancel your cover, you may have to pay a cancellation fee plus the cost of any cover you have had so far. If you cancel before the start date of your policy, you won't need to pay any additional fees.

For Textphone: first dial 18001. Car, home, travel, caravan, classic car and motorcycle: Mon-Fri 8am-9pm, Sat 8am-5pm, Sun 9am-5pm.
Pet: Mon-Fri 8am-8pm, Sat 9am-5pm. Life: Mon-Thurs 9am-8pm, Fri 9am-5pm. Calls may be recorded.
LV= and Liverpool Victoria are registered trade marks of Liverpool Victoria Friendly Society Limited and LV= and LV= Liverpool Victoria are trading styles of the Liverpool Victoria group of companies. Liverpool Victoria Insurance Company Limited, registered in England and Wales number: 3232514, is authorised by the Prudential Regulation Authority and regulated by the Financial Conduct Authority and the Prudential Regulation Authority, registered number: 202965. Liverpool Victoria Friendly Society Limited (LVFS) is authorised by the Prudential Regulation Authority and regulated by the Financial Conduct Authority and the Prudential Regulation Authority, register number 110035. Registered address: County Gates, Bournemouth BH1 2NF.

FS21338554

LIVERPOOL VICTORIA

Customer discounts

 **UP TO 15% OFF**

 Home
0800 066 5252

 **10% OFF**

 Travel
0800 012 1079

 Pet
0800 022 3742

 Life
0800 066 5096

 5% OFF

 Multi Car
0800 171 2629

 Motorcycle
0800 316 0852

 Caravan
0800 066 5134

 Classic Car
0800 316 4861

LV.com

LV= LIVERPOOL VICTORIA

McGraths, and it was to Seamus McGrath that 14-year-old Pat was apprenticed in 1966. 'God knows what else I would have done. All of my life I have only dreamed of one thing and that is to be a top jockey. I couldn't wait to get out of school to get on a horse.' However, there were lots of promising boys in McGrath's yard and Eddery was well down the pecking order. After having his one and only ride in Ireland as an apprentice – on True Time in a six furlong handicap at the Curragh on 19 August 1967, finishing last just like Fordham and Archer – Eddery Junior was pointed towards England. A place with Sir Gordon Richards was mooted but didn't materialise. Instead, overtures were made to Frenchie Nicholson.

For as long as Nicholson practised the art he had no superior in the manufacture of jockeys. He had been taught by Stanley Wootton and he preached the gospel according to Wootton: 'Have style and cut a dash.' Nicholson's approach differed from most trainers of young jockeys because he chose to concentrate on the particular, not the general: instruction, not advice, was his guiding principle. Paul Cook, Tony Murray, Pat Eddery and Walter Swinburn became just four of many worthy disciples. Nicholson's influence on Eddery was immense in every respect. 'I thought I could ride as a kid but when I went to him I realised I was doing it all wrong. He was a great teacher. He was with you every day in the stables and he'd take you racing, and if you felt good after riding a treble or something like that, you'd soon feel pretty bad travelling home with him. He'd tell you what an idiot you were, what you'd done wrong and point out how badly you'd ridden. He didn't let you get too high and mighty. He taught you to be polite, he taught you how to ride properly and he taught you not to get too cocky. It was hard work but you never forget things like that.'

Nicholson's boys were always much sought after and it thus comes as no surprise to find that Pat Eddery's first winner was for an outside stable. On 24 April 1969 he and Michael Pope's Alvaro landed the Spring Apprentices' Handicap over the Derby course and distance. Within 29 days Alvaro carried Eddery to a further four victories and by the end of the season the youngster's total had reached 23. Among them were the Wokingham Stakes on Pope's Sky Rocket and Redcar's Vaux Gold Tankard on Philoctetes for Staff Ingham. The show was on the road. The winners started rolling in (he rode a five-timer at Haydock on 22 August 1970) and Eddery had lost his right to claim by the time he won the 1971 title of champion apprentice with 71 successes.

Eddery should have been crowned champion apprentice in 1970: Philip Waldron beat him 59 to 57, but Eddery twice incurred the wrath of the stewards which resulted in him receiving two seven-day suspensions. Senior jockeys dubbed him Polyfilla because of his inclination to go for impossible gaps. The story had a familiar ring to

Top: *The poise of a champion jockey. Eddery in 1976.*

Above: *Even a champion jockey must ride work.*

it. The kid wanted to win, badly. Fred Archer . . . Lester Piggott . . . Pat Eddery. Once again something special was brewing but youth's quixotic enthusiasm, which pays scant lip-service to either self-preservation or protocol, began to ensnare Eddery as frequently as it had Piggott. 'Christ, I was never out of the Stewards' Room. I was simply trying too hard. I was desperately keen to ride winners and went for every little gap. Then if I got into trouble I would try and push my way out of it. At that time I would risk anything to be the first over the line.' Tradition decreed Eddery learn his lesson the hard way. The two suspensions of 1970 were followed by a third seven-day ban in May 1972. Far worse was the punishment imposed when Eddery, Greville Starkey and Michael Goreham were all stood down for 'careless and improper riding' after filling the places in the Queen Anne Stakes at the Royal Ascot meeting of 1974. This suspension cost Eddery the winning mount on English Prince in the Irish Derby. Losing a Classic winner hurt. Eddery was now retained by Peter Walwyn's stable, one of the strongest in the land. Little fish are always sweet and accumulate championships, but Eddery was rapidly acquiring a taste for finer fare. In 1973, his first full season as Walwyn's jockey, he had been leading rider at Royal Ascot and already in 1974 he had won the Oaks on Walwyn's Polygamy to record his initial success in a Classic. Eddery's impetuosity would have to be curbed. Then, along came Grundy.

Shortly after Grundy had won the Dewhurst Stakes in the autumn of 1974 and earned himself top weight in the Free Handicap, Eddery bought an Afghan puppy which he christened in honour of the colt he was positive was going to be 'a good 'un'. How right he was. The Irish 2000 Guineas, the Derby, the Irish Derby, the King George VI and Queen Elizabeth Diamond Stakes: the creamy chestnut with the flaxen mane and tail won the lot. 'In the King George he gave me everything. He threw himself at the line and that's why I shall always love him.' Despite that regally-gained hat-trick of Classics, it is the half a length that separated him and Bustino at Ascot for which Grundy will be remembered. There have been all too many pennants run up the 'Race of the Century' flagpole but this one flutters proudly and indisputably. 'A battle worth more than all the diamonds in the world,' wrote John Oaksey in the *Sunday Telegraph*; 'Only those with iced water for blood could remain aloof from the excitement that flooded through the stands,' opined Hugh McIlvanney in the *Observer*. Bustino's trainer, Dick Hern, ran two pacemakers in a deliberate effort to burn off Grundy's speed and the audacious ploy almost succeeded. The track record was lowered by over two seconds. Turning into the straight, Bustino was four lengths clear of Grundy. 'It was agony; all the way up the straight I thought I'd never get to him. Every time I got nearer he kept finding some more. It was only inside the final furlong that I caught him and then he came and headed me again. It could still have gone either way but Grundy wouldn't give in. He really was a lovely horse.'

Polygamy and Grundy alone would have made the years 1974 and 1975 burn bright in Eddery's memory but an extra glow lay in the fact that they also signified his first two jockeys' titles. At the start of 1974 Coral's offered 11–8 on Willie Carson, 6–4 Lester Piggott and 8–1 Eddery about the championship, odds reflecting their position the previous season. By the end of May, Eddery was no more than a 2–1 shot after a blistering early season onslaught yet, although Eddery recorded his quickest 50 and passed the century mark on 23 August, a peak-form Lester Piggott still enjoyed a cushion of 11. However, Eddery drew level on 5 September and had put together a lead of five by the end of the season for a championship-winning total of 148. Over the next three seasons he kept a firm grip on the title with scores of 164, 162 and 176; the runner-up on each occasion was William Fisher Hunter Carson.

In contrast to his Irish rival, Stirling-born Carson boasted no blue-blooded racing pedigree (his father was a warehouse foreman for Fyffe's bananas) but, inheriting his mother's tiny stature, he set about making himself into a jockey. 'I'm not a natural rider. It has taken very hard work to learn the business. The one thing you can say about

PAT

Above: *'It has taken very hard work to learn the business.' Willie Carson as champion jockey, 1972.*

Right: *Carson notches another big win, on Known Fact in the Queen Elizabeth II Stakes, on his way to a fourth championship in 1980.*

me as a kid was that I was a good newspaper boy.' The path to the top was rocky: Carson did not ride his first winner until he was nearly 20 and suffered bouts of gloom during which he frequently contemplated giving up; when his appointment to succeed Doug Smith as first jockey to Lord Derby for the 1968 season put him on the verge of a breakthrough into the big league, he was involved in an horrific car smash that almost killed him. 'I broke my femur, jaw, wrist and had to have 27 stitches in my face. I was a wee bit mangled. The front wheel of the car was in the radio, the windscreen was gone, my broken leg was touching my chin and my head was out in the open. I kept going in and out of consciousness but I could hear one of the ambulance men say, "Have a look at the driver, he looks a goner." I couldn't move or say anything but I remember thinking, "I'm not gone yet . . . I'm still here." ' Carson was made of stern stuff. Although unable to walk without the aid of callipers for some months, he was back in the saddle in time to win the 1968 Dee Stakes on Laureate for his new patron. Nor could a crashing fall at York in May 1972, which left him nursing a fractured cheekbone and a cracked wrist, foil his surge toward a first jockeys' championship. Informed he would be out of action for six weeks, he rode again in four and became the first Scot to land the title, riding 132 winners.

PAT

A pensive moment for racing's cackling jester.

Improving his total by 31 in 1973 Carson easily retained the championship. However, there was always the spectre of you-know-who. 'Lester is the real champion. We all know that. All the time he wants to be champion the title is his. Lester is always able to pinch the best horses. I seemed doomed to play second fiddle to him for life. At Sam Armstrong's he used to get the best rides because he was the son-in-law. When I went to Bernard van Cutsem I was only number one rider for one owner, Lord Derby. I missed out when it came to the others and the big races, like Park Top in the King George and Karabas in the Washington International. By the time Lester goes, somebody else will probably come along.' The 'somebody else' turned out to be Eddery, who had youth on his side. He was ten years younger than Carson; by way of compensation the Scot went to scale at 7st 9lb, some 6lb lighter than Eddery. With or without serious opposition from an increasingly less committed Piggott, battle lines were drawn for a seemingly never-ending struggle between the two Celts for the right to call himself top dog.

The balance tipped back in Carson's favour after he and Eddery accepted new posts. From 1977 Carson held down the coveted job of stable jockey to Dick Hern; Eddery's fortunes meanwhile began to hit a sticky patch. The stream of winners from Peter Walwyn's yard dried up as a result of persistent outbreaks of the virus. The 110 Walwyn winners of 1977 which helped Eddery to his fourth consecutive title dropped to 70 in 1978 and a calamitous 44 in 1979, so that when Eddery was approached by the Sangster–O'Brien operation in the summer of 1980 to replace Lester Piggott, his answer (though he initially rejected the offer) was a foregone conclusion. His five-year contract entailed regular trips to Ireland, which brought him the Irish championship in 1982 but cost him any genuine hope of regaining the English version that Carson took from him in 1978. Besides this championship – and two more in 1980 and 1983 – there was another immediate benefit for Carson. Prior to 1977 he had ridden just one Classic winner, High Top in the 2000 Guineas of 1972, but West Ilsley was chock full of classically-bred animals and the Queen's Dunfermline won both the 1977 Oaks and St Leger to set the new trainer–jockey association on the right track. Over the next 13 seasons Hern's stable provided Carson with ten English Classic winners (Minster Son's St Leger coming in Neil Graham's name due to Hern's spell of incapacitation in late 1988), thereby establishing him as a Classic race jockey of the highest order instead of the mere puncher-home of lesser lights. Carson became fashionable and other victories for Jeremy Tree, Richard Hannon and John Dunlop raised his total of Classics to 16, twice as many as Eddery and more than any 20th century jockey bar Piggott. Only six men have ridden a greater number.

Nevertheless, whether aboard a Nashwan in the Derby or a plater at Folkestone, the Carson style was identical and, what's more, inimitable. 'Sam Armstrong told me to model myself on Doug Smith. I don't see a lot of Doug in myself now except that I like to keep chasing. I keep pushing, that's all. I don't think I really niggle at them that much, but the other day I said I had been quiet on one to somebody and he said, "If that is quiet, no wonder they run a bit when you get disturbed."' Bernard van Cutsem likened Carson to Tommy Weston, a previous wearer of Lord Derby's black jacket ('Both rugged little men with strong hands') and praised his indomitable desire to win. So, too, would Dick Hern: 'I continually see Willie win races from positions where there was every justification for him to drop his hands – he simply never gives up.' The Carson persona astride a horse is a fair reflection of the man himself: a bundle of energy anxious to exert itself. 'I always have wanted to dig in, and never get defeated. Be on the winning side.' When the moment is ripe, the angle of Carson's head drops a notch, his teeth seem to grip the horse's mane in tangible determination and his arms begin to pump ever more furiously. This head-down technique may occasionally lead to directional problems but this is easily compensated by the whole crouching ensemble acting in total concert with the animal's rhythm. Carson seldoms wins cheekily: his

Nashwan winning the Derby: 'Nash the Dash was some machine.'

mounts are invariably driven out, whatever the race, challenged or not. Troy's Derby was won by seven lengths (the widest margin for half a century), Nashwan's by five; Sun Princess won her Oaks by a record 12 lengths, Salsabil hers by five.

Out of the saddle Carson often chooses to put a similar amount of distance between himself and his pursuers. The cap and bells of racing's cackling jester are as likely to be replaced with a suit of armour when the media come calling. Carson, like his boss, has been bruised by the fourth estate more often than he would prefer and is not always able to disguise the fact. Carson has known insecurity and is quick to fend off all attacks, imagined or actual. When Hern suffered a broken neck in 1984, heart problems in 1988 and eviction in 1989, Carson's supply of good horses looked to be in jeopardy and he considered retirement. 'I made up my mind that the end of the road had come and it was time to call it a day. I was becoming resigned to the fact, although it was hard and painful to accept. Everybody was half telling me I was finished.' Adversity brought the melancholy-prone jockey and the wheelchair-bound trainer closer and closer together – and together they fought and survived. Sheikh Hamdan Al-Maktoum was the catalyst. He began building a new yard for Hern and signed Carson on a personal retainer. 'One of the greatest things in life is to be wanted. If you're wanted, you'll give your all.' Instead of doom and despondency cloaking the seasons 1989–91 they were filled by the wonderful exploits of Sheikh Hamdan's Nashwan, Salsabil, Dayjur, Elmaamul and Shadayid. 'Good horses make good trainers and good jockeys as well,' said a rejuvenated Carson. 'They also make good friends. You become a better friend to yourself and everybody wants to be friends with you.'

Nashwan meant an awful lot to owner, trainer and jockey. He was the first Derby winner owned by one of Dubai's ruling band of four brothers; he was the Derby winner Dick Hern might never have seen; and he was, according to Carson, not only the best of his three Derby winners but the best horse he had ever ridden. 'Troy was a very good horse – a relentless galloper. He went from A to B quickly but he couldn't do it in the same fashion as Nashwan who had a fantastic turn of foot. Nashwan just changed gears – that is why he is possibly the best horse I will ever ride. Nash the Dash was some machine.'

However, if Nashwan made 1989 a golden year in Carson's life, 1990 surely defied description. Salsabil and Dayjur provided the star quality and 187 winners provided the kind of quantity which propelled Carson towards all sorts of records. His best ever total; his 3000th winner (Kawtuban at Salisbury) on 22 May, followed on 24 August by the 3112th (Joud at Newmarket) which edged him past Doug Smith into third position in the all-time list behind Richards and Piggott. 'This is a great moment and I'll always remember it. There were times when I thought I'd never make a jockey, let alone

Dayjur takes the sprint honours in 1990, with Carson aboard.

ride 3000 winners. It took me at least five or six years to get going and it's even further back since I used the money from my paper round to ride a Shetland pony called Wings at Mrs McFarlane's riding school in Stirling.' And at Newcastle on June 30 Carson rode six winners (from seven rides) to match the sextets recorded by Richards and Alec Russell, the only six-timers in Britain this century. 'In India I rode eight out of nine one day and was only just beaten on the loser, but it's obviously a great feat and one which I'll never forget.' With that, Carson jetted over to Ireland and won the Irish Derby on Salsabil, the first filly to win the race since 1900. She had previously won the English 1000 Guineas and Oaks, and at The Curragh had the Derby winner Quest for Fame back in fifth which made Carson wonder whether she might even be superior to Nashwan. 'I wouldn't say that Salsabil is better . . . yet. Of course, she's the best filly I've ridden because she's the only filly I've won a Derby on. She's got the most pulverising turn of foot it makes your spine tingle. Let Salsabil

go on and win the Arc and her other races first before I say she's the best.' Alas, Salsabil was past her best on Arc day and finished a forlorn tenth.

While Salsabil enjoyed a holiday during the middle of the season, Dayjur was illuminating the racing sky like a firecracker to establish himself as one of the fastest sprinters seen since the war. No fancy-dan tactics were necessary: the sound of the stalls opening was enough to ignite Dayjur's fuse and he was never headed in winning the Temple Stakes by two lengths, the King's Stand by two and a half, the Nunthorpe (in record time) by four, the Ladbroke Sprint Cup by one and a half and the Prix de l'Abbaye de Longchamp by two. Dayjur was so quick that not even the daunting prospect of racing on dirt and round a bend – neither of which he'd encountered before – was thought likely to stop him adding the Breeders' Cup Sprint at Belmont Park. Dayjur handled everything American racing could throw at him except the shadow emanating from the clocker's hut on the grandstand roof which extended across the bright orange track in front of the finish wire like a menacing black ditch. As Dayjur was about to draw clear of the filly Safely Kept, he tried to jump the shadow, lost his impulsion and with it with race. 'Everybody knows he should have won but, by an act of God, he didn't. The horse lost nothing in defeat. He was a very, very exceptional animal and will go down as one of the best I've ridden. He was a true champion – over five furlongs he was unbeatable.'

Dayjur contributed three Group I successes (Nunthorpe, Ladbroke Sprint Cup and Abbaye) to Carson's incredible 1990 haul of 13. Salsabil led the way with four (1000 Guineas, Oaks, Irish Derby and Prix Vermeille) while Elmaamul won the Eclipse and the Phoenix Champion Stakes in Sheikh Hamdan's colours. Other owners to benefit from Carson's midas touch were Lord Weinstock, for whom he won the Yorkshire Oaks on Hellenic; Wafic Said, whose Distant Relative won the Sussex Stakes; and Prince Faisal, whose Rafha won the Prix de Diane. The remaining Group I winner of 1990 was Sheikh Hamdan's Shadayid trained, like Salsabil, by John Dunlop: on Arc Sunday she emulated her stablemate by winning the Prix Marcel Boussac. The similarities did not cease there: in 1991 she, too, won the 1000 Guineas.

Pat Eddery's sojourn with Vincent O'Brien may have curtailed access to the jockeys' championship but it proved a singularly successful springboard to uniting him with prime horseflesh. By the time he regained his title in 1986 Eddery had built an impressive portfolio: Detroit, Golden Fleece, Sharpo, Lomond, Assert, Caerleon, El Gran Senor, Sadlers Wells, Pebbles, Rainbow Quest and Dancing Brave make an impressive list of thoroughbreds; English, Irish and French Classics, Arlington Million, Breeders' Cup Turf, Eclipse, Champion,

PAT

Previous page: Carson returns in triumph after his 1000 Guineas victory on Sheikh Hamdan's Salsabil. The Oaks would follow.

King George and Arc an equally outstanding catalogue of big races – several secured more than once. With some animals Eddery boasted an unbeaten relationship. Four out of four on 1982 Derby hero Golden Fleece; two from two on Pebbles; six from six on 1985 Arc winner Rainbow Quest – indeed, he was the only rider to win on the colt. Offsetting these enviable records were the two occasions he was beaten when, according to some commentators, he should not have been.

Dancing Brave's defeat in the 1986 Breeders' Cup Turf, however, was not laid directly at Eddery's door: the arduous journey to California at the conclusion of a seven-month European campaign took most of the blame. But the vivid memory of his last-furlong sprint down the centre of the track to win the Arc remains unsullied. 'The first time I rode Dancing Brave, in the King George, he came there cruising, so I let him off, thinking he'd win seven or eight lengths but he pulled up in front. So before the Arc I said to Guy (Harwood) that I'd be the last horse to challenge. I don't know whether he thought I was a bit bonkers but he left it to me. If I'd made a mistake I would have got a slating but I sat and sat and the horse did what I thought he would do. Brilliant he was.'

The principal skeleton in Eddery's cupboard belonged to El Gran

A master of every situation: no need for drastic measures from Eddery on Balla Jidaal at Doncaster.

Señor, on whom he won everything in 1983–4 with the exception of the Derby. The colt effortlessly captured the 2000 Guineas from as vintage a field as had ever contested the event, the trio who chased him (Chief Singer, Lear Fan and Rainbow Quest) all going on to win Group I races. Two furlongs out in the Derby, Eddery's hands were resting on El Gran Señor's withers and his eyes were flicking from opponent to opponent in vain search of danger. Secreto, the horse on his outside, was at full stretch. But incredibly, Secreto muscled El Gran Señor out of it by a short head. 'I couldn't believe you could be travelling as well on a horse as I was on him and still get beaten. I got plenty of stick afterwards but if I could ride the race again I wouldn't do it any differently. I'd just hope to get a lead for a bit longer. El Gran Señor had the ability to get past horses quick, real quick. But then he'd think he'd done enough and would pull up. At Epsom they just died and left me in front too soon. I wanted a horse to come and help me along but my fellow didn't concentrate enough that last bit and got done. Everyone said I waited too long but four weeks later I went out and rode exactly the same race to win on him in the Irish Derby.' However, O'Brien, for one, voiced the opinion that had Eddery kicked hard when he had all his rivals cold, instead of delaying the strike, the initiative would have discouraged Secreto's jockey from persevering or, at very least, the momentum so gained would have enabled El Gran Señor to hold on. After the race a mischievous Lester Piggott was reputed to have approached the trainer and whispered, 'Do you miss me?' In a slowly-run Irish Derby Eddery made no mistake. He sat on Rainbow Quest's tail until below the distance and then left him for dead. 'Whoosh, it was all over in two strides. If we'd had Rainbow Quest in the Derby we'd have won.'

Dancing Brave and El Gran Señor are the two horses Eddery unreservedly places on the top shelf. 'And Pebbles – she was incredible when she won the 1985 Breeders' Cup at Aqueduct because she didn't stay. It was only because it was such a tiny track and she got lucky up the inner that she won that day, but in the Champion Stakes before that she was fantastic, bloody unbeatable. She slaughtered the colts, she beat them, all those Group I horses – Slip Anchor, Commanche Run – on the bit.' Golden Fleece might have developed into the best of the bunch had he stood training after the 1982 Derby. For once in his life Eddery was on edge. 'The Derby gets to me. The Arc, the King George, the Guineas don't bother me. I knew how good Golden Fleece was and knew everyone at Ballydoyle expected him to win. He was a hard horse to ride – in fact he'd bolted with me when I rode him as a 2-year-old – and when he coughed in his box on the morning of the race I suddenly felt that things were destined to go wrong. I am not one to suffer from nerves but I did that day. My fears were unfounded as it turned out because as soon as he got out on the course he switched off. I couldn't believe

Right: Eddery pulls out all the stops on Benguela at Sandown in July 1986.

Bottom: Dancing Brave has just won the Arc. Quiet satisfaction for Eddery at a job well done.

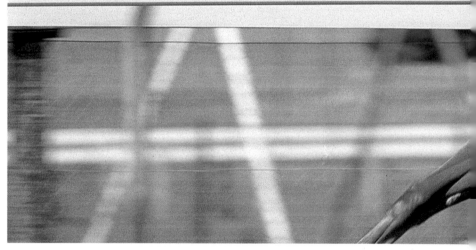

how relaxed he was and once the race was underway I just knew that when I let him go he would win. Had he pulled as hard as he had in previous races he wouldn't have won, because he wouldn't have been able to show that turn of speed. On that particular day he was probably as good a horse as I've ever ridden.'

The five years at Ballydoyle convinced any lingering doubters that Eddery was the man ready and waiting to don Piggott's mantle once it was irrevocably laid aside. Eddery rarely threatened to promote so much newspaper copy as Old Stoneface, but his equally uncanny gifts had rapidly won the same degree of respect from those whose lives

revolved around thoroughbreds. 'Quite simply, Pat has the best pair of hands in racing,' says Mark Beecroft, the chief riding instructor at the British School of Racing in Newmarket, where he uses Eddery's technique as a copybook example for aspiring young jockeys. 'He is the supreme master at settling a horse. Rainbow Quest was a prime example. He was a really hard puller and Pat was the only one who could settle him. Basically, having such good hands means he doesn't grab hold of horses and unsettle them. His hands are perfectly placed on the horse's withers and he is so beautifully relaxed and gentle, which communicates itself to the horse.'

Eddery does not dispute the exquisite contribution made by the hand of God ('I ride instinctively. There's not much time to think, so I just do what comes naturally') but has always been conscious of the fact that times change and apathy is a performer's most insidious enemy. 'Each year is different. You pick up something new, something that works for you, and you go along with it. You never stop learning in this game. When I first started, I was too high in the saddle. I felt I was hindering rather than helping a horse. Now I get a lot lower and chase 'em along. I always thought Lester got more out of a horse than anyone else and I have tried to get that way in a finish.' Eddery's *modus operandi* has evolved from the Piggott trick of lowering the backside right down onto the saddle and bumping up and down in an effort to induce maximum response from the horse. When Eddery premiered it before the Americans towards the climax of the 1983 Arlington Million on the eventual winner Tolomeo, the leading American race-caller Dave Johnson boomed, 'Ride him cowboy!' Retorts Eddery: 'Old style is old style. We are doing faster times, horses are getting better. The jockeys, I feel, are getting better and it's the way I ride and I'm not going to change.'

Tolomeo's success was Eddery's first in a Grade I event in the United States; he has also recorded Group I victories in Italy, Germany, Canada and Japan besides England, Ireland and France. Lester Piggott's innovatory globetrotting habits (he once rode in France, the United States and Japan within the space of four days) have now become commonplace among the top European jockeys. Gordon Richards, by contrast, hardly ever rode abroad: he won just three races in France during his entire career, failed to win an Irish Classic and never rode in the United States. Our weighing rooms have become increasingly cosmopolitan and not just on big-race days when a Sorrentino, Okabe, Shibata or Cordero may be spotted; Gianfranco Dettori, Alain Lequeux, Tony Cruz and South Africans John Gorton and Michael Roberts have all benefited from permanent links with English stables, in addition to the traditionally omnipresent Australians and Americans. However, in the 80 years since the Wootton–Maher era only one other Australian and one other American have managed to duplicate the championship-winning deeds of their countrymen. Lester Piggott had to overcome Scobie Breasley; Eddery and Carson had to contend with Steve Cauthen.

One day in the late 1970s, so the story goes, a visitor to Walton, Kentucky, searching for the home of Steve Cauthen, was advised: 'Drive 70 miles up the Interstate Highway and look at the sky – there's a star in the east.' The emergence of this jockey prodigy was indeed seized upon as nothing short of divine intervention. 'The Kid' was a natural. At the age of seven he astonished one Kentucky trainer by pacifying the most volatile resident of his barn and from the age of 12 he dedicated himself to becoming a jockey. Years of riding finishes

'The Kid': America's finest racing ambassador, Steve Cauthen.

PAT

Toes in the irons like he was taught, Cauthen steers Satin Flower down to the start of the 1991 Jersey Stakes at Royal Ascot.

on straw bales in his father's barn, sharing the clockers' stand and camera patrol shed, or picking up tips from stall handlers down at the track gave him balance, ambidexterity with the whip, tactical awareness and a superb sense of pace beyond his tender years, so that when he was allowed a licence on his 16th birthday, success was never going to be long in coming. He rode his first winner 17 days later, on 17 May 1976; the very next year he won 487 races worth $6 million, three of American racing's prestigious Eclipse Awards and was voted Sportsman of the Year by Associated Press, *Sporting News* and *Sports Illustrated*. In 1978 he partnered Affirmed to the American Triple Crown. Both trainers and horseplayers sang his praises. Affirmed's Cuban-born handler Laz Barrera, who often mangled his adopted country's language, was emphatic: 'He came here from outer space on a flying sausage. He is no 18-year-old, he's an old man. Sometimes he makes me believe in reincarnation. Maybe he had another life where he was a leading rider for 50 years.' A noted New York bettor delivered perhaps the ultimate citation: 'When you're betting against him, the kid is poison. Pure poison.'

However much Lester Piggott gradually assimilated the American style, the arrival of Steve Cauthen in March 1979 afforded the opportunity of witnessing the adaptation of the genuine article to English conditions. In that initial season, the contrast between Piggott and Cauthen was pronounced. Piggott, bottom high in the air when waiting to pounce and the image of controlled venom at daggers-drawn; Cauthen, low in the saddle, practically a second skin to the

Big-race specialist Walter Swinburn aboard Musical Bliss, his first 1000 Guineas success, in 1989. Of the English Classics, only the St Leger remains unconquered by Swinburn.

horse beneath, only the pumping elbows towards the finish line disturbing his motionless crouch. 'You could serve drinks on the kid's back at the furlong marker and you wouldn't spill a drop before he hits the wire,' is how one Belmont regular had phrased it. Obviously, Cauthen recognised the need to adapt his style to the disparate tracks and tactics of English racing. 'In America the horses jump off and go almost flat out from the start. They finish slower, whereas in England they often run the last quarter faster than any other. But the most fundamental adjustment is learning to balance horses over undulating courses. In America, as the tracks are flat, the jockey has to sit up the horses neck and balance himself so as not to slow its movement down. I had to learn to shift my weight wherever the horse was going uphill or downhill. It took me three years to really get comfortable on all the courses here.'

Ten years on, the Cauthen style has developed into a subtle blend of American and Anglo-Saxon. 'I'm three inches taller now than when I came over, so that means I have to ride a bit longer these days and I tend to use a longer rein now simply to keep horses better balanced.' However, he still rides 'acey deucy' – the left leg deeper down the horse, born of necessity on America's sharp, cambered left-handed tracks – but he sits up a little straighter than of yore and his whip is no longer carried in the forehand position like an aerial. Cauthen has given as well as received. More than any other he has revived the art of winning from the front, a tactic which few British jockeys could be guaranteed to reproduce at will. His acute grasp of pace enables him to select exactly the correct gear for the diverse underfoot conditions encountered in this country. The clock in Cauthen's head is most definitely a Rolex. 'I have never consciously thought about forcing the pace or making sure that races are run faster than before. But I know I am as good a judge of pace as anyone and I'm prepared to back that judgement in races . . . As long as I know the main thing about the horse I'm riding, I can react to the way the race goes and still get the best out of the horse in question.'

Having said that, it demands the 'reaction' of a jockey blessed with nerveless judgement to make every yard in a Derby as Cauthen did twice in three years. 'I had no special plans to make the running but after 50 yards it was obvious nothing was going my pace so I just had to let him go on,' he said after Slip Anchor's seven-length triumph in 1985. No Derby winner had led from the start since Coronach 'ran away' with Joe Childs in 1926. Two years later Cauthen elected to utilise the same tactics on Slip Anchor's stablemate Reference Point. 'I rode Reference Point to the front because it suited us to do that. I did not want to get caught in behind inferior horses. I wanted to keep clear of trouble and give the horse every chance.' The colt did not wave goodbye to his field as Slip Anchor had done but he was never headed, just as he had not been in the Mecca–Dante Stakes and would not be in the King George, Great Voltigeur or St Leger. In 1989 Cauthen once again excelled in this tricky art when landing the French Derby (by seven lengths) and the Irish Derby (by four) on Old Vic. He thus became the only man to have ridden the winner of a Kentucky, French and Irish Derby in addition to Epsom's original. Moreover, Oh So Sharp's 1000 Guineas, Oaks and St Leger sweep of 1985 makes him the only jockey to have achieved a Triple Crown in England and the United States.

If the velvet-gloved late swoop is deemed more suitable than mail-fisted front-running, Cauthen can still deliver, as he amply demonstrated on the marvellous fillies Triptych and In The Groove, both of whom needed to be dropped out and kidded along if they were to do their best. 'She's a bit of an enigma and does what she wants,' Cauthen said of Triptych after they had won the 1988 Coronation Cup. 'She dropped further and further back and I began to get a bit worried. But as we came down the hill she came back on the bridle. When the pace quickened up she decided she'd go and then I didn't want to hit the front too soon.' Cauthen had previously persuaded her to win the 1987 Matchmaker International at York, a race which, in its new guise as the Juddmonte International, he would

*Cauthen and Eddery fight it
out; no holds barred.*

win three years later, on In The Groove. Saving the big filly for a
stunning burst of speed inside the final quarter was Cauthen's
predicament. 'She was inclined to stop when hitting the front so I
think the secret is to get her relaxed.' Her authoritative victory at
York, and others in the Irish 1000 Guineas, Champion Stakes and
Coronation Cup, showed Cauthen at his tender best. The Group I
successes of Cormorant Wood, Time Charter, Pebbles, Oh So Sharp,
Indian Skimmer and Diminuendo underline Cauthen's way with the
ladies. 'He's now one of the top few riders in the world,' said Bill
Shoemaker in 1990 of his country's finest racing ambassador. 'When
he left the States he was a boy, gifted but immature. Now he is a man
and the complete jockey. And a very nice man.' Cauthen's
anglicisation, as jockey and man, was as complete as Danny Maher's.
Children, pensioners, pressmen and aristocrats were all treated alike –
politely and generously – and won over without reservation.

All bar one (the first) of Cauthen's ten English Classic winners
have been provided by Henry Cecil. Stable jockey at Warren Place is
the most prized appointment in racing. Richards, Piggott and, in 1985,
Cauthen: quite a line of succession. The job had made a champion
jockey of Joe Mercer in 1979 and Cauthen was anxious to retain the
crown he won in 1984 which had made him the first jockey to top the
lists in both the United States and England. 'If I want to be the best –
and I do – I have to do the job properly. If I want to be champion
jockey again – and I do – I have to ride enough horses.' With the
Cecil battalions behind him, the relatively modest winning total of
130 in 1984 (from 781 rides) increased to 195 (from 818 rides) in
1985. Cauthen required all the potent ammunition he could muster
because the severing of Pat Eddery's link with Vincent O'Brien
enabled the former champion to concentrate his attentions once more
on the jockeys' title. And Cauthen was no longer a slip of a boy:
1979's eight stoner was now tipping the scales at 8st 10lb.

Eddery wrested the title back. 'Not even people who shed surplus fat by the ton can appreciate what it's like to stay one stone under weight,' said Cauthen. 'Basically you just don't eat. Although I can get down to 9 stone without too much difficulty, everything after that is a real struggle. I prefer to diet rather than sweat because sweating is just a temporary thing.' Cauthen's summer menu consists of black coffee, lettuce leaves, slivers of tomato . . . 'Nothing worth having comes easy. I wish I could ride 9 stone – I'd feel terrific.' For 1987, however, he pared himself down to 8st 7lb, thereby clearing the decks for an epic championship duel with Eddery which ran and ran towards a nailbiting final day of the season reminiscent of the Piggott–Breasley days.

Monday 2 November saw both men ride a winner at Lingfield to make the score 192 to 189 in Cauthen's favour, but an Eddery treble to Cauthen's single at Leicester on the Tuesday reduced the gap to just one. The action then switched to Edinburgh where Eddery struck on Hopping Around to level the scores and Valtaki in the last to draw ahead as Cauthen's four mounts all ran unplaced. Thursday involved the comparatively short journey westward to Hamilton. The pendulum swings back to Cauthen; a double for him, no joy for Eddery in six rides. Friday means the long haul down to Doncaster for the final, debilitating two days of a campaign which had sprung into life on the selfsame Town Moor over seven months earlier. Cauthen wins the sixth race on Cecil's Proud Crest but a frustrating second and third is all Eddery can accumulate and he goes into the last day two behind. When Cauthen takes the nursery on Vague Discretion the pressure on the defending champion begins to soar. Neither man features in the next two finishes. The writing seems on the wall for Eddery. Three chances left: he needs them all to draw. The three o'clock, another 2YO contest; Eddery rides the 7–4 favourite Night Pass. It scoots in by three lengths. For probably the solitary occasion in its life, the 6-furlong Remembrance Day Stakes becomes essential viewing. Eddery is on the little Irish filly Vilushi; Cauthen on the grey Padre Pio. Two furlongs out, Vilushi moves into the lead but the Eddery body is never at a confident angle. For 100 yards or so she holds the pack at bay before it brushes her, and Eddery's championship hopes, contemptuously aside. Cauthen's title: 197–195. One for the history books.

Though delighted to have regained the title, Cauthen was disappointed not to have passed the magic 200 mark which had proved such an insuperable barrier to every jockey of the post-Richards era. Smith (168), Breasley (179), Piggott (191), Carson (182), Eddery (176), Mercer (164) constituted the highest championship-winning totals of the six individuals concerned, although Smith had recorded 173 when second to Richards in 1947 and, of course, Eddery had just got to within five of the double ton. However, in deference

PAT

Previous page: *The ladies' man – Cauthen comes home on Indian Skimmer, one of several outstanding fillies associated with him, at York in 1987.*

Below and opposite: *All smiles after Eddery and Toulon have secured the 1991 St Leger.*

to racing's ever increasing internationalism, it is unfair to speak of the 200 mark as not having been breached. In 1987, for example, both Cauthen and Eddery easily made up their shortfall with victories abroad – Cauthen with three Group I events in France alone. Even this was nothing new. Lester Piggott first achieved a global 200 in 1966, did so again in 1970 (when he won no less than 43 races in France in addition to 162 in Britain) and on several subsequent occasions. The days of a purely British-orientated champion like Richards were long gone. Nevertheless, a domestic double century, if for no other reason than its rarity value, remained a coveted prize. After prising the title away from Cauthen with totals of 183 (1988) and 171 (1989), Pat Eddery was determined to realise the dream in 1990.

A winner a day was the easy-sounding target, one made to seem all the more straightforward by the copious supply of evening fixtures and the fast cars and private planes which brought them within Eddery's compass. On 4 July 1981 Paul Cook had actually ridden a winner at three different courses in less than six hours: the 2.15 at Sandown, the 5.00 at Bath and the 7.50 at Nottingham (a scarcely credible feat yet one successfully emulated on 14 June 1991 by Gary Carter). 'It's everyday riding,' says Eddery. 'You go from day to day. You have a bad day yesterday, you forget it and think about tomorrow.' In 1990 Eddery went from 'day to day' with a vengeance. His 100th winner (Singing at Kempton) arrived on 27 June – his fastest ever century – and put him just ten days behind Richards' fastest ton of 1949. The bookies quoted him at 5–4 on to reach his goal. Eddery told reporters: 'I'm going all out for the double century even if it means going to Edinburgh at the end of the season.' It didn't. Any danger of Eddery missing the boat was removed by a five-timer at York on 10 October; the bookmakers stopped taking bets. Winner number 199 came up at Newmarket ten days later (Junk Bond in the Houghton Stakes) and the elusive 200th four rides after that, at Chepstow on Tuesday 23rd, fourteen racing days before the end of the Turf season. The horse was a 2-year-old filly called Miranda Jay, trained by Michael Jarvis; the race was the Offa's Dyke Maiden Stakes. 'It's a great relief to get the 200. I'm really chuffed. I first gave myself a chance when I found myself 28 ahead of schedule at Goodwood, but you've got to get through the second half of the season. You've got to work hard, doing two a day, and you've got to keep going right to the end.'

So Eddery (whose final total was 209) gained entry to an exclusive club frequented by just Richards, Archer and Tommy Loates. En route to his eighth title he'd passed some other notable statistical milestones. In May he equalled Archer's career total of 2748, and six winners at the Wolverhampton and Windsor meetings of July 16 lifted him past Joe Mercer's total of 2810 into fifth place on the all-

time list. Only Richards, Piggott, Carson and Smith lay ahead of him.

However, Eddery's 1990 season was not only a numbers game: there were seven Group I scalps. In Europe he won two Derbies inside four days: the French on Sanglamore and the English on Quest For Fame; the Irish 2000 Guineas on Tirol; the French 1000 Guineas on Houseproud; the Prix du Moulin on Distant Relative; in North America he landed Canada's Rothmans International on French Glory and the Man o'War Stakes at Belmont with Defensive Play.

Eddery's 3000th winner arrived at Bath on 22 July 1991. It had taken him 22 years and 3 months: two years less than Richards, five less than Piggott, six less than Carson and eleven fewer than Smith. Richards' progress, of course, was slowed by the onset of the Second World War and, as Eddery says, 'No one thought of having helicopters to ride at two meetings on the same day.'

Even though a certain Lester Keith Piggott had made a surprise return to the saddle, the mantle of champion jockey and master horseman now lay securely and indisputably on Pat Eddery's shoulders.

QUO VADIS?

QUO VADIS?

'Over the years, Britain has steadily produced the best jockeys in Europe, quite possibly the best in the world. But unless we devote more time to the apprentices, this flow of talent will dry up very rapidly and we could so very easily become just another horse-riding nation.'

When these reservations were voiced by former royal and Classic-winning jockey Harry Carr in 1973, the first ten in the jockeys' table comprised six Englishmen, two Irishmen, a Welshman and a Scot; in 1990 the list resembled a UN delegation featuring as it did three Irishmen, an American, an Italian, a South African, two Scots and just two Englishmen, Kevin Darley and Dean McKeown, whose father is half Irish. Attempts to arrest the rapid decline in the number of apprentices who establish themselves as senior jockeys led to a fundamental review of the system during 1991. As of 1992 apprentices will, for instance, benefit from an extension of the age limit from 24 to 25 (it was once as low as 21) and an increase in the 7lb allowance from 10 to 15 winners and in the 3lb allowance from 75 to 85. 'It's a great boost for an apprentice to ride out his claim but that hasn't been the trend in recent years,' commented Michael Caulfield, secretary of the Jockeys Association. 'The new measures should help and will give young riders confidence to go on.'

Quo vadis: whither now? It is not inconceivable that two centuries after Buckle ruled the roost another Frankie – albeit not a Francis but a Lanfranco – will sit on the sport's top perch as the first Italian-born champion jockey, because 19-year-old Lanfranco Dettori's 141 winners in 1990 made him the first teenager to score a century since Lester Piggott 35 years earlier. Alternatively, might the dawning of the 21st century witness the coronation of Alan Munro – of Scottish lineage, English upbringing but American style – or perhaps Darryll Holland, the dazzling apprentice find of 1991? Is it pure fantasy to imagine Alex Greaves, the only woman ever to ride out her claim, cutting the kind of swathe on this side of the Atlantic that Julie Krone has cleared in the United States?

Smart money suggests greatness awaits Dettori and Munro. Indeed, money has already talked, because Dettori was appointed stable jockey to Luca Cumani for 1990 while Munro, the elder by four years, was sensationally retained by Prince Fahd Salman to ride his 60 horses less than a month before one of them, Generous, embarked on a winning spree which encompassed the 1991 Derby, Irish Derby and King George VI & Queen Elizabeth Diamond Stakes. 'It is still like some kind of fairytale. Of course the money is a bonus, but it is the prestige of winning these sort of races that is tremendous,' said Munro, who wound up the season being voted Flat Jockey of the Year. 'Two years ago I was riding in the North for Mel Brittain. I've never had an experience like this.'

Previous page: 'Down low and go for dough' – Alan Munro wins the 1991 Irish Derby on Generous.

Munro did not have to wait long before he discovered that even the most lucrative geese occasionally lay eggs far from golden. Richard Quinn, the jockey Munro, through no fault of his own, so summarily displaced, had won Salman the Irish Oaks and St Leger of 1990 and was well liked by one and all. The press, in particular, thought him hard done by. Here was Munro walking off with the glory which should have been Quinn's. At the post-Derby press conference, Munro's attitude displeased certain denizens of the press room accustomed to being spoon-fed with the kind of bland fare they could have concocted themselves. The knives flashed and Munro went the way of Caesar on what should have been the greatest day of his life: in a *Daily Telegraph* piece entitled 'Derby jockey was far from Generous', even the habitually obliging and considerate John Oaksey was moved to call Munro 'a cocky stripling'. Fences had to be mended. A conciliatory interview appeared in the *Telegraph* ('John Oaksey reconsiders his Derby criticism of an intensely competitive jockey') while a Royal Ascot hat-trick on Salman's Dilum, Fair Cop and Magic Ring offered Julian Wilson the opportunity to invite

'This is how it's done': Munro receives Lester Piggott's pearls of wisdom prior to the Irish Derby.

Munro before the BBC cameras. 'It ruined the best day of my life. The big worry was that they'd criticise my riding, but they couldn't do that so they criticised my personality instead. Perhaps I did give the wrong impression and give them cause to write what they did, but I was on a high after the race and the questions were all coming too quickly. You've got to remember there are other people involved. When I said, "Look, my contract is none of your business," I was trying to protect the Prince's privacy as much as anything else. It was the same answering questions about Keith Piggott. The advice he gave me about riding in a Derby might be something he values very dearly. It's not for me to tell everybody about it. I should have been more pleasant, more diplomatic and full of smiles but it's been good for me in one sense. Without any shadow of doubt I've come out of this a lot wiser.'

When Sentimental Rose carried an 18-year-old Munro to his first success on 21 August 1985, any Derby-winning thoughts firing the jockey's imagination were certainly not advertised by any obviously apparent potential in the saddle. There were no horsey connections in the Munro family to smooth his path when he left school at 16 to join Barry Hills. That single contribution from Sentimental Rose was all Munro had to show for two years in Lambourn: he was going nowhere fast. He moved north to the Yorkshire stable of self-made millionaire Mel Brittain. The trainer's attitude rubbed off: 'If you can do anything to improve yourself, go and do it.' In the winter of 1986 Munro went to Italy but the following off-season, heeding the advice 'Go west, young man', he set out for the USA and a conversion akin to St Paul's. 'Before I went to America I didn't know how to ride. I was trying to ride like Lester Piggott. I was riding very, very short and, being weak as well, I was just so unbalanced.' After riding Brittain's Hot Ruler at Beverley in June 1986 he was called in by the stewards, who advised a drastic reappraisal of his style. Munro spent that winter working the farms of New Jersey where he met an old race-rider called Lyndon Hannigan, who was quick to assure him no American trainer 'would ever dream of employing a work rider with his ass stuck up in the air like yours'. Munro dropped his leathers a notch or two, got his knees below the pommel of the saddle, stuck his toes in the irons and his chest between his knees. The streamlined, aerodynamic Yankee crouch fitted him like a glove: 'Down low and go for dough'. Two more winters in California climbing over the fences into Santa Anita and Hollywood Park to hustle for work (and at one point living in a hotel which doubled as a place of assignation for ladies plying the 'oldest profession') completed the metamorphosis from ugly British duckling to sophisticated, Americanised swan. 'Over there it's all about balance, which is a big thing throughout a race. And with your knees dropped you automatically get more of a feel with the horse, which in turn helps your balance. If you can

balance a horse and get in rhythm with it you can, like the Americans, become part of the horse and provide it with so much assistance.'

As Munro sat down in the saddle, people in the stands began to sit up – and take notice. On this side of the Atlantic, Cash Asmussen was the only point of reference: even Steve Cauthen had abandoned the American crouch in its purest form. Munro was immediately, and unimaginatively, dubbed 'Cash' by the racing press. Having ridden one winner in his first three seasons, the Americanised Munro partnered 77 in the next three, which led to an offer from Bill O'Gorman to ride as his number one in 1990. Munro's season began tremendously with victory in the Lincoln on Evichstar and continued in like vein courtesy of Pattern race glory aboard Mac's Imp (including the Group I Heinz 57 Phoenix Stakes) and a record-equalling 16 victories on another O'Gorman 2-year-old colt, Timeless Times. By 30 October Munro's total had soared to 95, but a season of achievement which had passed at such breakneck speed now very nearly ended, quite literally, with a broken neck. Shortly after leaving the stalls in the Daily Telegraph Racecall Nursery at Redcar, Munro's mount Mystic Crystal stumbled and deposited him beneath the hooves of another horse: Munro's head was used as a football. He was not permitted to sit on a horse for three months. Instead, he worked out on the mechanical horse, called an Equicizer, he had brought over from the States. 'The fact is that if you're not trying to improve all the time, you're probably standing still. I know what I want. I don't dilly-dally around. I want to be the champion – the king. Nothing else matters to me.' Alan Munro placed his cards on the table face up:

Previous page: Alan Munro's fairytale begins, with the five-length victory of Generous in the Derby. In the winner's enclosure with horse and jockey is the owner, Prince Fahd Salman.

had Fahd Salman not picked them up, someone of equal patronage most definitely would have. 'Alan's one of the best around. He could soon be champion.' Who says so? No less an authority than Lester Keith Piggott.

Nor has Munro's most obvious challenger for championship honours escaped the knowing gaze of the man who increasingly belies his former description of Old Stoneface. In early 1991, Piggott had this to say on the inevitability of Frankie Dettori some day being champion. 'It looks that way. He's got everything one would want – he does everything right and has a good race-riding brain.' Luca Cumani was, understandably, even more effusive on the merits of a jockey he had been licking into shape since 1985. 'I've seen his potential from the very beginning. He's done nothing but improve. He's like a wonderful horse that shows potential the day you break him in as a yearling, wins all his races as a 2-year-old and then goes on to be a champion as a 3-year-old. He's probably not going to be a champion jockey for a few years yet but he's got all the potential there and I rate him as high as any young jockey there's ever been. He's got a good sense of pace, he understands horses very well and has a very good sense of timing for the winning post. He's extremely stylish. I love the way he pushes a horse out and goes for the whip. He's never hard on a horse with his whip and doesn't use it excessively, and I think everything really seems to fit together nicely in the making of a good jockey.'

Dettori has much in common with Munro. Though not as pronounced, he too employs the low-backed posture born of winters

Lanfranco Dettori demonstrates the lessons learned Stateside: flat back, short rein.

Left: '*I was more intent on becoming a petrol pump attendant*' – *Lanfranco Dettori.*

Stateside: both jockeys keep up to scratch using the mechanical horse popularised by the top American jockeys. However, whereas Munro's American experiences were confined to morning work-outs (up to the end of 1990 his one mount in a race was on O'Gorman's Timeless Times), Dettori has been winning $60 000 events thanks to the help of Neil Drysdale and Richard Cross. This kind of influential patronage begins to identify why the pair have trod different paths to the top, for while both these dark-haired, Latin-looking young men could be the sons of an Italian champion jockey, only one is. Connections open doors: Gianfranco Dettori had been champion of Italy 13 times and was still winning his country's Classics when his son hit the heights in 1989. Moreover, Dettori senior rode two English Classic winners (the 2000 Guineas on Bolkonski and Wollow) in the course of frequent visits to this country to ride for the Italian patrons of Henry Cecil, and Cecil's former assistant Luca Cumani, during the 1970s. At that time Dettori junior was far too young to contemplate a future aboard racehorses: 'I was more intent on becoming a petrol-pump attendant. I know it seems funny but the price of petrol was very high and it seemed the right job to be in.' But the gift of a pony and numerous excursions to the races with his father soon implanted the ambition. 'When I was 14 my father suggested that I should go and learn in

Below: *A rising star? Darryll Holland.*

another country, see how I managed and then maybe go back home. I was lucky to have 115 rides in Italy before I had my first in England. He thought here would be better than France and I've been here ever since.'

Dettori duly arrived at Cumani's Bedford House stables in 1985, but owing to his youth was not granted a licence to ride until 1987, by which time he'd won 17 races back in Italy, the first at Turin on 9 November 1986. As a result of those Italian successes Dettori began his English career with a 5lb claim instead of 7lb. Lizzy Hare broke the ice at Goodwood on 9 June and seven more winners had followed by November. In 1988 the shooting star gathered speed. Dettori's tally increased to 22, despite a couple of brushes with the stewards. In 1989 the Italian comet was the cynosure of all eyes. He recorded his first hat-trick, at Leicester on 5 June, and the winners came so thick and fast (seven trebles in all and a success rate of 16%) that he finished the season securing the apprentices' championship with a total of 75. En route, two significant milestones were passed. On 18 July he lost the last of his allowance after Versailles Road won at Beverley and, more importantly, on 28 August it was announced that he had stepped into the plum job – when still only 18 and barely two years after his first English winner – of Cumani's stable jockey for 1990 upon Ray Cochrane's switch to Guy Harwood. Had everything come too quickly, too soon? Since Pat Eddery had made the successful transition from champion apprentice to champion jockey, no one had got close and many a young hopeful (Dineley, Edmondson) had bitten the dust altogether. Eddery was only 20 when he became number one jockey to Peter Walwyn. However, he too was the son of a champion jockey, as was Walter Swinburn, just 19 in his first season with Michael Stoute. If any teenager was bred for the task ahead it was Dettori. 'It's a big responsibility but I'm ready to take it. It's a question of not doing silly things and concentrating on the job. I am going to grab the opportunity with both hands.'

Dettori certainly did that. Throughout 1990 he never wavered, despite the heavy pressure of his new position, three nasty falls and a motorway pile-up in his Mercedes. He rode his 100th winner of the season at Chepstow on 27 August, nearly four months before his 20th birthday, the first teenager to do so since Lester Piggott, whose 100th winner of 1955 beat his 20th birthday by only ten days. Dettori further improved the comparison by eventually riding 141 winners (at a percentage of 20.1) to Piggott's 103 (at 19.4) to occupy fourth place in the jockeys' table. He'd not emulated his father by winning a Classic, but at Ascot's British Festival of Racing he won both Group I races, the Queen Elizabeth II Stakes and Brent Walker Fillies Mile, on Markofdistinction and Shamshir respectively, his initial successes at this level of the sport. To round off a marvellous year, the Horserace Writers Association voted him Flat jockey of 1990, quite an accolade

A picture Darryll Holland never dreamed would be taken. He strides out alongside his idol Lester Piggott.

when one considers Pat Eddery had achieved the first double century in 38 years. The media warm to Dettori: its members find the endless banter delivered in a fractured version of the English language somehow endearing. Some think him too flippant but it is he whom the press love, not the pensive, sardonic Munro.

Perhaps in years to come 1991 will be remembered as the season in which Darryll Holland announced his arrival in the big time. The 19-year-old Mancunian took the racing world by storm. He had never even sat on a horse when he first entered Barry Hills' Lambourn stable in 1988 but within a month any thoughts of enrolling him at the British Racing School were deemed unnecessary. 'It is difficult to take away anything from the greats,' says Hills, 'but this boy has always been a bit of magic to me.' Holland's 51st winner of 1991,

Kirby Opportunity at Brighton on 25 July, placed him ninth in the jockeys' table (above Swinburn, Cochrane and Dettori) and saw the loss of his allowance just 15 months after winning his first race. By the close of the Turf season on 11 November his score had increased to a new post-war record for an apprentice of 83, which ensured his name remained in the list of 10 leading jockeys.

A minor debate arose concerning the validity of Holland's new record. He had beaten by eight the totals of Edward Hide (in 1956) and Frankie Dettori (in 1989) for instance, but the former maintained that the first 89 of his 131 winners in 1957 were achieved on an apprentice's licence. A rival school of thought, however, believed that the season in which the apprentice rides out his claim (in Hide's case 1954 not '56 or '57) counts as his last in that capacity. Thus Greville Starkey with 45 wins was the champion apprentice of 1957, not Hide with 89. By this yardstick, Charlie Elliott's 85 of 1922 is the all-time record, for this was the year he lost his allowance. The totals of 89 and 106 which he achieved in 1923 and 1924 to win the jockeys' championship itself were thus rendered inadmissible even though he was still indentured to Jack Jarvis.

This interpretation seems harsh in view of the modifications made to the system down the years. When an allowance was first introduced, for the 1894 season, it was an all-embracing 5lb restricted to selling races and lasted just one year from the date of a lad's initial winner. The need to nurture domestic talent in the face of American and Australian competition later prompted the Jockey Club, so it was said, to include handicaps and prolong the allowance until 40 winners had been ridden – the system as Elliott knew it. Although allowances assumed the more familiar three-tiered format after World War II, the 40-winner watershed remained in force till increased to 75 as of 1966. On this basis, therefore, Hide's best score was 53 in 1954. Further complicating the issue is the fact that 10 of Holland's 83 came courtesy of all-weather racing, an opportunity denied Elliott, Hide et al.

All the customary fireworks accompanied Holland's brief acquaintance with apprenticeship. July 1991 proved microcosmic. He sat out the first week owing to a neck injury sustained in a three-horse crash at Wolverhampton; at York on the 13th he recorded a pair of notable firsts – a treble and a two-day ban for excessive use of the whip; the following Wednesday he received a further seven days' holiday for a similar offence at Sandown, where he was adjudged to have struck Horizon 19 times (a dozen is the arbitrary guideline) before getting the 13–8 favourite home by a short head. 'I broke the rules and they were right in giving me a ban, but you don't really count how many times you hit a horse when you're riding him to win,' Holland explained. The next morning at exercise he felt a stinging blow across the leg from Hills' riding crop: 'Did that hurt? Good. Now you know what that horse felt like when you whopped it

Top and above: Alex Greaves' first major win, in the 1991 William Hill Lincoln Handicap on Amenable.

too much.' Amid all this unwelcome attention from the stewards, Holland encountered another of the jockey's traditional adversaries, having to forgo mounts as a result of feeling groggy after wasting too hard. At a willowy 5ft 6in there is already something about Holland that reminds one of the young Archer: something about the dark eyes, the line of the jaw and the shape of the front teeth, the faint suggestion of a stoop.

Holland assured everyone that his feet would be kept firmly on the ground; his master would see to it. Although revering Hills, the youngster attributed much of his improvement to a recent three-month stay with Californian trainer Gary Jones. The American trademarks were self-evident: the flat back, the periscopic whip carriage and acute judgement of pace. 'It took many weeks getting up at 6.30am and riding ten lots out to make me become more streamlined and tidy. The Americans are so advanced, they go over every aspect of the game. But I am nowhere near how I want to ride yet. It will take a long time.' It may indeed. But there is one thing for sure: Holland has both time and talent on his side.

The United States may have loaned us Steve Cauthen – and helped mould Alan Munro, Frankie Dettori and Darryll Holland in his image – but can the astonishingly successful career of Julie Krone act as a similar role model for budding female riders in this country? 'I used to sit in the showers at Pimlico and I would cry, "I can't believe this.

QUO VADIS?

I'm better than these guys," and I'd bang my head and try to drown
myself in the water. There were a lot of difficult times but it was
never a case of me fouling up. I just would never get the
opportunity,' says Krone, before adding venomously: 'I'm not
interested in being judged as a woman rider. I just want to be judged
on ability.' In ten years Krone has earned that right. Nearly 2000
winners, including six on one card; $20 million in purse money;
leading rider at Monmouth Park, Meadowlands, Atlantic City . . .
'She don't ride like no girl rider,' grunted Angel Cordero; 'She can
ride with any jockey in the country,' said 'The Shoe' after Krone had
beaten him in a match. Krone overcame a racing community every bit
as conservative as Britain's. Girls just weren't strong enough. To
breach this male bastion Kathy Kusner had gone to court in order to
gain her licence in 1968. Krone, too, was obliged to fight for her
chance (quite literally on occasions as fellow jockeys Turcotte, Rujan
and Nied could testify) but surviving a broken back and a smashed
arm she has triumphed gloriously.

What odds of a British Julie Krone emerging in the near future?
When Alicia Meynell rode in a series of matches at York against
members of the opposite sex in 1804 and 1805, crowds flocked in
their thousands to enjoy the spectacle ('A jockey in petticoats – a
phenomenon,' declared one chronicler) and in one contest she
actually humbled no less a personage than Frank Buckle. However, in
spite of Meriel Tufnell's historic victory on Scorched Earth in the
first race for lady jockeys – the Goya Stakes at Kempton on 6 May
1972 – the Jockey Club did not permit women to compete against
male amateurs until 1974, or ride against professionals until 1976.
When the subject of female jockeys was aired, most treated it as a
joke. 'Their bottoms are the wrong shape,' observed Lester. To Karen
Wiltshire in 1978 went the honour of being the first to get the better
of professional male riders on the Flat. Yet in 1991 a woman was
leading the jockeys' championship a month after the Lincoln
Handicap – traditionally the start of the Flat season – had come and
gone. To boot, that same woman had actually won the Lincoln. Her
unlikely position in the table, however, derived from an innovation
no less revolutionary than professional lady jockeys: all-weather
racing. Enter Alex Greaves, 'The Queen of the Sands'.

Alex Greaves broke more new ground by forfeiting her claim with
a double at Hamilton on 31 May 1991. It had taken her a fraction less
than 18 months, not much longer than Darryll Holland and faster
than either Munro or Dettori, but though various awards did come
her way (Lanson Lady of the Month for January 1990 after eight
winners on the Southwell fibresand, Lady Jockey of 1990 from the
Jockeys Association and the Aberlour Outstanding Achievement
Award from the Federation of British Racing Clubs), that vital
acceptance into a male-dominated world was still slow in coming.

'We are still regarded as novelties,' Greaves told the *Sunday Times*. 'You have to be as tough and ruthless as the men are, and a bit more besides. They'll take liberties with you because you're a girl and you could be intimidated by it all. And there is an awful lot of hypocrisy, too. Trainers will come up and tell you you rode a brilliant race but they'd never dream of putting you up on their horses. I would like to think that I could get further than girls have done in the past. But the chances of me or any other successful lady jockey getting into the big league is nil.' Greaves owes virtually all her success to the patronage of Yorkshire trainer David Barron. Her first success, in December 1989, came at Southwell as did the next 22 (all bar one for Barron). 'If this had happened on the grass it would have been unbelievable but because it is on fibresand a lot of people think it's a fluke,' said the trainer, 'but I don't. Most of the girls were too weak but I never had any such doubts about Alex – she was always a strong rider.'

Greaves recognised that Southwell provided an unnatural – albeit profitable – habitat with its gentle terrain and consistent going encouraging a tactic-free, flat-out gallop in most races, and the opening of her grass account at Catterick the following March on Joe Bumpas was consequently greeted with some relief. A steady if unspectacular flow of winners during the summer preceded another oustanding campaign on the sand which culminated in her being crowned champion of the all-weather season after finishing five ahead of John Williams. On 18 January 1991, for example, she rode a four-timer at Southwell (all for Barron) to increase her amazing record at the Nottinghamshire track to 36 wins from 90 rides. The last of that quartet was a 6-year-old bay gelding called Amenable, on whom she would make more racing history two months later by winning the Lincoln. 'From the stands could you have picked out Amenable's jockey as a girl during the race?' Barron asked the press. 'Would you have recognised her as a girl in the finish? Of course you wouldn't. If she had been a man her career would have taken off completely by now.' Alex Greaves had little left to prove and, like Julie Krone, was now able to say with justifiable pride and not a little feeling, 'Out there you're a jockey not a woman.'

Whether she will ever attract the same quantity and quality of rides as her American alter ego remains to be seen. At least one prominent English trainer thinks women jockeys do have a future in the sport. Before coming to Newmarket as private trainer to Sheikh Mohammed, John Gosden operated Stateside and observed Ms Krone at close quarters. 'She showed what women riders can do and I would say emphatically that they are every bit as capable as men. In 50 years' time maybe 30% of our jockeys will be women.'

As the 21st century beckons us, the prospect of Frank Buckle's legacy being disputed by a reincarnation of Alicia Meynell is possibly not so far-fetched after all.

APPENDIX: CLASSIC WINS

b = bay   br = brown   c = colt   ch = chestnut
f = filly   gr = grey   fav = favourite
jt fav = joint favourite

SAM CHIFNEY SENIOR

DERBY
1789 5th Duke of Bedford's b c SKYSCRAPER (4–7 fav) 11 ran

OAKS
1782 1st Earl Grosvenor's b f CERES (4–7 fav) 12 ran
1783 1st Earl Grosvenor's ch f MAID OF THE OAKS (4–1 fav) 10 ran
1789 3rd Earl of Egremont's b f TAG (5–2 jt fav) 7 ran
1790 5th Duke of Bedford's ch f HIPPOLYTA (6–1) 12 ran

FRANK BUCKLE

2000 GUINEAS
1810 2nd Earl Grosvenor's b c HEPHESTION (5–1) 9 ran
1820 4th Duke of Grafton's b c PINDARRIE (Evens fav) 5 ran
1821 4th Duke of Grafton's b c REGINALD (11–10 fav) 4 ran
1822 4th Duke of Grafton's b f PASTILLE (4–6 fav) 3 ran
1827 4th Duke of Grafton's br c TURCOMAN (5–1) 5 ran

1000 GUINEAS
1818 John Udney's br f CORINNE (7–1) 8 ran
1820 4th Duke of Grafton's ch f ROWENA (7–4 fav) 6 ran
1821 4th Duke of Grafton's b f ZEAL (4–6 fav) 6 ran
1822 4th Duke of Grafton's ch f WHIZGIG (2–5 fav) 4 ran
1823 4th Duke of Grafton's br f ZINC (4–6 fav) 5 ran
1827 4th Duke of Grafton's br f ARAB (8–1) 7 ran

DERBY
1792 1st Earl Grosvenor's ch c JOHN BULL (4–6 fav) 7 ran
1794 1st Earl Grosvenor's b c DAEDALUS (6–1) 4 ran
1802 3rd Duke of Grafton's b c TYRANT (7–1) 9 ran
1811 Sir John Shelley's b c PHANTOM (5–1) 16 ran
1823 John Udney's b c EMILIUS (5–4 and 11–8 fav) 11 ran

OAKS
1797 1st Earl Grosvenor's b f NIKE (15–8 fav) 5 ran
1798 John Durand's b f BELLISSIMA (6–4 fav) 7 ran

1799 1st Earl Grosvenor's ch f BELLINA (5–2) 4 ran
1802 John Wastell's gr f SCOTIA (5–4 and 6–4 fav) 6 ran
1803 Sir Thomas Gascoigne's b f THEOPHANIA (5–2) 7 ran
1805 2nd Earl Grosvenor's b f METEORA (7–2 and 3–1) 8 ran
1817 George Watson's b f NEVA (Evens fav) 11 ran
1818 John Udney's br f CORINNE (5–2) 10 ran
1823 4th Duke of Grafton's br f ZINC (Evens and 5–6 fav) 10 ran

ST LEGER
1800 Christopher Wilson's b c CHAMPION (2–1 jt fav) 10 ran
1804 Harry Mellish's b c SANCHO (2–1 fav) 11 ran

NB: Though no jockey is recorded it is highly probable that Buckle also partnered the following in the 1000 Guineas:
1819 4th Duke of Grafton's br f CATGUT (20–1) 7 ran
1825 4th Duke of Grafton's ch f TONTINE walked over

WILLIAM CLIFT

2000 GUINEAS
1809 Christopher Wilson's ch c WIZARD (4–5 fav) 8 ran
1818 3rd Baron Foley's b c INTERPRETER (7–4 and 5–4 fav) 9 ran

1000 GUINEAS
1814 Christopher Wilson's b f CHARLOTTE (11–5 fav) 5 ran
1815 3rd Baron Foley's unnamed br f by Selim (3–1) 5 ran

DERBY
1793 Sir Ferdinando Poole's b c WAXY (12–1) 13 ran
1800 Christopher Wilson's b c CHAMPION (7–4 fav) 13 ran
1803 Sir Hedworth Williamson's b c DITTO (7–2) 6 ran
1810 3rd Duke of Grafton's b c WHALEBONE (2–1 fav) 11 ran
1819 4th Duke of Portland's br c TIRESIAS (2–1 and 5–2 fav) 16 ran

OAKS

1804   3rd Duke of Grafton's br f PELISSE (4–5 fav) 8 ran

1808   3rd Duke of Grafton's ch f MOREL (3–1 fav) 10 ran

ST LEGER

1807   4th Earl Fitzwilliam's b f PAULINA (8–1) 16 ran

1810   6th Duke of Leeds's ch c OCTAVIAN (12–1) 8 ran

JEM ROBINSON

2000 GUINEAS

1825   2nd Marquis of Exeter's ch c ENAMEL (7–4 fav) 6 ran

1828   5th Duke of Rutland's br c CADLAND (5–2) 5 ran

1831   5th Earl of Jersey's ch c RIDDLESWORTH (1–5 fav) 6 ran

1833   3rd Earl of Orford's gr c CLEARWELL (5–4 fav) 6 ran

1834   5th Earl of Jersey's ch c GLENCOE (6–1) 7 ran

1835   5th Earl of Jersey's br c IBRAHIM (1–7 fav) 4 ran

1836   5th Earl of Jersey's b c BAY MIDDLETON (4–6 fav) 6 ran

1847   Sir Robert Pigot's b c CONYNGHAM (4–1) 10 ran

1848   B Green's b c FLATCATCHER (4–1) 5 ran

1000 GUINEAS

1824   5th Earl of Jersey's b f COBWEB (5–2) 4 ran

1828   Arthur Molony's b f ZOE (6–5 fav) 7 ran

1830   5th Earl of Jersey's ch f CHARLOTTE WEST (5–1) 7 ran

1841   Stanlake Batson's ch f POTENTIA (6–4 jt fav) 5 ran

1844   George Osbaldeston's ch f SORELLA (10–1) 9 ran

DERBY

1817   John Payne's ch c AZOR (50–1) 13 ran

1824   Sir John Shelley's ch c CEDRIC (9–2) 17 ran

1825   5th Earl of Jersey's ch c MIDDLETON (7–4 fav) 18 ran

1827   5th Earl of Jersey's b c MAMELUKE (9–1) 23 ran

1828   5th Duke of Rutland's br c CADLAND (4–1) 15 ran

1836   5th Earl of Jersey's b c BAY MIDDLETON (7–4 fav) 21 ran

OAKS

1821   2nd Marquis of Exeter's b f AUGUSTA (20–11 fav) 7 ran

1824   5th Earl of Jersey's b f COBWEB (8–11 fav) 13 ran

ST LEGER

1827   Edward Petre's b f MATILDA (9–1 and 10–1) 26 ran

1832   John Gully's ch c MARGRAVE (8–1) 17 ran

SAM CHIFNEY JUNIOR

2000 GUINEAS

1812   3rd Earl of Darlington's br c CWRW (7–1) 7 ran

1000 GUINEAS

1843   Thomas Thornhill's b f EXTEMPORE (7–1) 9 ran

DERBY

1818   Thomas Thornhill's ch c SAM (7–2) 16 ran

1820   Thomas Thornhill's ch c SAILOR (4–1 and 7–2) 15 ran

OAKS

1807   Thomas Grosvenor's b f BRISEIS (15–1) 13 ran

1811   5th Duke of Rutland's b f SORCERY (3–1 fav) 12 ran

1816   John Leveson Gower's b f LANDSCAPE (2–1 fav) 11 ran

1819   Thomas Thornhill's b f SHOVELER (2–1) 10 ran

1825   Thomas Grosvenor's ch f WINGS (13–1) 10 ran

FRANK BUTLER

2000 GUINEAS

1849   Anthony Nichol's bl c NUNNYKIRK (5–6 fav) 8 ran

1853   John Bowes's b c WEST AUSTRALIAN (4–6 fav) 7 ran

1000 GUINEAS
1848 Baron Stanley's br f CANEZOU (5–1) 9 ran
1850 3rd Earl of Orford's ch f LADY ORFORD (5–6 fav)
      5 ran

DERBY
1852 John Bowes's ch c DANIEL O'ROURKE (25–1)
      27 ran
1853 John Bowes's b c WEST AUSTRALIAN (6–4 fav)
      28 ran

OAKS
1843 George Ford's ch f POISON (30–1) 23 ran
1844 George Anson's ch f THE PRINCESS (5–1) 25 ran
1849 6th Earl of Chesterfield's br f LADY EVELYN (3–1 jt
      fav) 15 ran
1850 George Hobson's b f RHEDYCINA (6–1) 15 ran
1851 Baron Stanley's ch f IRIS (4–1) 15 ran
1852 John Scott's b f SONGSTRESS (2–1 fav) 14 ran

ST LEGER
1845 George Watts's ch c THE BARON (10–1) 15 ran
1853 John Bowes's b c WEST AUSTRALIAN (6–4 fav)
      10 ran

WILLIAM SCOTT

2000 GUINEAS
1842 John Bowes's ch c METEOR (6–4 fav) 8 ran
1843 John Bowes's b c COTHERSTONE (1–3 fav) 3 ran
1846 William Scott's b c SIR TATTON SYKES (5–1) 6 ran

DERBY
1832 Robert Risdale's ch c ST GILES (3–1 fav) 22 ran
1835 John Bowes's ch c MUNDIG (6–1) 14 ran
1842 George Anson's b c ATILLA (5–1) 24 ran
1843 John Bowes's b c COTHERSTONE (13–8 fav) 23 ran

OAKS
1836 John Scott's b f CYPRIAN (9–4 fav) 12 ran
1838 6th Earl of Chesterfield's br f INDUSTRY (9–2)
      16 ran
1841 1st Marquis of Westminster's b f GHUZNEE (7–4 fav)
      22 ran

ST LEGER
1821 Thomas Orde-Powlett's br c JACK SPIGOT (6–1)
      13 ran
1825 Richard Watts's b c MEMNON (3–1 fav) 30 ran

1828 Edward Petre's ch c THE COLONEL (5–2 and 3–1
      fav) 19 ran
1829 Edward Petre's ch c ROWTON (7–2 fav) 19 ran
1838 6th Earl of Chesterfield's b c DON JOHN (13–8 fav)
      7 ran
1839 Mr Yarburgh's br c CHARLES XII (4–6 fav) 14 ran
1840 1st Marquis of Westminster's br c LAUNCELOT (7–4
      fav) 11 ran
1841 1st Marquis of Westminster's br c SATIRIST (6–1)
      11 ran
1846 William Scott's b c SIR TATTON SYKES (3–1 jt fav)
      12 ran

NAT FLATMAN

2000 GUINEAS
1845 2nd Earl of Stradbroke's b c IDAS (5–6 fav) 5 ran
1851 Viscount Enfield's br c HERNANDEZ (5–1) 10 ran
1856 14th Earl of Derby's b c FAZZOLETTO (5–1) 10 ran

1000 GUINEAS
1835 Charles Greville's ch f PRESERVE (1–3 fav) 3 ran

1847 George Payne's b f CLEMENTINA (5–2) 5 ran

1857 John Scott's b f IMPERIEUSE (100–8) 8 ran

DERBY

1844 Jonathan Peel's b c ORLANDO (20–1) 29 ran

ST LEGER

1848 3rd Viscount Clifden's b c SURPLICE (9–4) 9 ran

1856 Anthony Nichol's b c WARLOCK (12–1) 9 ran

1857 John Scott's b f IMPERIEUSE (100–6) 11 ran

GEORGE FORDHAM

2000 GUINEAS

1867 8th Duke of Beaufort's br c VAUBAN (5–2 fav) 18 ran

1868 William Graham's ch f FORMOSA (3–1) dead-heated; 14 ran

1880 8th Duke of Beaufort's bl c PETRONEL (20–1) 17 ran

1000 GUINEAS

1859 William Stirling-Crawfurd's b f MAYONAISE (9–2) 4 ran

1861 G Hilton's b f NEMESIS (10–1) 9 ran

1865 8th Duke of Beaufort's br f SIBERIA (3–1) 11 ran

1868 8th Duke of Beaufort's ch f SCOTTISH QUEEN (100–8) 9 ran

1881 William Stirling-Crawfurd's ch f THEBAIS (5–6 fav) 13 ran

1883 Joachim Lefevre's br f HAUTEUR (9–4 fav) 9 ran

DERBY

1879 Baron Lionel de Rothschild's br c SIR BEVYS (20–1) 23 ran

OAKS

1859 1st Baron Londesborough's br f SUMMERSIDE (4–1) 15 ran

1868 William Graham's ch f FORMOSA (8–11 fav) 9 ran

1870 William Graham's ch f GAMOS (100–8) 7 ran

1872 Joachim Lefevre's b f REINE (3–1) 17 ran

1881 William Stirling-Crawfurd's ch f THEBAIS (4–6 fav) 12 ran

JOHN WELLS

2000 GUINEAS

1858 Sir Joseph Hawley's ch c FITZROLAND (100–6) 14 ran

1000 GUINEAS

1854 Henry Padwick's ch f VIRAGO (1–3 fav) 3 ran

1864 Baron Meyer de Rothschild's b f TOMATO (10–1) 15 ran

DERBY

1858 Sir Joseph Hawley's br c BEADSMAN (10–1) 23 ran

1859 Sir Joseph Hawley's br c MUSJID (9–4 fav) 30 ran

1868 Sir Joseph Hawley's b c BLUE GOWN (7–2) 18 ran

ST LEGER

1855 Tom Parr's b c SAUCEBOX (40–1) 12 ran

1869 Sir Joseph Hawley's br c PERO GOMEZ (3–1) 11 ran

FRED ARCHER

2000 GUINEAS

1874 6th Viscount Falmouth's ch c ATLANTIC (10–1) 12 ran

1879 6th Viscount Falmouth's ch c CHARIBERT (25–1) 15 ran

1883 6th Viscount Falmouth's br c GALLIARD (9–2) 15 ran

1885 William Brodrick Cloete's b c PARADOX (1–3 fav) 7 ran

1000 GUINEAS

1875 6th Viscount Falmouth's b f SPINAWAY (10–1) 6 ran

1879 6th Viscount Falmouth's b f WHEEL OF FORTUNE (40–75 fav) 8 ran

DERBY

1877 6th Viscount Falmouth's b c SILVIO (100–9) 17 ran
1880 1st Duke of Westminster's ch c BEND OR (2–1 fav) 19 ran
1881 Pierre Lorillard's br c IROQUOIS (11–2) 15 ran
1885 20th Baron Hastings's b c MELTON (75–40 fav) 12 ran
1886 1st Duke of Westminster's b c ORMONDE (4–9 fav) 9 ran

OAKS

1875 6th Viscount Falmouth's b f SPINAWAY (5–4 fav) 7 ran
1878 6th Viscount Falmouth's b f JANNETTE (65–40) 8 ran
1879 6th Viscount Falmouth's b f WHEEL OF FORTUNE (1–3 fav) 8 ran
1885 5th Earl Cadogan's b f LONELY (85–40 fav) 10 ran

ST LEGER

1877 6th Viscount Falmouth's b c SILVIO (65–40 fav) 14 ran
1878 6th Viscount Falmouth's b f JANNETTE (5–2 fav) 14 ran
1881 Pierre Lorillard's br c IROQUOIS (2–1 fav) 15 ran
1882 6th Viscount Falmouth's br f DUTCH OVEN (40–1) 14 ran
1885 20th Baron Hastings's b c MELTON (40–95 fav) 10 ran
1886 1st Duke of Westminster's b c ORMONDE (1–7 fav) 7 ran

TOM CANNON

2000 GUINEAS

1878 4th Earl of Lonsdale's ch f PILGRIMAGE (2–1 fav) 10 ran
1882 1st Duke of Westminster's ch f SHOTOVER (10–1) 18 ran
1887 Douglas Baird's ch c ENTERPRISE (2–1 fav) 8 ran
1889 Douglas Baird's ch c ENTHUSIAST (25–1) 9 ran

1000 GUINEAS

1866 4th Marquis of Hastings's b f REPULSE (1–2 fav) 9 ran
1878 4th Earl of Lonsdale's ch f PILGRIMAGE (4–5 fav) 9 ran
1884 George Baird's b f BUSYBODY (85–40 fav) 6 ran

DERBY

1882 1st Duke of Westminster's ch f SHOTOVER (11–2) 14 ran

OAKS

1869 Sir Frederick Johnstone's b f BRIGANTINE (7–2) 15 ran
1873 James Merry's ch f MARIE STUART (2–1 fav) 18 ran
1882 7th Earl of Stamford's br f GEHEIMNISS (4–6 fav) 5 ran
1884 George Baird's b f BUSYBODY (100–105 fav) 9 ran

ST LEGER

1880 Charles Brewer's b c ROBERT THE DEVIL (4–1) 12 ran

MORNY CANNON

2000 GUINEAS

1899 1st Duke of Westminster's b c FLYING FOX (5–6 fav) 8 ran

DERBY

1899 1st Duke of Westminster's b c FLYING FOX (2–5 fav) 12 ran

OAKS

1900 6th Duke of Portland's b f LA ROCHE (5–1) 14 ran
1903 Jack Joel's b f OUR LASSIE (6–1) 10 ran

ST LEGER

1894 1st Baron Alington's b f THROSTLE (50–1) 8 ran
1899 1st Duke of Westminster's b c FLYING FOX (2/7 fav) 6 ran

JACK WATTS

2000 GUINEAS

1894 5th Earl of Rosebery's b c LADAS (5–6 fav) 8 ran
1895 Sir John Blundell Maple's b c KIRKCONNEL (10–1) 8 ran

1000 GUINEAS

1886 12th Duke of Hamilton's b f MISS JUMMY (3–1) 10 ran
1890 6th Duke of Portland's b f SEMOLINA (1–2 fav) 10 ran
1896 HRH Prince of Wales's br f THAIS (5–1) 19 ran
1897 5th Earl of Rosebery's b f CHELANDRY (9–4) 9 ran

DERBY
1887 George Baird's b c MERRY HAMPTON (100–9) 11 ran
1890 Sir James Miller's ch c SAINFOIN (100–15) 8 ran
1894 5th Earl of Rosebery's b c LADAS (2–9 fav) 7 ran
1896 HRH Prince of Wales's b c PERSIMMON (5–1) 11 ran

OAKS
1883 5th Earl of Rosebery's b f BONNY JEAN (5–1) 14 ran
1886 12th Duke of Hamilton's b f MISS JUMMY (Evens fav) 12 ran
1890 6th Duke of Portland's br f MEMOIR (100–30) 7 ran
1893 6th Duke of Portland's b f MRS BUTTERWICK (100–7) 17 ran

ST LEGER
1883 12th Duke of Hamilton's b c OSSIAN (9–1) 9 ran
1884 Robert Vyner's b c THE LAMBKIN (9–1) 13 ran
1890 6th Duke of Portland's br f MEMOIR (10–1) 15 ran
1892 Baron Maurice de Hirsch's br f LA FLECHE (7–2) 11 ran
1896 HRH Prince of Wales's b c PERSIMMON (2–11 fav) 7 ran

TOD SLOAN
1000 GUINEAS
1899 Lord William Beresford's b f SIBOLA (13–8 fav) 14 ran

DANNY MAHER
2000 GUINEAS
1910 5th Earl of Rosebery's ch c NEIL GOW (2–1 fav) 13 ran
1912 Herman Duryea's ch c SWEEPER (6–1) 14 ran
1000 GUINEAS
1901 Sir James Miller's b f AIDA (13–8 fav) 15 ran
DERBY
1903 Sir James Miller's br c ROCK SAND (4–6 fav) 7 ran
1905 5th Earl of Rosebery's ch c CICERO (4–11 fav) 9 ran
1906 Eustace Loder's b c SPEARMINT (6–1) 22 ran
OAKS
1906 16th Earl of Derby's b f KEYSTONE (5–2 fav) 12 ran

ST LEGER
1903 Sir James Miller's br c ROCK SAND (2–5 fav) 5 ran
1909 Alfred Cox's b c BAYARDO (10–11 fav) 7 ran

FRANK WOOTTON
OAKS
1909 William Cooper's ch f PEROLA (5–1) 14 ran
ST LEGER
1910 17th Earl of Derby's br c SWYNFORD (9–2) 11 ran

FRANK BULLOCK
1000 GUINEAS
1925 2nd Viscount Astor's br f SAUCY SUE (1–4 fav) 11 ran
OAKS
1925 2nd Viscount Astor's br f SAUCY SUE (30–100 fav) 12 ran

BROWNIE CARSLAKE
2000 GUINEAS
1920 Dermot McCalmont's gr c TETRATEMA (2–1 fav) 17 ran
1000 GUINEAS
1918 17th Earl of Derby's b f FERRY (50–1) 8 ran
1922 Barney Parr's ch f SILVER URN (10–1) 20 ran
OAKS
1934 5th Earl of Durham's br f LIGHT BROCADE (7–4 fav) 8 ran
ST LEGER
1919 17th Earl of Derby's br f KEYSOE (100–8) 10 ran
1924 HH Aga Khan III's b c SALMON TROUT (6–1) 17 ran
1938 James Rank's b c SCOTTISH UNION (7–1) 9 ran

JOE CHILDS
2000 GUINEAS
1918 Lady James Douglas's b c GAINSBOROUGH (4–1) 13 ran
1931 Arthur Dewar's b c CAMERONIAN (100–8) 24 ran

1000 GUINEAS
1928 HM King George V's b f SCUTTLE (15–8 fav) 14 ran
1933 William Woodward's b or br f BROWN BETTY (8–1) 22 ran

DERBY
1916 Sir Edward Hulton's ch f FIFINELLA (11–2) 10 ran
1918 Lady James Douglas's b c GAINSBOROUGH (8–13 fav) 13 ran
1926 1st Baron Woolavington's ch c CORONACH (11–2) 19 ran

OAKS
1912 Jean Prat's b f MIRSKA (33–1) 14 ran
1916 Sir Edward Hulton's ch f FIFINELLA (8–13 fav) 7 ran
1919 Lady James Douglas's b f BAYUDA (100–7) 10 ran
1921 Joseph Watson's b or br f LOVE IN IDLENESS (5–1 fav) 22 ran

ST LEGER
1918 Lady James Douglas's b c GAINSBOROUGH (4–11 fav) 5 ran
1921 7th Marquis of Londonderry's ch c POLEMARCH (50–1) 9 ran
1925 Sir John Rutherford's b c SOLARIO (7–2 jt fav) 15 ran
1926 1st Baron Woolavington's ch c CORONACH (8–15 fav) 12 ran

STEVE DONOGHUE

2000 GUINEAS
1915 Solly Joel's b c POMMERN (2–1 fav) 16 ran
1917 Alfred Cox's b c GAY CRUSADER (9–4 fav) 14 ran
1925 Henry Morriss's b c MANNA (100–8) 13 ran

1000 GUINEAS
1937 Sir Victor Sassoon's b f EXHIBITIONNIST (10–1) 20 ran

DERBY
1915 Solly Joel's b c POMMERN (11–10 fav) 17 ran
1917 Alfred Cox's b c GAY CRUSADER (7–4 fav) 12 ran
1921 Jack Joel's ch c HUMORIST (6–1) 23 ran
1922 1st Baron Woolavington's ch c CAPTAIN CUTTLE (10–1) 30 ran
1923 Ben Irish's br c PAPYRUS (100–15) 19 ran
1925 Henry Morriss's b c MANNA (9–1) 27 ran

OAKS
1918 Alfred Cox's b f MY DEAR (3–1 fav) 15 ran
1937 Sir Victor Sassoon's b f EXHIBITIONNIST (3–1 fav) 13 ran

ST LEGER
1915 Solly Joel's b c POMMERN (1–3 fav) 7 ran
1917 Alfred Cox's b c GAY CRUSADER (2–11 fav) 3 ran

GORDON RICHARDS

2000 GUINEAS
1938 Henry Morriss's b c PASCH (5–2 fav) 18 ran
1942 HM King George VI's b c BIG GAME (8–11 fav) 14 ran
1947 Arthur Dewar's br c TUDOR MINSTREL (11–8 fav) 15 ran

1000 GUINEAS
1942 HM King George VI's b f SUN CHARIOT (Evens fav) 18 ran
1948 Sir Percy Loraine's br f QUEENPOT (6–1) 22 ran
1951 Henry Tufton's b f BELLE OF ALL (4–1 fav) 18 ran

DERBY
1953 Sir Victor Sassoon's b c PINZA (5–1 jt fav) 27 ran

OAKS
1930 1st Baron Glanely's br f ROSE OF ENGLAND (7–1) 15 ran
1942 HM King George VI's b f SUN CHARIOT (1–4 fav) 12 ran

ST LEGER

1930 1st Baron Glanely's b c SINGAPORE (4–1 jt fav)
13 ran

1937 1st Baron Glanely's b c CHULMLEIGH (18–1) 15 ran

1940 HH Aga Khan III's b c TURKHAN (4–1) 6 ran

1942 HM King George VI's b f SUN CHARIOT (9–4) 8 ran

1944 HH Aga Khan III's b c TEHRAN (9–2) 17 ran

CHARLIE ELLIOTT

2000 GUINEAS

1923 5th Earl of Rosebery's b c ELLANGOWAN (7–1)
18 ran

1928 Sir Laurence Philipps's b c FLAMINGO (5–1) 17 ran

1940 Marcel Boussac's b c DJEBEL (9–4 fav) 21 ran

1941 2nd Duke of Westminster's b c LAMBERT SIMNEL
(10–1) 19 ran

1949 Mrs Marion Glenister's b c NIMBUS (10–1) 13 ran

1000 GUINEAS

1924 5th Earl of Rosebery's ch f PLACK (8–1) 16 ran

1931 4th Earl of Ellesmere's b f FOUR COURSE (100–9)
20 ran

1932 Evremond de Saint-Alary's b f KANDY (33–1) 19 ran

1944 Jim Joel's b f PICTURE PLAY (15–2) 11 ran

DERBY

1927 Frank Curzon's ch c CALL BOY (4–1 fav) 23 ran

1938 Peter Beatty's br c BOIS ROUSSEL (20–1) 22 ran

1949 Mrs Marion Glenister's b c NIMBUS (7–1) 32 ran

OAKS

1931 Charles Birkin's b f BRULETTE (7–2 jt fav) 15 ran

1943 James Rank's ch f WHY HURRY (7–1) 13 ran

CHARLIE SMIRKE

2000 GUINEAS

1948 HH Maharajah of Baroda's b c MY BABU (2–1 fav)
18 ran

1950 HH Aga Khan III's gr c PALESTINE (4–1) 19 ran

1000 GUINEAS

1957 HH Aga Khan III's b f ROSE ROYALE (6–1) 20 ran

DERBY

1934 HH Maharajah of Rajpipla's b c WINDSOR LAD
(15–2) 19 ran

1936 HH Aga Khan III's gr c MAHMOUD (100–8) 22 ran

1952 HH Aga Khan III's br c TULYAR (11–2 fav) 33 ran

1958 Sir Victor Sassoon's b c HARD RIDDEN (18–1) 20 ran

ST LEGER

1934 Martin Benson's b c WINDSOR LAD (4–9 fav) 10 ran

1935 HH Aga Khan III's b c BAHRAM (4–11 fav) 8 ran

1952 HH Aga Khan III's br c TULYAR (10–11 fav) 12 ran

1954 Robert Sterling Clark's ch c NEVER SAY DIE
(100–30 fav) 16 ran

HARRY WRAGG

2000 GUINEAS

1944 17th Earl of Derby's br f GARDEN PATH (5–1)
26 ran

1000 GUINEAS

1934 Sir George Bullough's b f CAMPANULA (2–5 fav)
10 ran

1943 17th Earl of Derby's b f HERRINGBONE (15–2)
12 ran

1945 17th Earl of Derby's ch f SUN STREAM (5–2 fav)
14 ran

DERBY

1928 Sir Hugo Cunliffe-Owen's b c FELSTEAD (33–1)
19 ran

1930 HH Aga Khan III's br c BLENHEIM (18–1) 17 ran

1942 17th Earl of Derby's b c WATLING STREET (6–1)
13 ran

OAKS

1938 Sir Hugo Cunliffe-Owen's br f ROCKFEL (3–1 fav)
14 ran

1941 Arthur Dewar's b f COMMOTION (8–1) 12 ran

1945 17th Earl of Derby's ch f SUN STREAM (6–4 fav)
16 ran

1946 Sir Alfred Butt's b f STEADY AIM (7–1) 16 ran

ST LEGER

1931 6th Earl of Rosebery's b c SANDWICH (9–1) 10 ran

1943 17th Earl of Derby's b f HERRINGBONE (100–6)
12 ran

LESTER PIGGOTT

2000 GUINEAS

1957 Sir Victor Sassoon's ch c CREPELLO (7–2) 14 ran

1968 Raymond Guest's b c SIR IVOR (11–8 fav) 10 ran

1970 Charles Englehard's b c NIJINSKY (4–7 fav) 14 ran

1985 Maktoum Al-Maktoum's b c SHADEED (4–5 fav) 14 ran

1000 GUINEAS

1970 Jean, Lady Ashcombe's gr f HUMBLE DUTY (3–1 jt fav) 12 ran

1981 Jim Joel's b f FAIRY FOOTSTEPS (6–4 fav) 14 ran

DERBY

1954 Robert Sterling Clark's ch c NEVER SAY DIE (33–1) 22 ran

1957 Sir Victor Sassoon's ch c CREPELLO (6–4 fav) 22 ran

1960 Sir Victor Sassoon's b c ST PADDY (7–1) 17 ran

1968 Raymond Guest's b c SIR IVOR (4–5 fav) 13 ran

1970 Charles Englehard's b c NIJINSKY (11–8 fav) 11 ran

1972 John Galbreath's b c ROBERTO (3–1 fav) 22 ran

1976 Nelson Bunker Hunt's b c EMPERY (10–1) 23 ran

1977 Robert Sangster's ch c THE MINSTREL (5–1) 22 ran

1983 Eric Moller's b c TEENOSO (9–2 fav) 21 ran

OAKS

1957 HM Queen Elizabeth II's br f CARROZZA (100–8) 11 ran

1959 Prince Aly Khan's gr f PETITE ETOILE (11–2) 11 ran

1966 Charles Clore's br f VALORIS (11–10 fav) 13 ran

1975 James Morrison's b f JULIETTE MARNY (12–1) 12 ran

1981 Mrs Diana Firestone's ch f BLUE WIND (3–1 jt fav) 12 ran

1984 Sir Robert McAlpine's b f CIRCUS PLUME (4–1) 16 ran

ST LEGER

1960 Sir Victor Sassoon's b c ST PADDY (4–6 fav) 9 ran

1961 Mrs Vera Lilley's b c AURELIUS (9–2) 13 ran

1967 Charles Englehard's b c RIBOCCO (7–2 jt fav) 9 ran

1968 Charles Englehard's b c RIBERO (100–30) 8 ran

1970 Charles Englehard's b c NIJINSKY (2–7 fav) 9 ran

1971 Mrs Ellen Rogerson's b c ATHENS WOOD (5–2) 8 ran

1972 Ogden Phipps's ch c BOUCHER (3–1) 7 ran

1984 Ivan Allan's b c COMMANCHE RUN (7–4 fav) 11 ran

SCOBIE BREASLEY

2000 GUINEAS

1951 Ley On's br c KI MING (100–8) 27 ran

1000 GUINEAS

1954 Arthur Dewar's ch f FESTOON (9–2) 12 ran

DERBY

1964 John Ismay's b c SANTA CLAUS (15–8 fav) 17 ran

1966 Lady Zia Wernher's b c CHARLOTTOWN (5–1) 25 ran

DOUG SMITH

2000 GUINEAS
1955 David Robinson's b c OUR BABU (13–2) 23 ran
1958 HM Queen Elizabeth II's ch c PALL MALL (20–1) 14 ran

1000 GUINEAS
1946 HM King George VI's b f HYPERICUM (100–6) 13 ran
1959 Prince Aly Khan's gr f PETITE ETOILE (8–1) 14 ran

EDWARD HIDE

1000 GUINEAS
1972 Mrs Susan Stanley's ch f WATERLOO (8–1) 18 ran
1977 Mrs Edith Kettlewell's b f MRS McARDY (16–1) 18 ran

DERBY
1973 Arthur Budgett's ch c MORSTON (25–1) 25 ran

OAKS
1967 Countess Margit Batthyany's br f PIA (100–7) 12 ran

ST LEGER
1959 William Hill's b f CANTELO (100–7) 11 ran
1978 Marcos Lemos' b c JULIO MARINER (28–1) 14 ran

GEOFF LEWIS

2000 GUINEAS
1969 Jim Brown's b c RIGHT TACK (15–2) 13 ran

1000 GUINEAS
1973 George Pope's ch f MYSTERIOUS (11–1) 14 ran

DERBY
1971 Paul Mellon's b c MILL REEF (100–30 fav) 21 ran

OAKS
1971 Roger Hue-Williams's ch f ALTESSE ROYALE (6–4 fav) 11 ran
1973 George Pope's ch f MYSTERIOUS (13–8 fav) 10 ran

JOE MERCER

2000 GUINEAS
1971 Mrs Jean Hislop's b c BRIGADIER GERARD (11–2) 6 ran

1000 GUINEAS

1974 HM Queen Elizabeth II's b f HIGHCLERE (12–1)
15 ran

1979 Helena Springfield Ltd's b f ONE IN A MILLION
(Evens fav) 17 ran

OAKS

1953 3rd Viscount Astor's b f AMBIGUITY (18–1) 21 ran

ST LEGER

1965 Jakie Astor's b c PROVOKE (28–1) 11 ran

1974 Lady Beaverbrook's b c BUSTINO (11–10 fav) 10 ran

1980 Jim Joel's b c LIGHT CAVALRY (3–1) 7 ran

1981 Sir Jakie Astor's b c CUT ABOVE (28–1) 7 ran

WILLIE CARSON

2000 GUINEAS

1972 Sir Jules Thorn's b c HIGH TOP (85–40 fav) 12 ran

1980 Khalid Bin Abdulla's b c KNOWN FACT (14–1)
14 ran

1987 Jim Horgan's b c DON'T FORGET ME (9–1) 14 ran

1989 Hamdan Al-Maktoum's ch c NASHWAN (3–1 fav)
14 ran

1000 GUINEAS

1990 Hamdan Al-Maktoum's b f SALSABIL (6–4 fav) 10 ran

1991 Hamdan Al-Maktoum's gr f SHADAYID (4–6 fav)
14 ran

DERBY

1979 Sir Michael Sobell's b c TROY (6–1) 23 ran

1980 Mme Etti Plesch's b c HENBIT (7–1) 24 ran

1989 Hamdan Al-Maktoum's ch c NASHWAN (5–4 fav)
12 ran

OAKS

1977 HM Queen Elizabeth II's b f DUNFERMLINE (6–1)
13 ran

1980 Dick Hollingsworth's ch f BIREME (9–2) 11 ran

1983 Sir Michael Sobell's b f SUN PRINCESS (6–1) 15 ran

1990 Hamdan Al-Maktoum's b f SALSABIL (2–1 fav) 8 ran

ST LEGER

1977 HM Queen Elizabeth II's b f DUNFERMLINE (10–1)
13 ran

1983 Sir Michael Sobell's b f SUN PRINCESS (11–8 fav)
10 ran

1988 Dowager Lady Beaverbrook's ch c MINSTER SON
(15–2) 6 ran

PAT EDDERY

2000 GUINEAS

1983 Robert Sangster's b c LOMOND (9–1) 16 ran

1984 Robert Sangster's b c EL GRAN SEÑOR (15–8 fav) 9 ran

1000 GUINEAS

1975 Carlo Vittadini's ch c GRUNDY (5–1) 18 ran

1982 Robert Sangster's b c GOLDEN FLEECE (3–1 fav)
18 ran

1990 Khalid Bin Abdulla's b c QUEST FOR FAME (7–1)
18 ran

OAKS

1974 Louis Freedman's b f POLYGAMY (3–1 fav) 15 ran

1979 James Morrison's b f SCINTILLATE (20–1) 14 ran

ST LEGER

1986 Lavinia, Duchess of Norfolk's b c MOON MADNESS
(9–2) 8 ran

1991 Khalid Bin Abdulla's b c TOULON (5–2 fav) 10 ran

STEVE CAUTHEN

2000 GUINEAS

1979 Tony Shead's ch c TAP ON WOOD (20–1) 20 ran

1000 GUINEAS

1985 Sheikh Mohammed's ch f OH SO SHARP (2–1 fav)
17 ran

DERBY

1985 9th Baron Howard de Walden's b c SLIP ANCHOR
(9–4 fav) 14 ran

1987 Louis Freedman's b c REFERENCE POINT (6–4 fav)
19 ran

OAKS

1985 Sheikh Mohammed's ch f OH SO SHARP (6–4 fav)
12 ran

1988 Sheikh Mohammed's ch f DIMINUENDO (7–4 fav)
11 ran

1989 Saeed Maktoum Al-Maktoum's ch f SNOW BRIDE
(13–2) 9 ran

ST LEGER

1985 Sheikh Mohammed's ch f OH SO SHARP (8–11 fav)
6 ran

1987 Louis Freedman's b c REFERENCE POINT (4–11 fav)
7 ran

1989 Charles St George's b c MICHELOZZO (6–4 fav) 8 ran

APPENDIX: CLASSIC WINS

TOP 10 ENGLISH CLASSIC WINNERS

	2000	1000	Derby	Oaks	St Leger	Total
1 Lester Piggott (1954–85)	4	2	9	6	8	29
2 Frank Buckle (1792–1827)	5	6	5	9	2	27*
3 Jem Robinson (1817–48)	9	5	6	2	2	24
4 Fred Archer (1874–86)	4	2	5	4	6	21
5 Bill Scott (1821–46)	3	0	4	3	9	19
Jack Watts (1883–97)	2	4	4	4	5	19
7 Willie Carson (1972–91)	4	2	3	4	3	16
John Barham Day (1826–41)	4	5	0	5	2	16
George Fordham (1859–83)	3	7	1	5	0	16
10 Joe Childs (1912–33)	2	2	3	4	4	15

Figures up to and including 1991.

Years refer to date of first and last Classic winner.

Frank Buckle's total excludes the 1000 Guineas of 1819 and 1825 which are unauthenticated.

TOP 10 BRITISH CAREER TOTALS

Wins		Best season	Titles
4870	Sir Gordon Richards (1921–54)	269 (1947)	26
4400	Lester Piggott (1948–91)	191 (1966)	11
3310	Willie Carson (1962–91)	187 (1990)	5
3111	Doug Smith (1932–67)	173 (1947)	5
3071	Pat Eddery (1969–91)	209 (1990)	9
2810	Joe Mercer (1950–85)	164 (1979)	1
2748	Fred Archer (1870–86)	246 (1885)	13
2591	Edward Hide (1951–83)	137 (1974)	0
2587	George Fordham (1851–83)	166 (1862)	14
2313	Eph Smith (1930–65)	144 (1947)	0

Figures complete to the end of the 1991 Turf season.

Years refer to date of first and last winner.

British wins only.

ACKNOWLEDGEMENTS

Illustrations

The Authors and Publisher would like to express
their thanks to the following for kind permission
to reproduce their paintings and photographs.

The Jockey Club
The National Horseracing Museum
The York Racing Museum
The Halifax Collection
The Earl of Derby
The Hulton-Deutsch Collection
The Illustrated London News Picture Library
WW Rouch & Co.
Sport and General
Mrs G Wragg
Phil Smith
Michael Tanner's Collection
Gerry, Mark and Paul Cranham

Memorabilia

Mr PB Taylor
Mr JO Taylor
Mr ET Foster
Mrs CK Wiles
Mrs G Wragg
Mrs CZ Sawbridge

Thanks also to the following for all their
kind help and advice.

The Marquess of Hartington
The Earl of Halifax
Robert Fellowes, agent of the Jockey Club
Dr Alice Hills, curator of the National Horseracing Museum
Dede Marks, curator of the York Racing Museum
Guy Wilmot
Gregory Way

Bibliography

In addition to contemporary newspapers, annuals,
periodicals and magazines the principal secondary sources
consulted were as follows:

Axthelm, The Kid, Paddington Press, 1978
Baerlein, Joe Mercer, Macdonald/Queen Anne Press, 1987
Blyth, The Pocket Venus, Weidenfeld & Nicolson, 1966
Britt, Post Haste, Muller, 1967
Browne, History of the English Turf, Virtue, 1931
Carr, Queen's Jockey, Stanley Paul, 1966
Cawthorne & Herod, Royal Ascot, Treherne, 1902
Childs, My Racing Reminiscences, Hutchinson, 1952
Cook, History of the English Turf, Virtue, 1904
Curling, The Captain, Barrie and Jenkins, 1970
Custance, Riding Recollections, Edward Arnold, 1894
Darling, Sam Darling's Reminiscences, Mills & Boon, 1914
Dixon, From Gladiateur to Persimmon, Grant Richards, 1901
Donoghue, Just My Story, Hutchinson, 1923
Donoghue, Donoghue Up, Collins, 1938
'Druid, The', Post and Paddock, Rogerson & Tuxford, 1856
'Druid, The', Silk & Scarlet, Rogerson & Tuxford, 1859
'Druid, The', Scott and Sebright, Frederick Warne, 1862
Duval, Lester, Stanley Paul, 1972
Duval, Pat on the Back, Stanley Paul, 1976
Duval, Willie Carson, Stanley Paul, 1980
Fairfax-Blakeborough, The Analysis of the Turf, Philip Allan,
    1927
Fitzgeorge-Parker, Jockeys of the Seventies, Stanley Paul,
    1980
Fitzgeorge-Parker, The Guv'nor, Collins, 1980
Fletcher, The History of the St Leger Stakes, Hutchinson, 1926
Francis, Lester, Michael Joseph, 1986
Galtrey, Memories of a Racing Journalist, Hutchinson, 1934
Gilbey, Champions All, Hutchinson, 1971
Good, Good Days, Hutchinson, 1941

Good, The Lure of the Turf, Odhams, 1957
Herbert, Vincent O'Brien's Great Horses, Pelham, 1985
Hislop, Of Horses and Races, Michael Joseph, 1961
Hughes, My Greatest Race, Michael Joseph, 1979
Humphris, The Life of Fred Archer, Hutchinson, 1923
Humphris, The Life of Mat Dawson, 1928
Jarvis, They're Off, Michael Joseph, 1969
Laird, Royal Ascot, Hodder and Stoughton, 1976
Lambton, Men and Horses I Have Known, Thornton
    Butterworth, 1924
Lawton, Lester Piggott, Arthur Barker, 1980
Marsh, A Trainer to Two Kings, Cassell, 1925
Mortimer, The History of the Derby Stakes, Michael Joseph,
    1973
Mortimer, The Flat, George Allen & Unwin, 1979
Morton, My Sixty Years on the Turf, Hutchinson, 1930
Onslow, Headquarters, Great Ouse Press, 1983
Poole, Scobie, Macdonald/Queen Anne Press, 1984
Porter, John Porter of Kingsclere, Grant Richards, 1919
Portland, Memories of Racing and Hunting, Faber and Faber,
    1935
Pryor, Lester, Sidgwick & Jackson, 1985
Radcliffe, The Life and Times of John Osborne, Sands, 1900
Richards, My Story, Hodder and Stoughton, 1955
Seth-Smith, Steve, Faber and Faber, 1974
Seth-Smith, Knight of the Turf, Hodder and Stoughton, 1980
Smirke, Finishing Post, Oldbourne, 1960
Smith, Five Times Champion, Pelham, 1968
Smith, Vincent O'Brien, Virgin, 1990
Tanner, Great Racing Partnerships, Sportsman's Press, 1987
Tanner, The Major, Pelham, 1991
Taunton, Famous Horses, Sampson Low, Marston & Co,
    1895
Welcome, Fred Archer, Faber and Faber, 1967

INDEX

Page references in italics denote illustrations.

INDEX